Teen Finance Series

College Financing Information For Teens, Second Edition

College Financing Information For Teens, Second Edition

Tips For A Successful Financial Life

Including Facts About Planning, Saving, And Paying For Postsecondary Education. With Information About College Savings Plans, Grants, Loans, Scholarships, Community And Military Service, And More

Edited by Elizabeth Magill

Omnigraphics

155 W. Congress, Suite 200
Detroit, MI 48226

Bibliographic Note

Because this page cannot legibly accommodate all the copyright notices, the Bibliographic Note portion of the Preface constitutes an extension of the copyright notice.

Edited by Elizabeth Magill

Teen Finance Series

Karen Bellenir, *Managing Editor*
Elizabeth Collins, *Research and Permissions Coordinator*
Cherry Edwards, *Permissions Assistant*
EdIndex, *Services for Publishers, Indexers*

* * *

Omnigraphics, Inc.

Matthew P. Barbour, *Senior Vice President*
Kevin M. Hayes, *Operations Manager*

* * *

Peter E. Ruffner, *Publisher*

Copyright © 2012 Omnigraphics, Inc.

ISBN 978-0-7808-1214-7

Library of Congress Cataloging-in-Publication Data

College financing information for teens : tips for a successful financial life including facts about planning, saving, and paying for postsecondary education, with information about college savings plans, grants, loans, scholarships, community and military service, and more / edited by Elizabeth Magill. -- 2nd ed.
    p. cm.
  Includes bibliographical references and index.
  Summary: "Provides information for teens about planning, saving, and paying for post-secondary education, with facts about government aid, private loans and scholarships, and other sources of financial assistance. Includes index and resource information"--Provided by publisher.
    ISBN 978-0-7808-1214-7 (hardcover : alk. paper) 1. College costs--United States. 2. Student aid--United States. 3. Finance, Personal--United States. I. Magill, Elizabeth. II. Title.
  LB2342.C63316 2011
  378.30973--dc23
                                                                                                    2011034082

Table of Contents

Part Four: Financial Aid And The Federal Government

Part Five: Other Sources Of Financial Aid

Part Six: If You Need More Information

Preface

About This Book

The federal government is actively encouraging people to attend college in these troubling economic times. The U.S. Department of Education awards about $100 billion a year in grants, work-study assistance, and low-interest loans, and the amount of the federal Pell grant has increased. In spite of the many options for federal aid, however, many teens feel overwhelmed by the idea of going to college. The entire process, from taking the right tests in high school to making sure one gets enough financial aid, can be confusing. Many teens find themselves in a state of bewilderment when considering the vast amount of information they need to absorb in order to plan, pay for, and attend college.

College Financing Information For Teens, Second Edition provides information about planning and paying for a postsecondary education. It explains college costs and describes practical steps middle and high school students can take to begin to prepare themselves for meeting future challenges. It discusses the process of choosing among different types of colleges and vocational schools and describes the procedures involved in applying for and receiving federal financial aid. A separate section discusses alternative sources of aid, including scholarships, institutional grants, private loans, and aid associated with community service, military service, athletic pursuits, and careers in healthcare. The book concludes with directories of resources for additional information.

How To Use This Book

This book is divided into parts and chapters. Parts focus on broad areas of interest; chapters are devoted to single topics within a part.

Part One: Preparing For College addresses middle and high school students who may be wondering about postsecondary education. It explains steps that can be taken as early as the eighth grade to maximize the number of options available after high school graduation. It describes how to use the high school experience to prepare for college, and it concludes with a discussion of the various types of standardized tests students may encounter when they decide to apply for college admission.

Part Two: Your Role As An Education Consumer helps students understand the vast array of choices they will face when making decisions about higher education. It explains the differences in costs between public and private institutions, and it discusses different types of colleges and vocational schools. It also includes chapters about online education (a growing trend) and study abroad.

Part Three: Saving For College answers questions about various tools available to help families save for future college expenses. It compares the tax advantages of some plans against their potential impact on future offers of aid and it discusses the pros and cons of saving money in a student's name. It also considers the advantages and disadvantages of working during college.

Part Four: Financial Aid And The Federal Government discusses the process of applying for federal financial aid and explores the three types of federal aid: grants, loans, and work-study. It discusses a student's options for repaying federal loans, including the circumstances under which a loan can be deferred (postponed) or cancelled (forgiven). It concludes with a discussion of federal tax credits for postsecondary education.

Part Five: Other Sources Of Financial Aid discusses aid that is available from private sources (such as scholarships and institutional loans) and government service (such as the military, the Peace Corps, and AmeriCorps). It also examines the requirements of students with specialized interests or needs, such as athletes, aspiring nurses, and those with disabilities.

Part Six: If You Need More Information offers a directory of financial aid resources, including federal and national student aid organizations, online scholarship search services, and other resources for information about planning for higher education. A separate directory of state higher education agencies will help students seeking to locate additional resources within their state of residence or the state in which they plan to attend college.

Bibliographic Note

This volume contains documents and excerpts from publications issued by the following government agencies: AmeriCorps; Federal Trade Commission; Peace Corps; U.S. Department of Defense; U.S. Department of Education; U.S. Department of Health and Human Services; U.S. Department of the Treasury; U.S. Securities and Exchange Commission.

In addition, this volume contains copyrighted documents and articles produced by the following organizations: American Institute of Certified Public Accountants; Bankrate.com; The College Board; College Savings Plans Network; Distance Education and Training Council; eCampusTours.com; EducationDynamics, LLC; FinAid Page, LLC; Financial Industry Regulatory Authority, Inc.; Forefield 2011; Kaplan, Inc.; National Collegiate Athletic Association;

Sallie Mae, Inc.; Scholarships.com, LLC; Student Lending Analytics; Texas Guaranteed Student Loan Corporation; U.S. News & World Report; University of Washington.

The photograph on the front cover is from Design Pics/SuperStock.

Full citation information is provided on the first page of each chapter. Every effort has been made to secure all necessary rights to reprint the copyrighted material. If any omissions have been made, please contact Omnigraphics to make corrections for future editions.

Acknowledgements

In addition to the organizations listed above, special thanks are due to Liz Collins, research and permissions coordinator; Cherry Edwards, permissions assistant; Karen Bellenir, managing editor; and WhimsyInk, prepress services provider.

Part One
Preparing For College

Chapter 1

Assessing Yourself And Your Future

Assessing Yourself

Assessing your personality, interests, and skills now will help later when it's time to choose a career.

Set up an appointment with your guidance counselor. They can help you assess your skills and talents and suggest opportunities based on your interests. They'll talk to you about setting goals and reaching them. In time, you'll have a better idea of who you are and what you want after high school.

Personality

Your personality traits can determine which careers are best suited to you. For example:

- Are you shy or outgoing?
- Patient or impulsive?
- Good with children or adults?
- Do you like animals or machines?

Answers to questions like these can help pinpoint careers you might excel in.

Personality Inventories

For a closer look at yourself, take a personality inventory—a questionnaire that asks how you would think, act, and feel in specific situations.

About This Chapter: Information in this chapter is from "Assessing Yourself" and "Researching Occupations," © 2010 Sallie Mae, Inc. All rights reserved. Reprinted with permission. For additional information, visit www .collegeanswer.com or www.salliemae.com.

The most popular personality inventory is the Myers-Briggs Type Indicator® (MBTI). Unofficial versions of this personality inventory are available online and can be completed in 30 minutes. Your answers to the multiple-choice questions will be evaluated and you'll receive an explanation of your personality type.

- PersonalityType provides the most abbreviated version and also presents popular career options.

- Humanmetrics offers a longer, more personalized version.

- The official version of the MBTI is available in print. This official test is administered by qualified trainers, and trained professionals evaluate the answers. Check with a guidance counselor to see if this test is available.

Based on what you find in your personality inventory, you might realize that the job of your dreams may not be perfect after all. On the other hand, what you learn about your personality, coupled with your skills and interest, could point you to your perfect role in life.

Interests

What makes you happy? If you had a spare moment, what would you do?

- Do you like to paint or draw?

- Take dance classes?

- Like the mental challenge of chess?

- Do you love to read?

- What are your hobbies?

Your answers to questions like these can say a lot about you. Your interests and skills offer additional insight into your personality and what you really love to do. And knowing that is important when you start thinking about your future.

Quick Tip

Another way to understand your interests and how they relate to your career is to take the Strong Interest Inventory®. If this is not already part of your high school's career or college prep curriculum, check with your guidance counselor.

Source: "Assessing Yourself," © 2010 Sallie Mae, Inc. All rights reserved. Reprinted with permission. For additional information, visit www.collegeanswer.com or www.salliemae.com.

> ### It's A Fact!
>
> Taking the ASVAB does not mean you're enlisting in the Armed Services.
>
> Source: "Assessing Yourself," © 2010 Sallie Mae, Inc. All rights reserved. Reprinted with permission. For additional information, visit www.collegeanswer.com or www.salliemae.com.

Skills

What are you good at?

- Do you excel in sports?

- Do people call you when they're having computer problems?

- When it comes to literature, do you see beyond the writing and into the meaning intended by the author?

- Can you take a motor apart, put it back together, and have no extra parts left over?

Beyond just answering these and similar questions by yourself, you can learn more about your talent for career-related (or "vocational") skills by taking an aptitude test.

The Armed Services Vocational Aptitude Battery (ASVAB)

One particularly thorough test is the ASVAB. It is designed to measure your aptitudes while you're in high school.

As a bonus when you take the test, you'll get *Exploring Careers: The ASVAB Workbook*. It will help you interpret your ASVAB test results.

The ASVAB includes eight short tests that cover:

- General science

- Arithmetic reasoning

- Word knowledge

- Paragraph comprehension

- Mathematics knowledge

- Electronics information

- Auto and shop information

- Mechanical comprehension

While the U.S. Army, Air Force, Navy, Coast Guard, and Marines use the test to place recruits in a military career field, the Department of Defense, in cooperation with the Department of Education, developed a version for high school students.

Many high schools administer this test as part of their college preparation routine. If the test is not available at your school, talk to your guidance counselor to arrange a test date.

Researching Occupations

Do some research. Talk to your parents, friends, teachers, guidance counselors, and individuals in occupations that interest you. Search the internet for career websites and job descriptions. Consider these items:

Job Outlook

How competitive will the job market be in the future? What are your chances for getting a job in the fields you're interested in?

Get the facts at the U.S. Department of Labor website, which publishes 10-year projections for U.S. workers in its *Occupational Outlook Handbook*.

Starting Salary And Job Growth

Is how much you make right away important to you? Or are you willing to make less in the beginning, but with the potential to make more down the road? Learn about job growth possibilities by checking out the Department of Labor's Bureau of Labor Statistics. Its website lists:

- The 10 fastest growing occupations

- The 10 occupations with the largest job growth

- The 10 industries with the fastest wage and salary employment growth

Remember, these are projections. Keep them in mind, but money should not be the only thing to consider. It's important to like your job.

Education And Training Requirements

In your research, you may discover that some jobs require specific job skills. You may gain these skills in your high school classes. But if the skill is very specialized—specific computer programs, for example—you may find classes at community centers or through private companies.

There's no better way to gain experience and knowledge in your interests than on-the-job training.

- Looking to go into medicine? Volunteer in the lab of a local hospital.

- Want to be a software programmer? Find a summer job at a software company.

Whatever you choose, you'll be able to interact with professionals in your field and learn what they do on a daily basis.

Do the research on the many different occupations out there. Find out how many years of education and experience you'll need, what the best locations are for certain jobs, your projected income, etc.

Armed with this information, you'll be on the right track to find a career that fits you.

Chapter 2

Getting Ready For College

Basic Information For All Students

Are you thinking about going to college? Whether the decision has already been made or is still years away, please browse through our Planner Timeline, which we have designed to help you prepare for college. Please note that although you can complete most of the necessary tasks in your junior or senior years of high school, you should start planning as early as the eighth grade. Not only will this improve your chances of getting into the college of your choice, but it will also make applying much easier.

Below are some general steps you should follow while preparing for college.

Prepare For College Early

Vague advice, perhaps, but invaluable. Preparing early for your college education will help you position yourself to get into the college you want. We recommend that you start as early as the eighth grade, and start using the Student Planner in your freshman year of high school. Even if you are in your junior or senior year, however, you can still choose, apply, and get accepted to the college best for you, if you plan carefully.

Regardless of the grade you are in now, there are some general notes to remember and rules to follow:

- Pay attention to deadlines and dates.

About This Chapter: Information in this chapter is from "Planner Timeline," Federal Student Aid, U.S. Department of Education, 2010.

- Keep in mind that even though they may not be required for high school graduation, most colleges require at least three, and often prefer four, years of studies in math, English, science, and social studies.

- In addition to this, most colleges require at least two years of the same foreign language.

- Your grades are important but the difficulty of your coursework can also be a significant factor in a college's decision to admit you. In general, most colleges prefer students with average grades in tougher courses than students who opt for an easy A.

- You should also note that most high schools grade Advanced Placement (AP) courses on a five-point scale rather than the four-point scale used for other classes, essentially giving students a bonus point for tackling the extra difficulty (e.g., a B in an AP course is worth as much as an A in a non-AP course).

- College admission officers will pay the closest attention to your grade-point average (GPA), class rank, college credit, AP courses, and scores on standardized tests.

- Participation in extracurricular activities is also a good idea in high school. Activities that require time and effort outside the classroom (such as speech and debate, band, communications, and drama) indicate a willingness to cooperate with others and put forth the effort needed to succeed.

- Computer science courses or courses that require students to use computers in research and project preparation can also aid your future college performance.

Find The College That's Right For You

The U.S. Department of Education provides a free way to investigate colleges on the web available at http://studentaid2.ed.gov/gotocollege/collegefinder. On this website there are three ways to select and search for a college:

- **By Name**
- **By Preference:** Use the College Finder to identify campuses using preferences such as college type, location, size, cost, campus life, academics, etc.
- **By Wizard:** Using the College Matching Wizard allows you to explore the advantages/disadvantages and definitions of various factors affecting the college selection process.

Get information online about the school of your choice. Some schools have online admission applications for you to complete.

Take The Necessary Assessment Tests

Most colleges in the United States require that students submit scores from standardized tests as part of their application packages. The most commonly accepted tests are the American College Testing Program (ACT) Tests, Scholastic Aptitude Test (SAT) Reasoning, and SAT Subject Tests. For information about which you should take, talk to your high school counselor or to the admissions office(s) at the college(s) to which you will apply.

The ACT Tests: For detailed information about the ACT Tests, registering for these tests, how to prepare for the tests, what to take with you on test day, and understanding your scores, visit www.act.org.

The SAT Tests: For information on or to register for any of the tests described below, visit www.collegeboard.org.

- **SAT Reasoning (Formerly SAT I):** The SAT Reasoning Test is a three-hour test that measures a student's ability rather than knowledge. It contains three sections: writing, critical reading, and math. Most of the questions are multiple choice.

- **SAT Subject Tests (Formerly SAT II):** The SAT Subject Tests measure knowledge in specific subjects within five general categories: English, mathematics, history, science, and languages. The specific subjects range from English literature to biology to Modern Hebrew. SAT Subject Tests are primarily multiple choice, and each lasts one hour.

Other Common Tests

For information and registration for any of the tests described below, visit www.college board.org.

> **It's A Fact!**
> Both the SAT Reasoning and SAT Subject Tests are offered several times a year at locations across the country.

The Preliminary SAT/National Merit Scholarship Qualifying Test: Commonly known as the PSAT, this test is usually taken in the student's junior year. It's a good way to practice for the SAT tests, and it serves as a qualifying exam for the National Merit Scholarship Corporation's scholarship programs. The PSAT measures skills in verbal reasoning, critical reading, mathematics problem solving, and writing.

Advanced Placement (AP) Program: These two- to three-hour exams are usually taken after the student completes an AP course in the relevant subject. (Speak to your high school counselor about taking AP classes.) A good grade on an AP exam can qualify the student for college credit and/or "advanced placement" in that subject in college. For example, if a student scores well on the AP English Literature exam, he or she might not have to take the college's required freshman-level English course. Most AP tests are at least partly made up of essay questions; some include multiple-choice questions. The tests are offered each spring; each test is offered once, with a makeup day a few weeks later.

The College-Level Examination Program® (CLEP): This test offers students the opportunity to gain college credit by taking an exam. Usually, a student takes the tests at the college where he or she is already enrolled. Not all colleges offer credit based on CLEP tests, and different colleges offer different amounts of credit for the same test, so do your research before committing to an exam. Your best source of information is your college.

Learn More About The Colleges Of Your Choice

You can visit college campuses virtually at http://studentaid2.ed.gov/gotocollege/campustour. Once you have narrowed your selection, arrange to visit the campuses in person. This is an important step in the decision process, so whenever possible, plan a visit to the schools.

Discover Your Payment Options

You should look into scholarships, student loans, and other financial aid options before you apply to a particular college or university. The federal government has $80 billion available for funding education beyond high school.

> **Quick Tip**
>
> You can apply online at http://studentaid2.ed.gov/apply. If you currently are a high school senior, you should complete the FAFSA as early as possible, but no earlier than January 1st.

Grade 8

In addition to your research online, you should ask counselors, teachers, parents, and friends any other questions you have about college. Talk to your guidance counselor (or teachers, if you don't have access to a guidance counselor) about the following:

- Going to a four-year college or university
- Courses to start taking in grade nine
- The importance colleges and universities place on grades, and what year in school grades will start to be considered in the admissions process
- College preparatory classes you should be taking in high school (grades 9 through 12)
- Academic enrichment programs (including summer and weekend programs) available through your school or local colleges

> **It's A Fact!**
>
> Remember, you will have more options if you start planning now and keep your grades up. Also, think about pursuing extracurricular activities (such as sports, performing arts, volunteer work, or other activities that interest you).

Grade 9/Freshman Year

Talk to your guidance counselor (or teachers, if you don't have access to a guidance counselor) about the following:

- Attending a four-year college or university
- Establishing your college preparatory classes: Your schedule should consist of at least four college preparatory classes per year, including: four years of English; three years of math (through Algebra II or trigonometry); two years of foreign language; two years of natural science; two years of history/social studies; one year of art; and one year of electives.

- Keeping track of your courses and grades

- Enrolling in algebra or geometry classes and a foreign language for both semesters (most colleges have math and foreign language requirements)

Create a file of the following documents and notes:

- Copies of report cards

- List of awards and honors

- List of school and community activities in which you are involved, including both paid and volunteer work, and descriptions of what you do

- Start thinking about the colleges you want to attend. Once you have narrowed down the list of colleges and universities in which you are interested, start touring the campuses.

Grade 10/Sophomore Year

Talk to your guidance counselor (or teachers, if you don't have access to a guidance counselor) about the following:

- Reviewing the high school curriculum needed to satisfy the requirements of the colleges you are interested in attending

- Finding out about Advanced Placement courses: what courses are available; whether or not you are eligible for the classes that you want to take; how to enroll in them for your junior year

You should also do the following:

- Update your file, or start one if you haven't already.

- Continue extracurricular activities, as admissions officers look at students' extracurricular activities when considering them for admission.

- Continue participation in academic enrichment programs, summer workshops, and camps with specialty focuses such as music, arts, and science.

- Take the PSAT in October of your sophomore year. The scores will not count for National Merit Scholar consideration in your sophomore year, but it is valuable practice for when you take the P SAT again in your junior year (when the scores will count), as well as for the SAT I exam which you should also be taking in your junior year. You will receive your PSAT results in December.

- Register, in April, for the SAT II for any subjects you will be completing before June.

- Take the SAT II in June.

Grade 11/Junior Year

Fall Semester

Maintaining your grades during your junior year is especially important. You should be doing at least two hours of homework each night and participating in study groups. Using a computer can be a great tool for organizing your activities and achieving the grades you want.

Talk to your guidance counselor (or teachers, if you don't have access to a guidance counselor) about the following:

- Availability of and enrollment in Advanced Placement classes.

- Schedules for the PSAT, SAT Reasoning Test and SAT Subject Test, ACT, and AP exams.

- Discuss why you should take these exams and how they could benefit you.

- Determine which exams you will take. (You can always change your mind.)

- Sign up and prepare for the exams you've decided to take.

- Ask for a preview of your academic record and profile, determine what gaps or weaknesses there are, and get suggestions on how to strengthen your candidacy for the schools in which you are interested.

- Determine what it takes to gain admission to the college(s) of your choice, in addition to GPA and test score requirements.

August: Obtain schedules and forms for the SAT Reasoning Test, SAT Subject Test, ACT, and AP exams.

September: Register for the PSAT exam offered in October.

It's A Fact!

Remember that when you take the PSAT in your junior year, the scores will count towards the National Achievement Program (and it is good practice for the SAT Reasoning Test).

October: Take the PSAT. Narrow your list of colleges to include a few colleges with requirements at your current GPA, a few with requirements above your current GPA, and at least one with requirements below your GPA. Your list should contain approximately 8–12 schools you are seriously considering. Start researching your financial aid options as well.

Begin scheduling interviews with admissions counselors. If possible, schedule tours of the school grounds on the same days. You and your parent(s) may want to visit the colleges and universities during spring break and summer vacation, so that you do not have to miss school. Some high schools consider a campus visit an excused absence, however, so if need be, you may be able to schedule interviews and visits during the school year, without incurring any penalties.

November: Review your PSAT results with your counselor, in order to identify your strengths and to determine the areas that you may need to improve upon.

December: You will receive your scores from the October PSAT. Depending on the results, you may want to consider signing up for an SAT preparatory course. Many high schools offer short-term preparatory classes or seminars on the various exams, which tell the students what to expect and can actually help to boost their scores.

Spring Semester

January: Take campus tours online or in person to further narrow your list of colleges to match your personality, GPA, and test scores.

February: Register for the March SAT and/or the April ACT tests. Find out from each college the deadlines for applying for admission and which tests to take. Make sure your test dates give colleges ample time to receive test scores. It is a good idea to take the SAT and/or ACT in the spring to allow you time to review your results and retake the exams in the fall of your senior year, if necessary.

March: Take the March SAT Reasoning Test. If you are interested in taking any AP exam(s), you should sign up for the exam(s) at this time. If your school does not offer the AP exams, check with your guidance counselor to determine schools in the area that do administer the exam(s), as well as the dates and times that the exam(s) you are taking will be offered. Scoring well on the AP exam can sometimes earn you college credit.

April: Take the April ACT test. Talk to teachers about writing letters of recommendation for you.

May: Take the SAT Reasoning Test, the SAT Subject Test, and the AP exams.

Quick Tip

When talking to teachers about writing letters of recommendation for you, think about what you would like included in these letters (how you would like to be presented) and politely ask your teachers if they can accommodate you.

June: Take the SAT Reasoning Test, the SAT Subject Test, and the ACT tests. Add any new report cards, test scores, honors, or awards to your file. Visit colleges. Call ahead for appointments with the financial aid, admissions, and academic advisors at the college(s) in which you are most interested. During your visits, talk to professors, sit in on classes, spend a night in the dorms, and speak to students about the college(s). Doing these things will allow you to gather the most information about the college and the atmosphere in which you would be living, should you choose to attend. Some colleges have preview programs that allow you to do all of these; find out which of the schools that you will be visiting offer these programs and take advantage of them.

Quick Tip

If you go on interviews or visits, don't forget to send thank you notes.

Summer Between Junior And Senior Years

- Practice writing online applications, filling out rough drafts of each application, without submitting them. Focus on the essay portions of these applications, deciding how you would like to present yourself. Don't forget to mention your activities outside of school.

- Review your applications, especially the essays. Ask family, friends, and teachers to review your essays for grammar, punctuation, readability, and content.

- Decide if you are going to apply under a particular college's early decision or early action programs. This requires you to submit your applications early, typically between October and December of your senior year, but offers the benefit of receiving the college's decision concerning your admission early, usually before January 1st. If you choose to apply early, you should do so for the college/university that is your first choice in schools to attend. Many early decision programs are legally binding, requiring you to attend the college you are applying to, should they accept you.

- Read your college mail and send reply cards to your schools of interest.

Grade 12/Senior Year

Fall Semester

September: Check your transcripts to make sure you have all the credits you need to get into your college(s) of choice. Find out from the colleges to which you are applying whether or not they need official copies of your transcripts (transcripts sent directly from your high school) sent at the time of application.

- Register for the October/November SAT Reasoning Test, the SAT Subject Test, and the ACT tests.

- Take another look at your list of colleges, and make sure that they still satisfy your requirements. Add and/or remove colleges as necessary.

- Make sure you meet the requirements (including any transcript requirements) for all the colleges to which you want to apply. Double-check the deadlines, and apply.

- Give any recommendation forms to the appropriate teachers or counselors with stamped, college-addressed envelopes, making certain that your portion of the forms are filled out completely and accurately.

- Most early decision and early action applications are due between October 1st and November 1st. Keep this in mind if you intend to take advantage of these options and remember to request that your high school send your official transcripts to the college to which you are applying.

October: Make a final list of schools that interest you and keep a file of deadlines and required admission items for each school.

- Take the SAT and/or ACT tests. Have the official scores sent by the testing agency to the colleges/universities that have made your final list of schools. Register for December or January SAT Reasoning Test and/or SAT Subject Test, if necessary.

- Continue thinking about and beginning writing (if you have not already started) any essays to be included with your applications.

November: Submit your college admission applications.

December: Early decision replies usually arrive between December 1st and December 31st.

- If you haven't already done so, make sure your official test scores are being sent to the colleges to which you are applying.

- Schedule any remaining required interviews.

Spring Semester

January: Submit the Free Application for Federal Student Aid (FAFSA) on or after January 1st. Contact the Financial Aid Office to see if you need to complete additional financial aid forms and check into other financial aid options. In order to be considered for financial aid, you'll need to submit these forms even if you haven't yet been notified of your acceptance to the college(s) to which you applied. For more information about the FAFSA, see Chapter 21.

- Request that your high school send your official transcripts to the colleges to which you are applying.

- Make sure your parents have completed their income tax forms in anticipation of the financial aid applications. If they haven't completed their taxes, providing estimated figures is acceptable.

- Contact the admissions office of the college(s) to which you have applied to make sure that your information has been received, and that they have everything they need from you.

February: If you completed the FAFSA, you should receive your Student Aid Report (SAR) within two to three weeks if you applied via paper. If you applied online, you can receive results via e-mail by the next business day after electronic submission. If corrections are needed, correct and return it to the FAFSA processor promptly.

- Complete your scholarship applications.

- Contact the financial aid office of the college(s) to which you have applied to make sure that your information has been received, and that they have everything they need from you.

March/April: If you haven't received an acceptance letter from the college(s) to which you applied, contact the admissions office.

- Compare your acceptance letters, financial aid, and scholarship offers.

- When you choose a college that has accepted you, you may be required to pay a nonrefundable deposit for freshman tuition (this should ensure your place in the entering freshman class).

May: Take Advanced Placement (AP) exams for any AP subjects you studied in high school.

- You should make a decision by May 1st as to which college you will be attending and notify the school by mailing your commitment deposit check. Many schools require that your notification letter be postmarked by this date.

- If you were placed on a waiting list for a particular college, and have decided to wait for an opening, contact that college and let them know you are still very interested.

June: Have your school send your final transcripts to the college which you will be attending.

- Contact your college to determine when fees for tuition, room, and board are due and how much they will be.

Summer After Senior Year

- Participate in any summer orientation programs for incoming freshmen.
- Now that you know you will be attending college in the fall, it is a good idea to evaluate whether to get student health insurance in case of any unforeseen emergencies or whether your family's insurance coverage is sufficient.

Chapter 3

Taking College Preparatory Courses

Selecting Your Courses

Recommended Classes For College Success

The academic rigor of your high school courses is an important factor in the college admission process. College admission officers see your high school course schedule as a blueprint of your education. They're looking for a solid foundation of learning that you can build on in college.

To create that foundation, take at least five solid academic classes every semester. Start with the basics and then move on to advanced courses. Challenging yourself is part of what makes school fun; but you need a firm grasp of the fundamentals before going on to more advanced work.

The following subjects and classes are standard fare for success in high school and beyond, whether you plan to attend a four-year or two-year college.

English (Language Arts): Take English every year. Traditional courses, such as American and English literature, help you improve your writing skills, reading comprehension, and vocabulary.

About This Chapter: Information in this chapter is from "Selecting Your Courses," http://www.collegeboard.com/student/plan/high-school/33.html. Copyright © 2011 The College Board. Reproduced with permission. The chapter also includes "Choose AP," http://www.collegeboard.com/student/testing/ap/about.html. Copyright © 2011 The College Board. Reproduced with permission. The chapter ends with material from "Innovations in Education: Connecting Students to Advanced Courses Online," a publication of the U.S. Department of Education, 2009.

Math: You need algebra and geometry to succeed on college entrance exams and in college math classes—and in many careers. Take them early on. That way, you'll be able to enroll in advanced science and math in high school, and show colleges you're ready for higher-level work.

Most colleges look for students who have taken three years of math in high school. The more competitive ones require or recommend four years. Each school has its own program, but some of the courses typically offered are:

- Algebra I
- Geometry
- Calculus
- Algebra II
- Trigonometry

Science: Science teaches you to think analytically and apply theories to reality. Colleges want to see that you've taken at least three years of laboratory science classes. A good combination includes two semesters of each of the following sciences:

- Biology
- Earth/space science
- Chemistry or physics

More competitive schools expect you to take four years of lab science courses. You can add two semesters in one of the following subjects:

- Chemistry or physics (the science you didn't already study)
- Advanced chemistry
- Advanced biology
- Advanced physics

Social Studies: You can better understand local and world events that are happening now by studying the culture and history that has shaped them. Here is a suggested course plan:

- U.S. history (two semesters)
- U.S. government (one semester)
- World history or geography (one semester)
- One additional semester in the above or other areas

Foreign Languages: Solid foreign language study shows colleges you're willing to stretch beyond the basics. Many colleges require at least two years of study in the same foreign language, and some prefer more.

The Arts: Research indicates that students who participate in the arts often do better in school and on standardized tests. The arts help you recognize patterns, discern differences and similarities, and exercise your mind in unique ways, often outside a traditional classroom setting.

It's A Fact!

Many colleges require or recommend one or two semesters in the arts. Good choices include studio art, dance, music, and drama.

Source: From "Selecting Your Courses," http://www.collegeboard.com/student/plan/high-school/33.html. Copyright © 2011 The College Board. Reproduced with permission.

Advanced Placement Program® (AP®): To be sure you are ready to take on college-level work, enroll in the most challenging courses you can in high school, such as honors or AP courses. Research consistently shows that students who score a three or higher on an AP Exam typically experience greater academic success and college graduation rates than students who don't take AP.

Success in AP can also help you in other ways. AP helps you stand out in the admission process and offers the opportunity to learn from some of the most inspiring teachers in the world.

Quick Tip

If you have concerns about your class schedule or progress in school, set up a meeting with your school counselor, teacher, or adviser. There are many resources to help you with this process, and with achieving your personal, college, and career goals.

Source: From "Selecting Your Courses," http://www.collegeboard.com/student/plan/high-school/33.html. Copyright © 2011 The College Board. Reproduced with permission.

Choose AP

Are you ready for a unique learning experience that will help you succeed in college? Through AP's college-level courses and exams, you can earn college credit and advanced placement, stand out in the admission process, and learn from some of the most skilled, dedicated, and inspiring teachers in the world.

A Different Kind Of Class

From the moment you enter an AP classroom, you'll notice the difference—in the teacher's approach to the subject, in the attitude of your classmates, in the way you start to think. In AP classrooms, the focus is not on memorizing facts and figures. Instead you'll engage in intense discussions, solve problems collaboratively, and learn to write clearly and persuasively.

Find Your Passion

With 34 AP courses to choose from, including Chinese Language and Culture, Environmental Science, and Psychology, you'll be able to explore your interests and discover new passions. In AP classes, you'll study fascinating topics and ideas that just might become the foundation of your future college major or career.

Prepare To Succeed In College

AP courses can help you acquire the skills and habits you'll need to be successful in college. You'll improve your writing skills, sharpen your problem-solving abilities, and develop time management skills, discipline, and study habits.

Earn College Credit And Placement

More than 90 percent of four-year colleges in the United States and colleges in more than 60 other countries give students credit, advanced placement, or both on the basis of AP Exam scores. By entering college with AP credits, you'll have the time to move into upper level courses, pursue a double-major, or study abroad.

Enrollment

Once you've decided to take the AP challenge it's easy to enroll. Talk to an AP teacher or the AP Coordinator at your school about the course you want to take. Discuss the course's workload and any preparation you might need.

Innovations In Education

Dual-Enrollment Courses

Dual-enrollment courses, also known as dual-credit courses, give students the opportunity to earn college credit while still in high school. In developing these courses, providers work with a local college or university to ensure that the courses meet that institution's requirements for students to receive college credit. In some cases, students may choose to take these courses for high school credit only, but those seeking college credit are given additional work (e.g., more writing-intensive assignments) and their performance is evaluated against higher standards (e.g., dual-credit students may be expected to use a greater number of resources or references in a research project). For example, Colorado Online Learning (COL), based in Lakewood, Colorado, offers a dual-enrollment option for several of its existing courses. Based on conversations with faculty from Colorado colleges and universities, the program developed an additional set of assignments (and guidelines for the instructor) for those students who want to earn college credit. The course rigor and grading rubric are preapproved by the credit-granting university or college. Should a dual-enrollment student later apply for admission to a different institution than the one that granted the credits, the second institution can accept the credits at its discretion.

Honors Courses

Honors courses are similar to dual-enrollment courses in that they require students to complete assignments of greater difficulty and often at a faster pace than in regular high school courses. Similarly, they require instructors to evaluate students' work against higher standards. Unlike dual-credit courses, however, completion of an honors course does not result in college credit. Instead, students typically receive additional grade points for passing honors courses, and honors courses are considered to strengthen a student's transcript for college application purposes.

International Baccalaureate (IB) Courses

IB courses are offered as part of the International Baccalaureate Diploma Programme, a rigorous two-year curriculum (geared primarily to students aged 16 to 19) that leads to a qualification (i.e., degree) that is widely recognized internationally. The Diploma Programme—operated by the IB, a nonprofit education foundation—prepares students for a university education, with a specific focus on helping them develop the ability to communicate with and understand people from other countries and cultures.

While the IB program itself is well established internationally, it is not yet as well known or as widely used in the United States. as the AP program. But when several American-based international schools that are members of the Maynard, Massachusetts-based Virtual High School (VHS) expressed an interest in an online IB economics course, VHS picked up on it. In 2004, VHS became the first online course provider to pilot an online IB course, in economics. During the two-year pilot phase (i.e., 2004–06), the course was offered entirely online to 11 students at schools in the United States, Brazil, and Ecuador. The primary goal was to find out whether students could successfully complete an IB course online. Because IB courses are designed to be extremely hands-on and interactive, with emphasis on inquiry, communication, and collaboration, the challenge of delivering them online is to create this same type of experience in a virtual classroom. As it turned out, all 11 students passed the IB economics examination. Promising findings from evaluation surveys of participating students and school leaders resulted in expansion of the pilot, which, for the 2007–08 and 2008–09 school years, included additional offerings. IB also is considering expanding its online presence by partnering with additional providers, such as Florida Virtual School (FLVS).

Chapter 4

Colleges Care About Your Extracurricular Activities

Extracurricular Activities

Life Outside The Classroom

Sure, life in school is pretty interesting. You've got algebraic equations, Bunsen burners, and vocabulary lists. But chances are you've got commitments outside school, too. Maybe you play on a sports team, perform in a band, do volunteer work, or hold a part-time job.

Colleges Care

The good news is that colleges pay attention to your life both inside and outside the classroom. Yes, your academics come first, but your activities reveal a great deal about you. In addition to demonstrating your interests, they can show that you are able to:

- Make a meaningful contribution to something.
- Manage your time and priorities.
- Maintain a long-term commitment.

Maintaining A Balance

Colleges are not necessarily interested in students who do everything. "We're looking for a commitment to and a passion for an activity outside of the academic setting—we're looking for depth rather than breadth," explains Nanci Tessier, a college admission director.

About This Chapter: Information in this chapter is from "Extracurricular Activities," http://www.collegeboard.com/student/plan/high-school/113.html. Copyright © 2011 The College Board. Reproduced with permission. The chapter also includes "Volunteer Opportunities," http://www.collegeboard.com/student/plan/high-school/7813.html. Copyright © 2011 The College Board. Reproduced with permission. The chapter ends with "How To Find An Internship," http://www.collegeboard.com/student/plan/high-school/8382.html. Copyright © 2011 The College Board. Reproduced with permission.

Getting Involved

Many school, community, and religious organizations give you chances to explore your interests and talents. There are lots of opportunities to try different things.

School Activities

It's easy to find out about activities available at school. The challenge may be figuring out how much to do. Here are some quick tips:

- When you find something you like to do, stick with it.
- Don't worry about being president of the club, or captain of the team. The key is whether you've done something significant—center stage or behind the scenes.
- Give your all to each activity, and, most importantly, to your schoolwork.

Work Experience

Work experience—paid or volunteer, year-round or summer—can help you identify career interests and goals, gain skills, and apply classroom learning to the real world. It's also a great way to earn money for college. Consider arranging for an internship or to shadow some people at their workplaces.

Community Service

You can also gain skills and experience through volunteer work, such as by tutoring elementary school kids or spending time at a local hospital. Some schools even offer academic credit for volunteer work.

Volunteer Opportunities

Helping Others Can Help You

Volunteering has a meaningful, positive effect on your community. It can have many benefits for you, too. It can help you give back to society, break down barriers, and even have fun.

You may have heard that volunteer experience is a plus on your college applications. Keep in mind, though, that colleges are not just looking for a list of organizations and dates. They want to see a complete picture of you, and real examples of your commitment, dedication, and interests.

Reasons To Volunteer

Gain Valuable Life Experiences And Skills: Whether you build houses for the homeless or mail flyers for a local politician, you can experience the real world through hands-on work. You can also use this experience to explore your major or career interests.

Meet Interesting People: Volunteering brings together a variety of people. Both the recipients of your volunteer efforts and your coworkers can be rich sources of insight. For example, maybe you'll learn about the legal profession from a former lawyer you visit at a convalescent center.

Get Academic Credit: Some schools and colleges offer academic credit for volunteer work through service-learning. This teaching method integrates hands-on learning (through service to the community) into the curriculum. To find out if your school offers service-learning, talk to your school counselor.

Send A Signal To Colleges: Colleges pay attention to your life inside and outside the classroom. Your extracurricular activities reveal a great deal about you, such as what your interests are, whether you can manage your priorities and maintain a long-term commitment, what diversity you'd bring to the student body, and how you've made a contribution to something.

Keep in mind, colleges are not interested in seeing you do it all. It's more meaningful to colleges to see your dedication to one or two activities than to see that you've spread yourself thin.

"Community service, which was required at my high school, was a big wow with interviewers. It's even better if you can match your service with your career interest. For example, volunteer at a hospital if you're planning on med school," says Faith, a college student.

How To Get Involved

There are many people, places, and organizations that need volunteers. Here's how to get started:

- Look for programs based in your community. Call and ask if they need help.
- Visit your town's website. It may list volunteer opportunities in your area.
- Contact your local United Way, a local cultural arts association, your student organization, or similar associations that can point you in the right direction.
- Ask libraries, religious organizations, and community colleges if they sponsor any volunteer groups.

Before You Volunteer

It's important that you enjoy the type of service you choose and that you have the time to stick with it. Ask yourself these questions before you get involved with an organization.

- How much time do I have to commit?
- Do I want an ongoing regularly scheduled assignment, a short-term assignment, or a one-time assignment?
- Am I willing to participate in a training course?
- What talents or skills can I offer?
- What would I most like to learn by volunteering?
- What don't I want to do as a volunteer?
- Do I want to work alone or with a group?
- With what kind of people do I want to work—both in terms of who is receiving my services and who my coworkers might be?

How To Find An Internship

Not Just Any Internship—One That Fits Your Needs

Internships come in all shapes and sizes. Some are paid and some are unpaid. Some last for a summer while others continue through the school year. Some internships are local, but others offer employment abroad. For example, you could help set up video shoots for a local film company, or you could work on an organic banana farm in Costa Rica.

Many people think internships are for college students, but opportunities for high school students exist as well. A high school internship can open the doors to the working world, showing you what it's like to have a boss, attend meetings, and meet deadlines. Internships also introduce you to experienced people who can help guide you toward a career.

Real Deal: Environmental Organization: It was the end of his sophomore year in high school, and Sufiyan needed something to do for the summer. He also wanted to earn a little money, so he visited his school career counselor for advice. The counselor suggested an internship with a local nonprofit environmental organization. Sufiyan had never worked in an office before, but he decided to try it. Today, he is still interning with the organization as a senior in high school. He even helped a friend get hired.

Sufiyan assists with clerical work like filing and copying. Sometimes he pitches in on special projects, such as conducting internet research on hotels for a conference. He says what he values most are the people who've taught him new skills. "My supervisors taught me how to behave in an office, how to be organized and speak in a professional manner."

He feels these skills will help him in many areas, such as college and job interviews, even asking a bank for a loan. Sufiyan wants to be a filmmaker, and he says working at an environmental group has helped him appreciate nature and incorporate it into his films.

How To Start Your Search

How do you find the right internship for you? Start by answering these questions:

- What interests you? Do you like photography? Flying? Computers?

- What kind of internship do you seek? Do you want to work during the summer or the school year? Do you need to earn money or could you work for free?

- What do you want out of an internship? If you're interested in the legal field, your search should start with law firms, not banana farms.

Use A Variety Of Resources

Many resources exist for finding internships. Employers often advertise internship positions through schools. Ask your high school counselor or career coordinator about these opportunities. You might also find out about internships through a school club. And don't forget family and friends. You may want to know more about the accounting field, and your friend's accountant mom might welcome your help.

If there's a specific company or organization you'd like to work for, don't be afraid to inquire directly. Even if they've never had an intern, you might be able to convince them they need one by being clear about how you could help.

To cast your net even wider, look for recent internship guidebooks. *Peterson's Internships* lists hundreds of opportunities for high school students. *The Best 109 Internships* and *The Internship*

Bible also list high school positions. More specific guides can help you find internships in the arts or those available to minorities. Many libraries have a career or education center that can help.

The internet also provides a wealth of resources. Helpful sites include:

- www.internshipprograms.com

- www.internabroad.com

- www.idealist.org allows you to search for internships at nonprofits such as environmental groups

- www.volunteerinternational.org lists volunteer opportunities abroad.

Real Deal: Local Newspaper: Kristen wasn't sure she wanted to be a journalist. She liked writing for her high school newspaper, and the field seemed exciting, but she didn't know much about it. To help make up her mind, Kristen landed an internship at the local newspaper through her high school business club. Her job was to help out in the office, but she also convinced the editor to let her do some reporting.

To her surprise, the editor gave her an assignment right away: report on Friday's high school football game. Kristen wasn't really interested in football, so she spent the game interviewing parents of players. When she typed up her story, she realized she didn't even know the final score! That taught her to make sure she got all the facts, and during her junior and senior years, Kristen covered everything from rodeos to a local burglary.

As an intern in the office, she processed subscription checks, wrote classified ads, and worked in the pressroom stuffing advertising inserts into newspapers. She learned every aspect of the newspaper business and decided to major in journalism in college.

Evaluate Opportunities

To make sure you get the most out of your internship, ask lots of questions. Find out exactly what your duties will be, and who will help teach you the skills you want to learn. You can even ask to speak to previous interns about their experiences. All this preparation will ensure the internship you land is right for you.

Sufiyan thinks every student should try interning. "Go outside your boundaries, outside your neighborhood, do something you've never done before," he says. He also recommends building relationships with those who can teach new skills. "Find someone to learn from," says Sufiyan. That way, no matter what you do, your internship will be worthwhile.

Chapter 5

Taking Standardized Tests

Testing Information

Most colleges in the United States require that students submit scores from standardized tests as part of their application packages. The most commonly accepted tests are the American College Testing Program (ACT) Tests and the Scholastic Aptitude Test (SAT) and SAT Subject Tests. For information about which you should take, talk to your high school counselor or to the admissions office(s) at the college(s) to which you will apply.

The ACT Tests

The ACT (No Writing) consists of four multiple-choice tests: English, reading, mathematics, and science reasoning. The ACT Plus Writing includes the four multiple-choice tests and a writing test. These tests are offered several times a year at locations across the country—usually at high schools and colleges.

For detailed information about the tests, including information about preparing to take the tests, what to take with you on test day, and understanding your scores, visit www.act.org.

The SAT Tests

SAT (Formerly SAT I): The SAT Test is a three-hour and 45-minute test that measures a student's ability rather than knowledge. It contains three sections: writing, critical reading, and math. Most of the questions are multiple choice.

About This Chapter: This chapter begins with information from "Testing Information," a publication of the U.S. Department of Education, January 2011. Additional information from Kaplan, Inc. and from Scholarships.com, LLC is cited separately within the chapter.

SAT Subject Tests (Formerly SAT II): The SAT Subject Tests measure knowledge in specific subjects within five general categories: English, mathematics, history, science, and languages. The specific subjects range from English literature to biology to Modern Hebrew. SAT Subject Tests are primarily multiple choice, and each lasts one hour.

It's A Fact!

Both the SAT and SAT Subject Tests are offered several times a year at locations across the country. For detailed information about these tests, including information about preparing to take the test, what to take with you on test day, and understanding your scores, visit www.collegeboard.org.

Source: From "Testing Information," a publication of the U.S. Department of Education, January 2011.

Other Common Tests

The Preliminary SAT/National Merit Scholarship Qualifying Test: This test, commonly known as the PSAT, is usually taken in the student's junior year. It's a good way to practice for the SAT tests, and it serves as a qualifying exam for the National Merit Scholarship Corporation's scholarship programs. The PSAT measures skills in critical reading, mathematics problem solving, and writing.

Advanced Placement (AP) Tests: The two- to three-hour Advanced Placement (AP) Program exams are usually taken after the student completes an AP course in the relevant subject. (Speak to your high school counselor about taking AP classes.) A good grade on an AP exam can qualify the student for college credit and/or advanced placement in that subject in college. For example, if a student scores well on the AP English Literature exam, he or she might not have to take the college's required freshman-level English course. Most AP tests are at least partly made up of essay questions; some include multiple-choice questions. The tests are offered each spring; each test is offered once, with a makeup day a few weeks later.

Quick Tip

For information and registration for any of the tests described here, visit www.collegeboard.org.

Source: From "Testing Information," a publication of the U.S. Department of Education, January 2011.

The College-Level Examination Program (CLEP): This program offers students the opportunity to gain college credit by taking an exam. Usually, a student takes the tests at the college where he or she is already enrolled. Not all colleges offer credit based on CLEP tests, and different colleges offer different amounts of credit for the same test, so do your research before committing to an exam. Your best source of information is your college.

Deciding Which Test To Take: The ACT Or The SAT

Source for information under this heading: "Should You Take the ACT or the SAT?" © Kaplan, Inc. All rights reserved. Reprinted with permission.

Both the ACT and the SAT are nationally administered standardized tests that help colleges evaluate candidates. All schools accept either test interchangeably. So as you begin to think about college and creating the best application package possible, your admissions plan should begin with the question, "Which test should I take?"

Differences Between The ACT And SAT

Table 5.1. Test Structure And Format

	ACT	SAT
Length	3 hours, 25 min (with Writing Test)	3 hours, 45 minutes
Structure	4 Sections (English, Math, Reading, Science) plus an optional Writing Test	10 Sections (3 Critical Reading, 3 Math, 3 Writing, and 1 Experimental, which is unscored)

Table 5.2. Scoring

	ACT	SAT
Score	Composite of 1–36 based on average scores from the four test sections; four scores of 1–36 for each test; Optional Writing Test score of 0–12 (not included in the overall score)	Total score range of 600–2400 based on adding scores from three subjects; three scores of 200–800 for each subject; Score of 0–12 for the Essay
Wrong Answer Penalty	No penalty for wrong answers	¼ point subtracted from your raw score for each wrong answer (except for Math Grid-Ins)
Sending Score History	You decide which score is sent	You decide which score is sent; Some colleges require you to send all scores, check with the college to be sure

Table 5.3. Content

	ACT	SAT
Reading	Reading Comprehension	Reading Comprehension; Sentence Completions
Math	Arithmetic; Algebra; Geometry; Algebra II; Trigonometry	Arithmetic; Algebra; Geometry; Algebra II
Science	Analysis; Interpretation; Evaluation; Basic Content; Problem Solving	Not applicable
Essay	Optional Final Section; 30 Minutes; Not Included in Composite Score; Topic of importance to high school students	First Section; 25 Minutes; Factored into overall score; More abstract topic

Tips For Taking Standardized Tests

Source for the information under this heading: The chapter ends with "Tips for Taking Standardized Tests," © Scholarships.com, LLC. Reprinted with permission.

Taking standardized tests can be very stressful. Following these standardized test taking tips can reduce your anxiety and enhance your performance.

Before The Test

- Spend time working through standardized test practice items for several weeks before your scheduled test date.

- Find out if there is a score penalty for wrong answers so that you will know whether you should guess at answers you don't know.

- Get a good night's sleep the evening before the test.

- Eat a healthy, protein-rich breakfast the morning of your test.

- Arrive at the testing facility a few minutes early.

- Relax your mind before the test begins.

During The Test

- Read the instructions carefully.

- Read each question carefully, paying attention to details.

- Pay attention to time passing in relation to the time allotment.

- Don't get distracted by other testers in the room.

- If you come across a question that is difficult, don't spend all of your time on it. Move on and come back to it at the end.

- Don't second guess yourself by changing your first answers unless you are 100 percent certain.

- Don't fall into the trap of looking for patterns in the answers. There really can be three (or more) "C" answers in a row.

- When you are finished, look closely to make sure that you haven't overlooked any questions.

Part Two
Your Role As An Education Consumer

Chapter 6

The Value Of Education

Education Pays

Students who attend institutions of higher education obtain a wide range of personal, financial, and other lifelong benefits; likewise, taxpayers and society as a whole derive a multitude of direct and indirect benefits when citizens have access to postsecondary education. Accordingly, uneven rates of participation in higher education across different segments of U.S. society should be a matter of urgent concern not only to the individuals directly affected, but also to public policymakers at the federal, state, and local levels.

This report presents detailed evidence of the private and public benefits of higher education. It also sheds light on the distribution of these benefits by examining both the increases and the persistent disparities in college participation and completion.

This Executive Summary highlights some of the key ideas in the report.

The Benefits Of Higher Education

Individuals with higher levels of education earn more and are more likely than others to be employed.

- Median earnings of bachelor's degree recipients working full time year-round in 2008 were $55,700, $21,900 more than median earnings of high school graduates.

- Individuals with some college but no degree earned 17% more than high school graduates working full time year-round. Their median after-tax earnings were 16% higher.

About This Chapter: Information in this chapter is from "Education Pays 2010 Executive Report," http://trends .collegeboard.org/education_pays/about/index. Copyright © 2011 The College Board. Reproduced with permission. Text under the headings "Talking To Your Family: Make Your Case" and "Talking To Your Family: Point Out Resources" is from "Why Go: Lift Your Family," U.S. Department of Education, 2010.

- For young adults between the ages of 20 and 24, the unemployment rate in the fourth quarter of 2009 for high school graduates was 2.6 times as high as that for college graduates.

It's A Fact!

Of the 20 fastest-growing occupations, more than half require an associate's degree or higher.

Source: From "Why Go: Boost Your Earnings," a publication of the U.S. Department of Education, 2010.

The financial return associated with additional years of schooling beyond high school and the gaps in earnings by education level have increased over time.

- In 2008, median earnings for women ages 25 to 34 with a bachelor's degree or higher were 79% higher than median earnings for women with a high school diploma. The earnings premium for men was 74%. These earnings differentials were 60% and 54%, respectively, a decade earlier.

- The median hourly wage gain attributable to the first year of college, adjusted for race, gender, and work experience, increased from an estimated 8% in 1973 to about 10% in 1989, and 11% in 2007.

Federal, state, and local governments enjoy increased tax revenues from college graduates and spend less on income support programs for them, providing a direct financial return from investments in post-secondary education.

- In 2008, 8% of high school graduates ages 25 and older lived in households that relied on the Food Stamp Program, compared to just over 1% of those with at least a bachelor's degree. The pattern was similar for the National School Lunch Program.

- Spending on social support programs and incarceration costs are much lower for college graduates than for high school graduates. Estimated lifetime savings range from $32,600 for white women to $108,700 for black men. The gains in tax revenues produced by a more educated population are even greater.

College-educated adults are more likely than others to receive health insurance and pension benefits from their employers and be satisfied with their jobs.

- In 2008, about 58% of college graduates and individuals with some college education or an associate degree reported being very satisfied with their jobs, while 50% of high school graduates and 40% of individuals without a high school diploma reported being very satisfied.

It's A Fact!

Substantial evidence indicates that the associations described in the *Education Pays* report are the result of increased educational attainment, not just of individual characteristics.

Source: From "Education Pays 2010 Executive Report," http://trends.collegeboard.org/education_pays/about/index. Copyright © 2011 The College Board. Reproduced with permission.

Adults with higher levels of education are more active citizens than others.

- Both the percentage of people who donate their time to organizations and the number of hours people spend in volunteer activities are higher among individuals with higher levels of education.

College education leads to healthier lifestyles, reducing health care costs for individuals and for society.

- Within each age group, college-educated adults are less likely than others to be obese. In addition, children living in households with more educated parents are less likely than other children to be obese.

- During the decade from 1998 to 2008, the smoking rate declined from 14% to 9% among adults with at least a bachelor's degree, while the rate for high school graduates declined from 29% to 27%.

College-educated parents engage in more educational activities with their children, who are better prepared for school than other children.

- Among parents whose highest degree was a bachelor's degree, 68% read to their children daily in 2007. This compares to 57% of parents with an associate degree, 47% of parents with some college but no degree, 41% of high school graduates, and 26% of parents who did not complete high school.

It's A Fact!

There's more to a job than a paycheck. Jobs for college graduates typically offer more and better benefits than jobs requiring just a high school diploma. These can include health insurance and retirement plans you may not get at lower-skill jobs.

Source: From "Why Go: Boost Your Earnings," a publication of the U.S. Department of Education, 2010.

Participation And Success In Higher Education

Although college enrollment rates continue to rise, large gaps persist across demographic groups.

- The college enrollment rate of high school graduates from the lowest family-income quintile increased from 51% in 1998 to 55% in 2008. The rate for middle-income students declined from 63% to 61%, while 79% of the highest-income high school graduates enrolled in college in 1998 and 80% enrolled in 2008.

- From 1998 to 2004, the gap between the proportions of white and black high school graduates who enrolled in college within a year fluctuated between eight and 10 percentage points. By 2008, the gap had grown to about 14 percentage points.

- From 2000 to 2004, the gap between the proportions of white and Hispanic high school graduates who enrolled in college within a year narrowed from 19 to 10 percentage points. By 2008, the gap had declined to eight percentage points.

Enrollment patterns differ across income groups, and graduation rates vary by institution type.

- About 40% of dependent undergraduate students from families with incomes below $40,000 enrolled in public two-year colleges in 2007–08, and 8% enrolled in for-profit institutions. In contrast, 17% of undergraduate students from families with incomes of $120,000 or higher enrolled in public two-year colleges, and 1% attended for-profit institutions.

- Of first-time full-time students who began studying for a bachelor's degree at a four-year institution in 2002, 57% earned this degree within six years from the institution at which they began their studies. Completion rates averaged 65% at private not-for-profit, 55% at public four year, and 22% at private for-profit institutions.

College completion rates differ considerably by family income, parental education level, and type of institution attended.

- The proportion of adults in the United States between the ages of 25 and 34 with a four-year college degree held steady at 24% in the 1980s, but grew from 29% in 2000 to 32% in 2009.

Talking To Your Family: Make Your Case

Are you afraid your family might have concerns when you tell them you want to continue your education? That's totally natural. Here are some ideas to help make talking to them easier:

- **Do your research.** Explain how college or other postsecondary education will benefit you and possibly the whole family. If you have already started looking into schools or financial aid, share what you've learned.

- **Plan your pitch.** Don't just go in cold. Make an outline so you don't forget anything you want to say.

- **Anticipate their concerns.** Just because they have concerns doesn't mean you can't convince them. To do that, be ready to respond to their objections calmly and politely with facts that ease their fears.

- **Practice first.** If you're feeling really nervous, rehearse what you are going to say ahead of time. It can really help you feel more confident. You can even role-play. Ask a friend to play the part of the family member you will be talking to.

- **Promise to do your part.** Pledge to hold up your end of the bargain. Promise them that their efforts to help you will be worth it. That means you'll apply yourself in school. You'll share with them all information about applications, tests, and deadlines. You'll research schools. You'll participate in activities that will enhance your college resume. Then keep your word and follow through.

- **Stay positive.** If you're lucky, things will go great and your family will be on board immediately. But if they don't see things your way, hang in there. They may come around eventually.

- **Prepare to be surprised.** They may not react negatively at all. They may be thrilled and offer more help than you ever expected. The only way to find out is to tell them.

Talking To Your Family: Point Out Resources

If your family supports your college dreams, but they don't know what they can do, you can help them help you:

- **Take them to school.** Bring your parents to meet your high school counselor. Explain to your counselor that your family needs help helping you go to college. Together, you can create a plan outlining the steps everyone should take.

- **Visit the library.** Your local public library will have lots of good information for you and your family. Ask a librarian if you need help finding it.

- **Lead them online.** The internet is a great source of college information.

Even after you explain the benefits, your family may not understand why you want to continue your education. Maybe they don't believe it's possible financially. Maybe they don't understand how important it is to you. Don't give up hope. Try these tips:

- **Find mentors.** Tell your high school counselor and your favorite teachers that you want to continue your education. Ask for their guidance, help, and support. Having one or two key people on your side can make all the difference.

- **Enlist an advocate.** Find an adult to talk to your family on your behalf. It could be someone from your place of worship. It could be a family friend. It could be your high school mentor. Hearing it from another adult they trust can help your family understand how important going is, for all of you.

- **Be committed.** Form a plan to go as soon as possible, and stick to it. When your family sees how determined you are, they may come around. If not, at least you will have started on the path to get there yourself.

- **Think long term.** If you don't go to college with your family's support, you can still go. If you can't go right after high school, you can still go later. Many people do. Stay focused and you can do it.

Chapter 7

Understanding College Costs

The Cost Of College

Don't let the cost stop you from pursuing a higher education.

How Much Is College Going To Cost Me?

After spending some time in higher education, you've probably discovered a few things. Maybe your education is costing more than you thought it would, or your financial situation has changed. Maybe you thought you had enough to get through four years and you ran out at the end of three.

Whatever the reason, students in college often discover that they need financial aid when they didn't expect to. There's no perfect formula for figuring out how much money college will cost and whether you'll have enough. The costs for things like tuition and books change every semester and depend on the college or university you select.

So, How Much Does A College Education Cost?

That's a tough question—The answer depends on many different factors.

There's no college-cost formula that you can plug numbers into. Costs may change every semester and depend on the college or university you select.

About This Chapter: This chapter begins with "The Cost of College," © 2011 Texas Guaranteed Student Loan Corporation. Reprinted with permission. For additional information about financing a college education, visit the Adventures in Education website, www.aie.org, a public service of the Texas Guaranteed Student Loan Corporation. "Statistics On Financial Aid" is from "Fast Facts (Financial Aid)," U.S. Department of Education, 2009; and the chapter concludes with"30 Ways to Reduce College Costs," U.S. Department of Education, 2010. Additional information from The College Board is cited separately within the chapter.

It's A Fact!

- In both the public and private nonprofit sectors, the 2010–11 average tuition and fee charges at bachelor's colleges are 27% lower than the average charges at doctoral universities.

- Community college prices in California, where 16% of full-time students in the sector are enrolled, are unusually low. The average price of public two-year colleges outside of California is $3,076.

- About 12% of full-time public four-year college students study out of state, but many states have reciprocity agreements with neighboring states that allow students to pay less than the published prices.

Source: From "Trends in College Pricing," Copyright © 2010 The College Board. Reproduced with permission.

Tuition and fees are usually combined and range from $2,000 a year to more than $20,000. Community colleges usually offer the least expensive tuition costs, but many four-year colleges and universities are also relatively inexpensive, especially for resident or in-state students.

Figure 7.1 provides information about what it costs today for tuition and fees at national institutions.

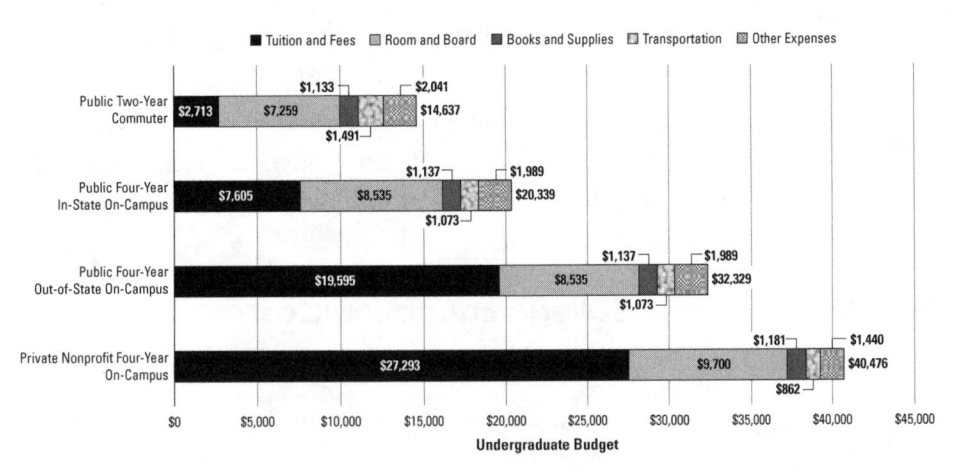

NOTE: Expense categories are based on institutional budgets for students as reported by colleges and universities in the *Annual Survey of Colleges*. They do not necessarily reflect actual student expenditures.

SOURCE: The College Board, *Annual Survey of Colleges*.

Figure 7.1. Average Estimated Undergraduate Budgets, 2010–11, Enrollment-Weighted. (Source: "Trends in College Pricing." Copyright © 2010 The College Board. Reproduced with permission.)

It's A Fact!

- Tuition and fees constitute 67% of the average total budget for full-time students at private nonprofit four-year colleges and universities.
- On average, tuition and fees at public four-year colleges are 2.8 times as high as at public two-year colleges. However, the total budget for a public four-year college student, including housing, food, transportation, books and supplies, and other expenses, is only about 40% higher than the total budget for a public two-year college student.

Source: From "Trends in College Pricing," Copyright © 2010 The College Board. Reproduced with permission.

Other Costs

As you can see, tuition and fees are not the only things factored into the cost of college. You also have to pay for books, supplies, and transportation. And don't forget room and board—the money you spend for a place to live and food to eat. These costs can also vary greatly. Also, whether you live at home, in a small town, in a big city, on campus, or share a place with friends, all help to determine how much you'll pay for room and board.

So, even though there's no exact answer to what it costs to go to college today, it is possible to make a good guess. Figure out what kind of school you want to attend and find out how much it costs to attend. From there, tack on an estimated percentage increase—five percent per year is a good guess.

Remember that even though you can expect the costs to go up by the time you go, the money you have available will probably increase along with it.

College Pays Off In The Long Run

College can be expensive, but this should not stop you from pursuing a higher education.

The money you invest in a college education will pay off in the long run. In fact, recent studies show that over the course of a person's working life, individuals with a bachelor's degree will earn $2.1 million on average—nearly twice as much as workers with only a high school diploma.

Statistics On Financial Aid

Sixty-six percent of all undergraduates received some type of financial aid in 2007–08. For those who received any aid, the total average amount received was $9,100. Fifty-two percent received grants averaging $4,900, and 38% took out an average of $7,100 in student loans.

Seven percent received aid through work-study jobs averaging $2,400 in wages, 2% received an average of $5,400 in veterans' benefits, and 4% of students had parents who took out an average of $10,800 in Parent PLUS loans. Parent PLUS loans are included in total aid but are not included in student loans because they are loans for parents of dependent students.

Forty-seven percent of all undergraduates received federal student aid in 2007–08, the average amount of which was $6,600. Sixteen percent received an average of $2,500 in state-funded grants and 20% received an average of $5,000 in grants funded by the postsecondary institution they attended.

In 2007–08, federal Pell Grants were awarded to 27% of all undergraduates at an average of $2,600, and 34% of all undergraduates took out federal Stafford loans averaging a total of $5,000. Subsidized Stafford loans were received by 30 percent of undergraduates and averaged $3,400, while 22% received an average of $3,200 in unsubsidized Stafford loans.

Thirty Ways To Reduce College Costs

1. Most colleges and universities offer merit or non-need-based scholarships to academically talented students. Students should check with each school in which they're interested for the criteria for merit scholarships.

2. The National Merit Scholarship Program awards scholarships to students based upon academic merit. The awards can be applied to any college or university to meet educational expenses at that school.

3. Many states offer scholarship assistance to academically talented students. Students should obtain the eligibility criteria from their state's education office.

4. Some colleges and universities offer special grants or scholarships to students with particular talents. Music, journalism, and drama are a few categories for which these awards are made.

5. Some students choose to attend a community college for one or two years, and then transfer to a four-year school. Tuition costs are substantially lower at community colleges than at four-year institutions.

6. Some parents may be financially able to purchase a house while their child is in school. If other students rent rooms in the house, the income may offset monthly mortgage payments. Families should make certain, however, that the property they purchase meets all of the requirements of rental property. If you have any questions, consult a tax professional.

7. Commuting is another way for students to reduce college costs. A student living at home can save as much as $6,000 per year.

8. Many schools provide lists of housing opportunities that provide free room and board to students in exchange for a certain number of hours of work each week.

9. Cooperative education programs allow students to alternate between working full time and studying full time. This type of employment program is not based upon financial need, and students can earn as much as $7,000 per year.

10. Another way to reduce college costs is to take fewer credits. Students should find out their school's policy regarding the Advanced Placement Program (APP), the College-Level Examination Program (CLEP), and the Provenience Examination Program (PEP). Under these programs, a student takes an examination in a particular subject and, if the score is high enough, receives college credit.

11. Some colleges give credit for life experiences, thereby reducing the number of credits needed for graduation. Students should check with the college for further information. You can also write to Distance Education and Training Council at 1601 18th Street, NW, Washington, DC 20009, or call (202) 234-5100.

12. Most schools charge one price for a specific number of credits taken in a semester. If academically possible, students should take the maximum number of credits allowed. This strategy reduces the amount of time needed to graduate.

13. In many cases, summer college courses can be taken at a less expensive school and the credits transferred to the full-time school. Students should check with their academic advisor, however, to be certain that any course taken at another school is transferable.

14. Most schools have placement offices that help students find employment, and all schools have personnel offices that hire students to work on campus. These employment programs are not based upon financial need, and working is an excellent way to meet college expenses.

15. Most colleges and universities offer their employees a tuition reduction plan or tuition waiver program. Under this type of arrangement, the school employee and family members can attend classes at a reduced cost or no cost at all. This type of program is based not upon financial need, but rather on college employment.

16. Most colleges and universities sponsor resident advisor programs that offer financial assistance to students in the form of reduced tuition or reduced room and board costs in exchange for work in resident halls.

17. The Reserve Officers Training Corps (ROTC) Scholarship Program pays all tuition, fees, and textbook costs, as well as providing a monthly living stipend. Students should be certain, however, that they want this type of program before signing up because there is a service commitment after graduation.

18. Service Academy Scholarships are offered each year to qualified students to attend the U.S. Military Academy, the U.S. Air Force Academy, the U.S. Naval Academy, the U.S. Merchant Marine Academy, or the U.S. Coast Guard Academy. The scholarships are competitive and are based upon a number of factors, including high school grades, Scholastic Aptitude Test (SAT) or the American College Testing Program (ACT) scores, leadership qualities, and athletic ability. Students receive their undergraduate education at one of the service academies. They pay no tuition or fees, but there is a service commitment after graduation.

19. One of the most obvious ways of reducing college costs is to attend a low-cost school, either public or private. There are many colleges and universities with affordable tuition and generous financial assistance. Students should investigate all schools that meet their academic and financial needs.

20. Some schools offer combined degree programs or three-year programs that allow students to take all of the courses needed for graduation in three years, instead of four, thereby eliminating one year's educational expenses.

21. Partial tuition remission for the children of alumni is a common practice. Parents and students should investigate their alma mater's tuition discount policy for graduates.

22. Some colleges and universities offer special discounts if more than one child from the same family is enrolled.

23. Some schools offer a tuition discount to student government leaders or to the editors of college newspapers or yearbooks.

24. Some colleges offer bargain tuition rates to older students.

25. Some colleges and universities convert nonfederal school loans into nonfederal grants if the student remains in school and graduates.

26. Some schools offer reduced tuition rates to families if the major wage earner is unemployed.

27. Some colleges and universities have special funds set aside for families who do not qualify for federal or state funding.

28. Some private colleges will match the tuition of out-of-state institutions for certain students. Check with your college to determine whether you qualify for this option.

29. Some companies offer tuition assistance to the children of employees. Parents and students should check with the personnel office for information.

30. Students should try to buy used textbooks.

Chapter 8

Traditional College Options

Types Of Schools

Most postsecondary schools can be described as public or private, two year or four year.

Public institutions are state supported. Private for-profit institutions are businesses. Private not-for-profit institutions are independent—for instance, the school might have been established by a church or through local community donations rather than by the state government.

Four-year institutions offer bachelor's degrees, and some offer advanced degrees. Two-year institutions offer associate's degrees. Less-than-two-year institutions offer training and award certificates of completion.

Here's a more detailed description of the kinds of schools you might hear about as you plan for your post-high-school education:

- **College:** A four-year college grants bachelor's degrees (Bachelor of Arts; Bachelor of Science). Some colleges also award master's degrees.

- **University:** A university grants bachelor's and master's degrees, and sometimes includes a professional school such as a law school or medical school. Universities tend to be larger than colleges, focus more on scholarly or scientific research, and might have larger class sizes.

- **Community College:** A public two-year college granting associate's degrees and sometimes certificates in particular technical (career-related) subjects. Many students

About This Chapter: This chapter begins with information from "Types of Schools," a publication of the U.S. Department of Education, 2010. The final section of the chapter is from "Career Colleges and Technical School—Finding Schools That Match Your Interests and Goals," a publication of the U.S. Department of Education, 2010. Other information from Sallie Mae, Inc. is cited separately within the chapter.

start their postsecondary education at a community college and then transfer to a four-year school, either because a community college tends to be more affordable than a four-year college, or because of the open admissions policy at community colleges.

- **Junior College:** Similar to a community college, except that a junior college is usually a private school.

- **Career School, Technical School, Or Vocational/Trade School:** These terms are often used interchangeably. May be public or private, two year or less than two year. Career schools offer courses that are designed to prepare students for specific careers, from welding to cosmetology to medical imaging, etc. The difference between technical schools and trade schools is that technical schools teach the science behind the occupation, while trade schools focus on hands-on application of skills needed to do the job.

Quick Tip

You can use the U.S. Department of Education's search tool at http://nces.ed.gov/college navigator/ to find information about all types of schools.

Source: From "Types of Schools," a publication of the U.S. Department of Education, 2010.

Learning About College Degrees

© 2010 Sallie Mae, Inc. All rights reserved. Reprinted with permission. For additional information, visit www.collegeanswer.com or www.salliemae.com.

A degree is a credential awarded by a college to a student who has completed a required course of study.

When you earn a bachelor's degree, it means you have passed examinations in a broad range of courses and have studied one or two subject areas in greater depth.

A graduate degree is usually earned through two or more years of advanced studies beyond four years of college.

Credentials You Could Earn

- **Associate's Degree:** Awarded upon completion of a specific program; usually requires two years of full-time study and 60–70 credits.

- **Bachelor's Degree (Baccalaureate Degree):** Granted upon completion of a specific program; usually requires four years of full-time study and 126–132 credits.

- **Master's Degree:** Granted upon completion of a specific program; usually requires one to three years and approximately 30–40 credits beyond a bachelor's degree.

- **Doctoral Degree:** Awarded upon completion of a specialized program of study; usually requires three to five years beyond a bachelor's degree.

- **Certificate:** Granted upon completion of a specific program; generally a trade or technical specialty. Usually requires fewer than 18 months of training.

- **Professional License:** Required for some career fields. May or may not require a college degree.

B.A. Versus B.S.

A Bachelor of Arts is the traditional liberal arts degree that exposes you to a wide variety of disciplines—literature, history, social sciences, and laboratory sciences—before requiring you to specialize by selecting a major.

Studying for a B.A. degree doesn't mean you're stuck majoring in the humanities. You can get your B.A. in laboratory sciences like physics, chemistry, and biology. The "Arts" refers to the fact that you have studied a broad range of disciplines, not to the subject that you studied.

The Bachelor of Science degree, on the other hand, leaves little room for courses outside your major. You usually select your major before entering the program or, in some cases, after your first year.

As with the B.A. degree, the name of the B.S. degree refers to how much time you focused on your major area of study, not its content. This means you can get your B.S. in disciplines such as journalism, economics, linguistics, and international relations.

B.A. Versus A.B.

Some four-year colleges and universities give their bachelor's degrees the initials A.B. instead of B.A. They're the same degree. A.B. refers to the original Latin name of the degree: artium baccalaureatus.

This is different from the two-year associate's degree (or an "A.A.") awarded by community colleges.

Community College

For many, community colleges (also known as "junior" or "two-year" colleges) provide a bridge from high school to college, offering courses for transfer toward a bachelor's degree at a four-year school.

Students have different reasons for attending a community college: They often cite low tuition, convenient locations, class schedules, open admissions policies, and comprehensive course offerings.

It's A Fact!

More than 11 million students, about 44% of all undergraduate students, attend community colleges throughout the United States.

Source: From "Community College," © 2010 Sallie Mae, Inc. All rights reserved. Reprinted with permission. For additional information, visit www.collegeanswer.com or www.salliemae.com.

What Community Colleges Can Offer

- Entry-level career training to prepare students for the job market.
- Job re-entry or career-advancement courses for adult students wanting to upgrade their skills.
- Advanced placement classes for ambitious high school students that count for credits toward their college degrees.
- English as a Second Language (ESL) classes for adults with varying levels of education in their native countries who need English-language instruction.
- Courses not offered by local four-year colleges.
- Distance learning programs for students wishing to learn at home to accommodate to their schedules.

Community College Benefits

Is getting your education at a community college right for you? Here are some popular reasons students go.

> ### It's A Fact!
>
> Community colleges offer the ability to continue education at any point in your life, close to home, and at an affordable price.
>
> Source: From "Community College," © 2010 Sallie Mae, Inc. All rights reserved. Reprinted with permission. For additional information, visit www.collegeanswer.com or www.salliemae.com.

Lower Tuition: Costs are often significantly lower than public and private four-year colleges and universities.

Convenient Locations: Many students are able to attend college while living at home, saving on campus-living costs.

Small Class Size: Students receive personal attention from their instructors. The average class at a community college has fewer than 30 students.

Flexible Class Schedules: Classes are offered during the day, evening, and weekends to accommodate work schedules. More than 80% of community college students work part- or full-time jobs and many have family responsibilities.

Transfer To A Four-Year College Or University: Students frequently begin their undergraduate studies at a community college and finish at a four-year school.

Professors Concentrate On Teaching: The instructors focus on teaching students and tend not to be distracted by research and publishing. Professors also have extensive practical experience in the subjects they teach. Full-time community college faculty spend more hours in the classroom than faculty in any other sector of higher education.

Direction For High School Students Still Seeking A Career Path: At a community college, students can explore different subject areas before committing to a program or enrolling in a certificate program in preparation for a specific career, trade, or profession.

Promote Skill Building And Job Advancement: Students can take continuing education courses to meet specific needs and interests for job advancement, job placement, and personal development.

Career Colleges And Technical Schools

Education beyond high school at a career or technical school can lead to a degree, diploma, or certificate in a variety of programs like computer programming, automotive technology, business administration and management, cosmetology, and interior design. Think carefully about what you want to do with your life. Find out as much as you can about the occupations that interest you by using the library and internet, or by talking to your high school guidance counselor.

With so many options, you'll want to find the program that best matches your natural skills, abilities, and interests in order to prepare for a successful career in the field of your choice. Here are some good resources:

- Career Onestop, at http://www.careeronestop.org/CareerTools/CareerTools.asp, provides information on determining your training needs and assessing your skills.

- *Occupational Outlook Handbook*, at http://www.bls.gov/oco/home.htm, describes the education and training needed, earnings, and expected job prospects in a wide range of occupations.

Finding A School

The Department of Education's College Navigator website (http://nces.ed.gov/college navigator/) can help you search for career colleges and technical schools. Only schools accredited by an agency recognized by the U.S. Department of Education are able to enroll students who receive federal student financial aid.

Also, contact the licensing agency in the state where you want to go to school to find information on schools offering the training or program you're interested in. Those agencies can tell you whether the school you are considering is operating legally in the state or if the state requires the school to be licensed or certified in order to offer instruction.

Preparation

Do you need to complete a specific education program to get an entry-level job in the field you are interested in? Do you need to get a license or certificate in order to work in your field of choice?

To get the answers to these questions, check with your high school guidance counselor, people already working in the field, and professional licensure agencies or certification organizations in your state.

Quick Tip

To find the certification requirements, and the certifying agencies for a variety of occupations, take a look at Career OneStop at http://www.acinet.org.

Source: From "Career Colleges and Technical School—Finding Schools That Match Your Interests and Goals," a publication of the U.S. Department of Education, 2010.

Find out if any special license or certification is needed to get a job in the field of your choice. If you need a certificate or license, ask any school you are considering if its graduates are eligible for licensure or certification after they complete its program.

It is also good to ask the school for the number of students who take and pass their licensing exams. Also, ask the school what percentage of its graduates find jobs in their field.

For more information about the skills and training you'll need for a particular job, look at O*NET OnLine (http://www.onetonline.org/), an interactive web-based tool providing information on skills and training required for different occupations.

Quick Tip

Call the employment office or human resources department of some businesses or companies where you might like to work. Ask if they expect employees to have a certificate or license in order to be hired. Also ask if they can recommend a career college or technical school that provides the training required for employment.

Source: From "Career Colleges and Technical School—Finding Schools That Match Your Interests and Goals," a publication of the U.S. Department of Education, 2010.

Chapter 9

Online Education

Is Distance Education For You?

An estimated eight million Americans are currently enrolled in distance learning programs. Because it relies so heavily on internet-related technology, distance learning is frequently called "online learning." The flexible study schedules, self-paced courses, and technological advances are attracting more students now than ever before, and educational opportunities in online education increase all the time. In fact, enrollments in online courses and degree programs are increasing by about 25 percent each year.

If you are interested in enrolling in a distance learning school, you probably have a lot of questions. Choosing the correct school is an important decision, and the well-informed student is the most likely to succeed in distance study.

A great place to start your research on which distance education institution and program best fits your personal needs is to spend some time with the Distance Education and Training Council (DETC)'s user-friendly, information-rich website at www.detc.org.

What are the benefits of distance education?

Distance learning students experience the freedom of studying when and where they choose. This flexibility allows each student to create his own study schedule. Students can accelerate through courses very quickly, or they can move at a slower pace if necessary. For many students, this individual approach to education promotes a more productive learning

About This Chapter: This chapter begins with "Is Distance Education for You?" © 2009 Distance Education and Training Council (www.detc.org). Reprinted with permission. The chapter also includes "Diploma Mills: Degrees of Deception," a publication of the Federal Trade Commission, April 2009.

environment. Distance learning also allows a student to maintain his career, family, and personal commitments while taking courses. Students who live in rural areas find that distance education permits them to enroll in programs that otherwise would not be available in their locations. And with the cost of commuting to a classroom increasing these days, studying at home makes even more sense than ever for those who must watch their expenses.

What types of students seek out distance learning?

Distance learners are often independent, industrious students eager to gain more knowledge in a chosen field. Often, they are older than "traditional students," and their ages typically range from 25–55 years old. Adult learners tend to be more experienced and are highly motivated to earn a degree or gain valuable job skills. Of course, any hardworking, goal-oriented, mature person who shows enthusiasm to study on his or her own is an excellent candidate for distance education.

What types of distance learning courses are available?

A wide variety of distance learning courses are available, including high school diploma programs, vocational courses, and college degree programs from an associate's to a professional doctoral degree. DETC schools currently offer more than 500 fields of study with an array of programs ranging from accounting to yacht design. DETC accredits schools offering courses at the kindergarten through professional doctoral degree level.

What should I look for in a distance learning school?

First and foremost, find out which U.S. Department of Education-recognized accrediting agency accredits the school. Then find out how long the school has been in operation, make sure the school's courses are up to date, that it maintains competent staff and instructors, that it adheres to ethical standards, that it is truthful in its advertising methods, and that it is financially responsible and can continue to meet its obligations to students. All of this information can be found by contacting the school's accrediting agency directly. The most important factor to check is this: "Is the institution accredited by a nationally recognized accrediting association?" The quickest way to check on any U.S. institution's accreditation status is to log onto www.chea.org and click on the Database of Institutions.

What methods of learning will I use as a student at a school?

This depends on which school you enroll in. Some distance learning schools are still primarily "correspondence based," which means you send and receive materials through the mail. Other institutions operate entirely online—information is provided through websites, online libraries, threaded discussions, live chats, web-based videos, podcasts, and more. Currently, many schools offer a combination of correspondence and online materials. Some schools still use textbooks and give students the option of mailing assignments instead of completing or submitting them online. Your preference of learning methods, be it correspondence, online, or a combination of both, is personal, and you should find the school that best suits your needs.

As a distance learning student, what degree of communication can I expect from my instructor or fellow students?

Again, this depends on the school, but accredited institutions are motivated to engage in frequent interactions with students, and it is common to see frequent written, e-mailed, and telephoned communication between faculty, staff, and students. Institutions usually mail study texts with the schedule of assignments to the student. Professors and instructors communicate via e-mail with students. One of the internet's most important roles in distance education may be the facilitation of communication between students and faculty. Video conferencing, live chats, threaded discussion boards, and e-mail help the student develop a sense of community when taking a distance learning course. With the internet, the student does not have to feel like a completely solitary learner—a classmate or instructor is only an e-mail message away.

I'm concerned that a distance education school could really be a "fly by night" operation. How can I protect myself?

Make sure the school you're interested in is accredited by a legitimate, nationally recognized accrediting association. "Nationally recognized" indicates that the accrediting association is recognized by either the United States Department of Education, the Council for Higher Education Accreditation (CHEA), or both. Accreditation is a voluntary process and ensures that the school has submitted to a thorough evaluation process, and that its academic, business, and ethical standards have been assessed. You can also check with the Better Business Bureau in the institution's state to learn about complaints filed against the school. If the school is accredited by a recognized accrediting association, you shouldn't have to worry about any scams or dishonest procedures. Be alert, however, to the many dozens of unrecognized accrediting associations plying the waters of the internet. The easiest way to check on an accrediting association's status is to go to www.chea.org which lists all recognized (Federal and CHEA recognized) accrediting bodies in its database.

How do I recognize a diploma mill?

It can be difficult to determine whether a school is actually a "diploma mill"—an institution granting degrees for a set price with little or no work required. Accreditation can assure students that the school is not a diploma mill, but not all unaccredited schools are suspect. Remember, accreditation is voluntary on the part of the educational institution. You should be very cautious, however, if an unaccredited school exhibits any of the following warning signs: the school claims to be accredited when it is not, or its accrediting agency is not recognized; degrees are granted solely or mostly on life or work experience; the school lacks state or federal licensure to operate; the "university" charges a single fee for an entire degree program; when degrees can be purchased for little work; the school fails to provide a list of faculty and their qualifications; the school does not provide a physical address or business location; degrees can be earned in a very short period of time. [Ed. Note: Additional information from the Federal Trade Commission can be found at the end of this chapter.]

What exactly does accreditation mean?

Accreditation is a nongovernmental, peer review process designed to determine whether an educational institution meets specific standards of academic quality and ethical practice. The school voluntarily submits to a thorough evaluation process to prove it can meet and maintain the accrediting agency's published standards. Accreditation can benefit a school by encouraging improvement through a self-evaluation process and by assuring the public that the school has clearly defined objectives and is working to improve and maintain all aspects of its operations. The United States Department of Education (ED) and the Council for Higher Education Accreditation (CHEA) are the two third-party agencies that recognize legitimate accrediting agencies in the United States. The DETC has operated since 1926, and is a nonprofit educational association that promotes sound education and good business practices in the field of distance education. DETC has emerged as the most experienced accrediting association in the United States of America for the accreditation of online and distance learning institutions.

How does DETC accreditation compare to regional accreditation?

One critical difference between regional agencies and the DETC is that the DETC specializes in accrediting distance learning institutions—those are the only institutions DETC accredits, while regional groups primarily are focused on and accredit residential institutions. DETC currently accredits dozens of institutions offering degree programs up through the professional doctoral degree. DETC's standards are extremely high, and institutions must submit to very thorough evaluations. Some institutions cling to the outdated notion that U.S.

regional accreditation is the only—or only acceptable—type of accreditation. This is simply no longer true. National accreditation—from a recognized agency like the DETC—has the same and even higher standards than regional bodies, and like them, enjoys both U.S. Department of Education and CHEA recognition. Distance education schools prefer DETC accreditation because the DETC is the oldest and most experienced distance education accrediting agency.

Does it matter if I live in one state and my school operates out of another state? What about foreign universities?

In general, a distance learning student can enroll in an accredited distance learning program located in any state, or even in another country. You may wish to check with your State Department of Education before enrolling to be sure your state does not have any specific regulations concerning distance education. If your prospective school is located outside of the United States, be sure it is accredited by a U.S. accrediting agency, such as the DETC. Accreditation standards and practices vary from country to country, and degrees earned at a foreign university may not be equivalent to those earned at a U.S. institution. The credits required to earn specific degrees may also vary in a foreign university. If you are unsure about the approval to operate status of a foreign institution, check www.chea.org and log onto the CHEA International Directory for a country by country listing of official quality assurance agencies in each country.

Will the credits I earn from a distance learning institution transfer to a college in my area?

That depends. If your school is accredited by a recognized agency in the United States, your college level credits should be transferable, but no one can guarantee acceptance in all cases. The decision to accept transfer of credit always lies with the receiving organization (college registrar, employer, etc.). Since there are more than 4,000 colleges and universities in the United States, the DETC is unable to provide a list of schools that accept credits from specific DETC institutions. When you explain that the institution is accrediting by a national or regional accrediting agency, the decision is often favorable. Surveys of DETC graduates indicate that students who attempt to have their academic credits accepted at regionally accredited institutions are successful 70% of the time.

Will my employer recognize a distance education certificate or degree?

Yes. Although almost all employers require that the institution be accredited, and some require a certain type of accreditation. Distance education is a popular method of earning a certificate or degree for a promotion and career advancement without leaving your current job. Thousands of leading companies provide tuition assistance to students attending DETC institutions, including the largest employer in the United States of America—the Federal Government. Through the U.S. Department of Defense and the voluntary education tuition program, the federal government pays the tuition for tens of thousands of military members at DETC institutions. DETC institutions rank in the very top tier of all colleges and universities in the support given to military students. For more information on DETC and corporate learning visit www.detc.org/coporate.

How do the expenses of distance learning schools compare to traditional schools?

Distance education institutions—DETC schools in particular—tend to be less expensive than traditional or residency schools. This is another encouraging factor for adult learners considering going back to school. The DETC recently completed a study comparing costs of college programs and found that students often pay about one half less in tuition for a similar degree program when attending a DETC school instead of a traditional institution.

What is the future of distance education?

Millions of students study via distance learning every year, and this method of learning is expected to continue to increase. DETC institutions have a healthy enrollment history—over 145 million Americans have enrolled in DETC institutions since 1890. More and more students are turning to distance education today to "go back to school" without being bound to one place or by a rigid study schedule. New technology continues to support and assist distance learning students. Currently, distance learning institutions are enjoying record enrollment rates around the world.

Diploma Mills: Degrees Of Deception

Are you ever tempted by an e-mail or an ad claiming you can "earn a college degree based... on life experience"? Don't be, say attorneys for the Federal Trade Commission (FTC), America's consumer protection agency. Chances are good that the ad is for a diploma mill, a company that offers degrees or certificates for a flat fee, requires little course work, if any, and awards degrees based solely on life experience.

Most employers and educational institutions consider it lying if you claim academic credentials that you didn't earn through actual course work. Federal officials say it's risky behavior: If you use a so-called degree from a diploma mill to apply for a job or promotion, you risk not getting hired, getting fired, and in some cases, prosecution.

Diploma mills may claim to be accredited. Colleges and universities accredited by legitimate organizations undergo a rigorous review of the quality of their educational programs. Although many diploma mills claim to be accredited, their accreditation is from a bogus, but official-sounding agency that they created. You can use the internet to check if a school is accredited by a legitimate organization at the database of accredited academic institutions posted by the U.S. Department of Education at www.ope.ed.gov/accreditation or at the Council for Higher Education Accreditation database at www.chea.org/search. (There are a few legitimate institutions that have not pursued accreditation.)

So how can you tell if the institution you're thinking about is legitimate? Here are some telltale signs of a diploma mill:

No Studies, No Exams: Diploma mills grant degrees for work or life experience alone. Accredited colleges may give a few credits for specific experience pertinent to a degree program, but not an entire degree.

No Attendance: Legitimate colleges or universities, including online schools, require substantial course work.

Flat Fee: Many diploma mills charge on a per-degree basis. Legitimate colleges charge by the credit, course, or semester, not a flat fee for an entire degree.

No Waiting: Operations that guarantee a degree in a few days, weeks, or even months aren't legitimate. If an ad promises that you can earn a degree very quickly, it's probably a diploma mill.

Click Here To Order Now: Some diploma mills push themselves through aggressive sales tactics. Accredited colleges don't use spam or high-pressure telemarketing to market themselves. Some diploma mills also advertise in newspapers, magazines, and on the web.

Quick Tip

Look out for sound alikes. Some diploma mills take on names that are very similar to well-known colleges or universities; a "dot edu" web address is no guarantee of legitimacy, either. Keep in mind that some diploma mills use credible-sounding foreign names. Researching the legitimacy of a foreign school can be a challenge, but is clearly worth the time. If you're having a tough time checking out a particular school, call the registrar of a local college or university and ask if it would accept transfer credits from the school you are considering.

Source: From "Diploma Mills: Degrees of Deception," a publication of the Federal Trade Commission, April 2009.

Advertising Through Spam Or Pop-Ups: If the school caught your attention through an unsolicited e-mail or pop-up ad, it may be a diploma mill. Legitimate institutions, including distance learning programs, won't advertise through spam or pop-ups.

It's A Fact!

The FTC works to prevent fraudulent, deceptive, and unfair business practices in the marketplace and to provide information to help consumers spot, stop, and avoid them. To file a complaint or get free information on consumer issues, visit ftc.gov or call toll-free, 1-877-FTC-HELP (1-877-382-4357); TTY: 1-866-653-4261. Watch a new video, How to File a Complaint, at ftc.gov/video to learn more. The FTC enters consumer complaints into the Consumer Sentinel Network, a secure online database and investigative tool used by hundreds of civil and criminal law enforcement agencies in the United States and abroad.

Source: From "Diploma Mills: Degrees of Deception," a publication of the Federal Trade Commission, April 2009.

Chapter 10

Searching For A College

College Selection

Selecting a school to educate you for your future is an important decision to make, especially when there are thousands of colleges, universities, and technical schools to choose from. It is imperative that there be a good fit between you and your college or university. Follow these steps to assist in the college selection process so you will pick the right school for you:

Step One: Identify Important School Attributes

You must first identify what is important to you in a school. Do you want to go to a large or small college? Do you want to go to an in-state or out-of-state school? Is money an issue? Are extracurricular activities and events important to you? Does the school have to have a wide variety of majors to choose from? Would you prefer a school in an urban or rural environment? Is it essential that the school have a good athletics program? These are the types of questions you need to ask yourself when deciding what factors are vital to you. Make a list of important school attributes and then move on to step two.

Step Two: Search For Schools That Fit Your Criteria

After you have identified what is important, you can begin researching schools that match your criteria. Meet with your guidance counselor to discuss your list of criteria and ask if he/she knows of schools that you might be interested in attending. Search the internet for schools

About This Chapter: This chapter begins with "College Selection," reprinted with permission from eCampusTours. com, a college planning website featuring 360-degree virtual tours of over 1300 campuses nationwide. Sponsored by Edsouth. Copyright 2010. All rights reserved. Additional information from the U.S. Department of Education and Sallie Mae, Inc. is cited separately within the chapter.

of interest. Visit a variety of websites so you can compare and contrast different schools. Make a list of the schools you could see yourself attending and prepare for the next step.

Step Three: Visit Campuses

Once you have a list of potential schools, you can begin visiting the campuses. If you are currently a senior, you probably spent a lot of time over the summer visiting various college campuses and may still have a few more campuses to visit. If you are a freshman, sophomore, or junior, the summer before your senior year is an opportune time to visit college campuses but feel free to visit schools beforehand if the opportunity arises. While you are on campus, be sure to ask any questions you have about the college. Talk to current students, instructors, admissions officers, and financial aid officers. Sit in on a couple of classes and eat the campus food. Try to experience as much as you can about the college while you are there and write down pros and cons of each campus so you can begin the next step of the college selection process.

Step Four: Compare Schools On Your List

After you have visited the campuses on your list, you need to compare them and try to narrow down your list. Are there aspects of some schools that you like but didn't like about others? If you didn't like the campus atmosphere of one of the colleges after you visited it, maybe you should delete that college from your list. Try to narrow down your list to about three reach schools and three safety schools in order to be ready for step five.

Step Five: Start Applying To Schools

Now that you have a final list of schools that you would like to attend, you can begin filling out applications for admission. If you are currently a senior, you're probably at this step right now or at least pretty close. Be sure to know the application deadlines for each college you are applying to. Try to send in your applications before winter break of your senior year at the latest. Be sure to fill the applications out carefully and have an impressive essay (if required). When this step is completed, you will have a waiting period until you can complete the final step.

Step Six: Decide Which School To Attend

If you are accepted to more than one school, you still have to make a final decision about which one to attend. If you qualify for financial aid, you will receive award letters from potential schools around March or April of your senior year. These letters will let you know if you have received any financial aid. You should compare the award offers from each school, which may help you make a final decision. The amount you are awarded at each school will vary depending on the cost of attendance. Go over all the factors and then make a final decision. Be sure to send a letter declining admission to schools you will not be attending. If you have questions or are confused about your acceptance information, call your contact at that school. He/she will be happy to help clarify.

Selecting the right college is critical because you will be spending the next four or more years of your life there. If you follow the above-mentioned steps, you will be able to make an informed decision about which school you would like to attend.

Quick Tip

No matter what kind of school you choose, it is important to make sure the school is accredited. It is also a good idea to check with the Better Business Bureau closest to where the school is located.

Source: From "Find Schools," a publication of the U.S. Department of Education, 2010.

Attending College Fairs

"Search for Specific Schools: Attending College Fairs," © 2010 Sallie Mae, Inc. All rights reserved. Reprinted with permission. For additional information, visit www.college answer.com or www.salliemae.com.

Before attending a college fair, have a plan. College fairs are especially helpful if you're unable to visit all the schools that interest you. Here's how to make the most of them.

Ready For Your Questions

Students and parents can go to these events for free. College fairs are a good chance for you to interact with admission representatives from a wide range of schools. Many of them will be ready to discuss:

• Course offerings

It's A Fact!

At college fairs, you can meet representatives from multiple schools without traveling far from home. They can tell you about their schools and answer your questions. Ask your high school counselor about college fairs in your area.

Source: From "Find Schools," a publication of the U.S. Department of Education, 2010.

- Admission and financial aid requirements
- Campus life
- Information pertinent to the college selection process

Expect Lots Of Information

You can catch college fairs at large convention centers as well as in high school gyms. Dozens—or even hundreds—of colleges and universities will have tables with information about their school and representatives to answer your questions.

If they're giving out bags at the entrance or the tables, use them to collect the materials from the colleges that interest you.

Your Plan Of Action

Be prepared before entering the college fair.

It's not unusual for thousands of students and parents to attend the larger events. So expect crowded halls and long lines at the booths of the more popular colleges.

Consider these tips as you prepare for and while you attend this event:

- Get a schedule from your guidance counselor.
- Find out which colleges will be represented.
- Prepare a short list of questions. (Bring a pen and small notebook.)
- Decide which colleges interest you, but talk with representatives from other schools.
- Dress appropriately—make a good impression.
- Collect brochures and business cards.
- Take notes before moving to the next booth.
- Prepare self-stick labels with your name, address, e-mail, phone, high school, year of graduation, intended major(s), and extracurricular activities. You will be asked to fill out interest cards at the booths; using these stickers will save you from writing the same information over and over.

Information Sessions And Open Houses

Most fairs present experts who cover a variety of topics about the college search process, admission applications, student financial aid, scholarships, and other issues. These sessions are a great place to ask questions about the college admission process and learn the things you need to know.

Another way to learn about colleges is to attend open houses. Open houses are held at the college itself so prospective students can explore the grounds and get a taste of campus life. Check with your guidance counselor or the schools' websites to find out when these events are.

Preparing For Campus Visits

It's important to visit schools you might want to attend. Visiting a school gives you a close-up look: a chance to focus on the details and actually experience the college before you make a commitment.

How many schools you visit depends on your time and money. You may not be able to visit every school you're considering, but try to at least visit schools that'll provide a variety of experiences.

For example, check out a large and a small school or go to one urban and one small-town campus. For those you can't visit, do the best you can with research and word of mouth. Consider visiting colleges in your area (even if you aren't interested in attending them) to get a feel for campus life.

Make The Most Of Campus Visits

- **Do some prep work.** Before the visit, decide what you want to learn about the school and put together a list of questions. Use a similar list for every school so you can make fair comparisons.

- **Schedule your visit at least two weeks in advance.** Call the admissions office to arrange your visit and inquire about campus tours. Ask to sit in on a class, eat in the cafeteria with students, spend the night in a dorm, and use the campus facilities.

- **Visit while classes are in session.** Fall is the ideal time to visit college campuses—classes are in session and campus activities are in full swing.

- **Set up interviews with faculty and admissions staff.** Arrange to meet with professors who teach subjects that interest you. Meet with an admissions rep to verify admission requirements and discuss costs and financial aid.

- **Take the campus tour.** Gain access to more of the campus—your tour guide can be a great source of candid information.

- **Attend information sessions.** Schedule your interviews after the information session and the campus tour. You'll speak more knowledgeably and have better questions.

- **Ask lots of questions.** Ask students what they like best and least about the school, what the campus is like on weekends, and which professors are best. Read the student newspaper and bulletin board postings.

- **Trust your instincts, take notes, and bring a camera.** Pay attention to your first impressions. Keep notes and take pictures to jog your memory as decision time approaches. After you've seen a few campuses, it's easy to confuse the details.

- **Send thank you notes.** After visiting a college, remember to send thank you notes. It's polite and could get you noticed.

The Power Of Observation

Pay attention to how you feel, especially first impressions. Each campus has a personality and atmosphere.

- Ask yourself: Is this where I want to live and study for four years?

- Drive or walk through surrounding neighborhoods and get a feel for the community.

- Take notes and, when something catches your interest, follow up with a phone call or e-mail.

Chapter 11

Choosing A College

Making The Final Decision

You've been accepted, maybe even to more than one school. You now have a big decision to make. What are you going to do?

If you're ready to begin school right away, consider these questions:

- Were you accepted by more than one school? If you were, which one is your first choice?

- If you were accepted at just one school, are you prepared to attend that school?

- Can you and your family afford each school?

- Is the value of the education at a school worth its cost?

There's a lot to consider, and some items will weigh more heavily when making this decision. So, review your options before making the final decision.

More Than Money

Cost is certainly an important factor, but you shouldn't decide on money alone. A recent online poll on student college selections revealed that academic reputation, location, and proximity to home are more important than affordability.

About This Chapter: This chapter begins with "Making the Final Decision," © 2010 Sallie Mae, Inc. All rights reserved. Reprinted with permission. For additional information, visit www.collegeanswer.com or www .salliemae.com. The chapter ends with "Sample Award Packages," and "How do I compare award packages?" publications of the U.S. Department of Education, 2010. Additional information from eCampusTours.com/ Edsouth is cited separately within the chapter.

Dollars And Sense

Money is an issue for most students, so carefully study each financial aid award letter. Work with your parents on this: They may have a vested, or invested, interest in your decision.

Think about life after graduation when selecting a school and a major.

- How much is a degree from each school really worth?
- Where will you work?
- How much can you earn?
- Your school should be able to provide postgraduation placement statistics.
- How much will the career you're considering pay?
- Research occupational outlook data at the Bureau of Labor Statistics.

If You Need More Time

Don't panic if attending school right away isn't the best choice for you. Not all high school graduates are ready for college.

Instead of jumping straight into a university setting, maybe you'd rather take some classes at a local community college. Or maybe the financial burden of enrolling now has you thinking that perhaps you'd be better off working and saving some money first.

The final decision is yours and yours alone.

Enrolling

Once you've made the decision to enroll, you need to:

- Formally accept the offer of admission.
- Follow the directions in the acceptance letter.
- Respond to the award letter by the deadline.

- Review instructions on housing, grants, scholarships, financial aid, orientation, etc.

- Read the letters carefully; you don't want to overlook any important details.

Congratulations! See you on campus!

Top Ten Reasons Not To Choose A College

Reprinted with permission from eCampusTours.com, a college planning website featuring 360-degree virtual tours of over 1300 campuses nationwide. Sponsored by Edsouth. Copyright 2010. All rights reserved.

Deciding where to attend college is a huge decision because you will probably be spending the next four or more years there. Students often choose a college for all the wrong reasons and end up transferring to a different college or maybe even dropping out of school altogether. Don't become one of those students. Here are the top ten reasons not to choose a college:

1. **Your boyfriend/girlfriend is going there.** Think of all the different people you are going to meet in college. You may get to college and realize that you want to focus more on developing new relationships. You may also decide you don't want to be distracted by a relationship and want to focus more on studying and earning your degree. You should give yourself the opportunity to experience college life and enjoy your educational experience so you can reach your maximum potential.

2. **Your best friend is going there.** If you and your best friend want to go to the same college because you both like the courses and extracurricular activities that are offered, then that's great. Just don't choose a college solely because you want to go to school with your best friend. Going away to college means meeting a lot of new, unique people. If you choose a college so you can be with your friend, the two of you may spend every day with each other, and you may not take the opportunity to meet other people and make new friends. Making new friends will help you grow as a person.

3. **It's a party school.** While school should be fun at times, it is more importantly a place for you to learn new ideas and earn a degree. While enjoying your time outside of the classroom is important, you can't spend all your time at school socializing. You need to pick a school that is conducive to your educational needs.

4. **You decided in the seventh grade that you wanted to go there.** While it is important to begin thinking about college early, you shouldn't choose a college solely because you decided when you were young that is where you wanted to go. You need to open yourself up to other possibilities and give yourself other options. If, after you've visited the campus,

spoken with college representatives, and found a suitable course of study, you're still convinced it's the right school for you, then you can begin making plans to attend. Just make sure you have considered a variety of possibilities before making your final decision.

5. **Your mom and dad are alumni.** Try to avoid letting your parents persuade you into going to their old alma mater if you're not interested. To be successful in school, you need to pick a college that is right for you based on a number of factors. If you share the same enthusiasm for your parents' school, still be sure to look around at other campuses to broaden your perspective. If you aren't excited by the prospect of becoming a legacy, have an open and honest conversation with your parents and offer reasonable examples of why you might be happier somewhere else. Chances are, when you work together as a family, you'll come up with a choice that makes everyone happy.

6. **It has a good football team.** Unless you want to be on the football team, don't choose a college just because you like the team. While school spirit is important to have, you need to base your decision on what the school can offer you in regards to academics, extracurricular activities, and so forth.

7. **Your school counselor told you to pick it.** Your school counselor can be a great resource when you are choosing a college. He or she can help guide you through the process and answer questions you might have about a college, based on valuable experience with former students. It is important for you to let your counselor know all of your interests in order to help you determine which colleges might be a fit, but you must also remember that this is your decision to make. It's best for you to take suggestions, research the schools, and then make a decision on your own.

8. **The school is prestigious.** Just because a school has the reputation of being prestigious, it does not mean that you are going to like it. What if the school doesn't offer the major that you want? What if it doesn't offer the extracurricular activity in which you want to be involved? You need to consider aspects that are important to you when choosing a school instead of worrying about whether or not it is a high-status school.

9. **The tuition is low.** Money is often a big factor when choosing a college, but keep in mind that a school that is more expensive may offer you a larger financial aid package with more gift aid (depending on your financial situation) than a school where the tuition is lower. Apply to the schools you really want to attend, including schools with high and low tuitions, and then compare their financial aid award letters in order to make a decision. Don't forget that you can also get a student loan to help you pay for tuition.

10. **It looks good in the guidebook.** Do not choose a college without visiting the campus first. While guidebooks and virtual tours will help you narrow down your choices, it is important to visit your top two or three schools in person so you can get a feel for what the campus atmosphere is like.

When it comes to choosing a college, students can give many good and bad reasons why they picked a certain school. Instead of choosing a college for the reasons listed above, take the time to research schools and find out what they have to offer. You want a school that will get you well prepared for the future, as well as one where you feel comfortable.

Sample Award Package

If your application for admission has been accepted, and you have taken all the steps to apply for financial aid, and your family demonstrates financial need, you are likely to receive a financial aid award.

Table 11.1 shows a sample of an award package that students may receive once their admission application is accepted. Interpreting the award letter can take time, and this sample may help you and your family interpret your aid award letter once you receive it. Be sure to ask all questions you have and get the answers before the acceptance deadline.

Table 11.1. Sample Financial Aid Award Package

Total Cost of Attendance	$20,000
Expected Family Contribution	$5,000
Outside Scholarship	$1,000
Financial Need	$14,000
Federal Pell Grant	$0
State Scholarship Grant	$1,500
Institutional Grant	$7,500
Federal Perkins Loan	$1,500
Federal Direct Loan	$1,500
Federal Work-Study	$2,000
Total Award	$14,000

In this award, the college is covering more than half of the demonstrated financial need with a grant. That certainly helps! But it would be important to ask the financial aid staff whether this level of grant can be expected in future years. (Unfortunately, some colleges do make large initial grants to encourage students to enroll, and may reduce or remove grants after the first year.)

You'll also want to ask about the continued availability of the state grant.

If the grants look to be stable over the time you'd be enrolled, you can estimate the total student loan indebtedness you would have after four years—in this case, around $12,000 if college costs remain the same. That's about the average level of indebtedness for students graduating nationwide.

You'll also want to look at the Federal Work-Study figure. Are you willing to work on campus to earn these funds? If not, you will be expected to come up with the $2,000 in some other way (either extra work beyond the summer earnings expectation, a gift from a relative, a loan, etc.).

Comparing Financial Aid Award Packages

If you've received more than one financial aid award package, this information will help you compare them.

Ratio Of Grant To Loan

In general, packages with higher percentages of grant aid than loan aid will be more appealing. You'll have less to pay while in college and fewer debts to repay when you graduate. This ratio may also give you a clue as to how much the college wants you, since colleges tend to award higher proportions of grant aid to the most desirable students in the accepted group.

Ratio Of Self Help To Grant

This looks at the big picture beyond just grant versus loan. How much of the total cost of attendance are you expected to cover through loans, the expected family contribution, and student employment on campus? You'll need to be realistic about whether you can meet the earnings expectations.

Loan Terms

Compare the types of loans you are expected to take on. Are the terms favorable in terms of interest and repayment? Student loans with low interest rates and no repayment until after college are preferable to private or unsubsidized loans with less attractive terms.

Gapping

Some colleges award aid that amounts to less than the difference between the Expected Family Contribution and the total cost of attendance. If you find you have been gapped in an award, only you can determine if you will be able to, and want to, come up with the additional money in order to attend.

Future Packages

You'll want to find out if all or part of your financial aid award is renewable if family circumstances stay the same (or worsen!). Beware of packages that seem too good to be true: often the terms will not be as favorable for subsequent years of enrollment.

Outside Scholarships

If you are applying for or will otherwise qualify for outside scholarships, be sure to find out how this money will be treated in each college's financial aid award package. At some colleges, an outside scholarship directly reduces the institutional grant by the same amount. Other colleges allow a certain amount to go first against any suggested loan, then, if the outside scholarship is greater than that amount, it will reduce equally institutional grant and loan.

Chapter 12

Study Abroad

Reasons To Study Abroad

Study abroad can be an enriching and eye-opening adventure, where learning extends to the world beyond the classroom walls. There is no substitute for living and studying in a foreign country if you want to gain in-depth knowledge of another culture's customs, people, and language. In addition, you will find that living and studying or working in another country can develop important transnational competencies that can be of interest to future employers.

Personal Growth

Students who return from a study abroad program often see it as an experience which matured them personally and intellectually. They praise being exposed to new ways of thinking and living, which encourages growth and independence. For many students, going abroad to study is the first time they have really been away from home, from familiar surroundings of the United States of America, as well as from friends and family. This is seldom an easy experience, but it is universally praised as worthwhile, often even life transforming. After immersing themselves in a new culture, mastering the challenges of learning in a new and different academic environment, and experiencing the many highs and lows of being a foreigner, students typically return home with increased self-confidence and justifiable pride in what they have achieved.

About This Chapter: This chapter contains "Study Abroad Student Guide—Part I: Reasons to Study Abroad," and excerpts from "Study Abroad Student Guide, Part II: Living Abroad," by Bill Hoffa, © 2011 EducationDynamics, LLC. All rights reserved. Reprinted with permission. To view the complete Study Abroad Student Guide, and additional information, visit www.studyabroad.com.

New Perspective On World Affairs

Study abroad can broaden your intellectual horizons and deepen your knowledge and understanding of international, political, and economic issues. It is almost certain that you will return from your sojourn abroad with a more informed and accurate perspective on world affairs. You will also have first-hand knowledge of how another culture approaches the tasks and challenges of everyday life, a sense of how global the international culture has become, and an appreciation of the importance of international cooperation.

You will probably also gain a broader understanding of, and appreciation for, the United States, its way of life, and its role in international affairs. Through your professors, the other students in your program, and people you meet, you'll learn how others view the United States and its world role. If you live in a country where English is not the native language, or is spoken only by some, you will learn the practical importance of learning another language and using it.

Career Enhancement

But study abroad does more than promote academic enrichment and personal growth. It also can enhance your employment prospects, especially in the fields of business, international affairs, and government service. Employers increasingly seek graduates who have studied abroad. They know that students who have successfully completed a study abroad program are likely to possess international knowledge and often second-language skills. Such students are also likely to have other transnational competencies that graduate and professional schools and employers value just as highly: cross-cultural communication skills, analytical skills, an understanding of and familiarity with local customs and cultural contexts, flexibility, resilience, and the ability to adapt to new circumstances and deal constructively with differences.

Quick Tip

There are a host of valid reasons for wanting to experience foreign study. Whatever your reasons, they should be positive ones. Study abroad should not be seen as an escape route from problems at home or on campus. Adjusting to life and learning in a foreign environment will have its stressful moments, and the more you are able to focus on your goals, the more you're likely to benefit from the experience.

Source: From "Study Abroad Student Guide—Part I: Reasons to Study Abroad," by Bill Hoffa, © 2011 EducationDynamics, LLC. All rights reserved. Reprinted with permission. To view the complete Study Abroad Student Guide, and additional information, visit www.studyabroad.com.

Reasons And Goals

After considering these potential benefits, you must still ask yourself why you, yourself, want to study abroad. Take some time to think about your reasons, for they will become your goals and your personal measures of success. Perhaps you want to learn a second language, or perfect one you already know. You might want to learn about another culture, diversify your studies, or prepare for graduate school. Maybe you want to travel and meet new people. Whatever your reasons are, write them down and share them with your professors, family, friends, and, most importantly, with your study abroad advisor.

Living Abroad

Choosing a study abroad program that is the right fit for you is the best way to achieve your personal and academic goals for study abroad, as well as assist you with your long-range career plans. Therefore, it is important to plan carefully. However, when selecting the program, you are likely to get the most from involved careful planning. Hundreds of opportunities exist, more than ever before. They differ in location, duration, curriculum, degrees of cultural immersion, language, cost, and many, many other ways. Because there is so much to consider, it's smart to begin planning a full year before you want to depart. In some cases colleges and universities expect you to declare your intent to study abroad a full year in advance.

Start by realistically assessing your academic and personal preparation and objectives:

- What do you want or need to study?
- Do you need to earn credit while abroad, or would a work abroad program not for credit be possible?
- Are you fluent enough in a foreign language to take classes in it, or will it be necessary for you to take some or all of your coursework in English?
- How much time can you afford to spend abroad, in terms of academic time and economic resources?
- Where do you want to go? Why?
- How structured or open of a program are you looking for?
- Do you want to live in a dorm with other Americans, stay with a local family, or have some other housing option?
- How much money can you spend on tuition and fees? On housing and food? On international transportation?

- Will you need to apply for financial aid? Is it available?

This chapter provides information that will help you answer these questions.

Quick Tip

Getting the most from any study abroad program requires open-mindedness, flexibility, dedication, independence, and above all, a spirit of adventure. Some programs, however, require more of these characteristics than others. Also keep in mind your adventure quotient when considering programs. Challenge yourself, but be realistic.

Source: From "Study Abroad Student Guide, Part II: Living Abroad," by Bill Hoffa, © 2011 EducationDynamics, LLC. All rights reserved. Reprinted with permission. To view the complete Study Abroad Student Guide, and additional information, visit www.studyabroad.com.

Your Study Abroad Office

Find out if your campus has a study abroad office. (It probably does if it sends more than just a few students abroad to study.) Study abroad advisors are experienced guides, especially in knowing what your campus supports and encourages. They can assist you in exploring all reasonable alternatives and help you sharpen your objectives for a foreign study program. He or she will help determine whether the courses you are considering will mesh with your educational goals—and whether you will receive academic credit for them. If your school doesn't have a study abroad advisor, consult the office of the academic dean, the office of academic advising, or a faculty member who is knowledgeable about foreign study programs. As described below, access to study abroad resources via written materials and the internet is easy.

Field Of Study

What do you want to study? The largest percentage of U.S. students abroad take some courses in their major, while others take a broader selection. The most prevalent course work available overseas is in social sciences and humanities areas, followed by business and management; third in popularity are foreign languages. But programs exist in nearly every subject, from art to zoology. There are courses in animation, classical studies, chemistry, development studies, historical preservation, literature, marine biology, mathematics, the performing arts, physics, social anthropology, TEFL/TESL (Teaching English as a Foreign (or Second) Language), and women's studies. You can learn or polish a foreign language, including Aramaic, French, Kannada, Russian, Spanish, Swahili, and Xhosa. And you can study the people and culture of another country or region.

It's A Fact!

Peterson's also publishes a large program guide and has a website listing programs. In addition, there are various other websites, such as www.studyabroad.com, which list programs and have hyperlinks to program web pages.

Source: From "Study Abroad Student Guide, Part II: Living Abroad," by Bill Hoffa, © 2011 EducationDynamics, LLC. All rights reserved. Reprinted with permission. To view the complete Study Abroad Student Guide, and additional information, visit www.studyabroad.com.

IIEPassport: Academic Year Abroad and *IIEPassport: Short Term Study Abroad*, published by Educational Directories Unlimited and the Institute of International Education, are comprehensive reference directories to international study for U.S. students. The books are updated annually, and contain information on thousands of program offerings. Programs are indexed by field of study—as well as cost ranges, sponsoring institutions, consortia, and special options—making these directories easy to use. All of the programs listed in these directories are also included in a very useful web directory, www.IIEPassport.org.

Explore A New Subject: You might like to take an opportunity to explore an entirely new subject. Some students go abroad to take courses that aren't available at their home campuses. Others want to pursue subjects that can offer a richer experience when they study in another country—political issues of the Middle East, for example, or the marine biology of Jamaica. If you are considering this option, find out how it will affect your graduation plans. Will you be able to meet your graduation and major departmental requirements? Will you need to spend an additional semester or year on campus?

Quick Tip

If you are interested in foreign language study, make sure any programs you consider are taught at your level of proficiency. Check program facilities: Is there a language lab? Is it well equipped? Will you have access to a multimedia center or library? Will the credits be accepted by the appropriate language department at your home university?

Source: From "Study Abroad Student Guide, Part II: Living Abroad," by Bill Hoffa, © 2011 EducationDynamics, LLC. All rights reserved. Reprinted with permission. To view the complete Study Abroad Student Guide, and additional information, visit www.studyabroad.com.

Foreign Language Courses: Many students take part in study abroad to learn a new language or to perfect their skills in a language that is their major or minor. Living in a foreign country can make learning the local language much easier, thanks to abundant opportunities to hear it and practice speaking it. In addition, you may want to study a language or a dialect that is rarely taught in the United States.

Academic Credit

It is as important to make sure you are able to earn the maximum academic credit for your program abroad as it is to decide what or where to study. With the ever-increasing cost of a college education, no one wants to discover upon return home that credit for a semester or academic year spent studying abroad will not be accepted. Even if the program is offered by your home university, having the credit accepted and counted toward graduation is seldom automatic.

It is essential to get approval in advance—and in writing. This may be routinely done on your campus or you may need to take an active role in getting approval for your study abroad program. Most colleges and universities only accept credit from programs that they authorize in advance. In fact, if you're receiving financial aid of any kind, preapproval is required.

Find out if your campus has a procedure (or a requirement) for arranging preapproval of the academic work you intend to take abroad. A study abroad advisor is the best source of help in this process. If your school doesn't have one, check with your registrar, faculty advisor, dean, or admissions officer. These are the questions to ask:

What can I earn credit for? This varies from institution to institution and obviously depends on the level and quality of your overseas courses. Once preapproval is given, this should make it clear if your overseas course work counts toward your academic major, or minor; or toward curricular electives; or simply as general degree credit. Be sure to find out before you leave where your credits fit in your domestic requirements for graduation. Ask if your school requires that you take a minimum course load in order to qualify for credit—it usually does.

What kind of documentation do I need to have a course approved? If you plan to enroll in a program offered by your home university, the description in the course catalog will probably be all your advisor (or registrar or dean) needs to approve it. If, however, you are considering a program offered by another U.S. university, you may need more in order to earn transfer credit—credit transferred from another school to your home university.

Your study abroad advisor may request all or some of the following before you are approved for participation:

- The number of contact hours of the program: hours spent in lectures, labs, field work, etc.

- The course format

- Course outline and reading list

- Information on the level of the course

- The academic credentials of the teaching faculty

- Method of course assessment (exams, essays, projects, etc.)

- The grading system (ABCDEF, numerical scale, etc.) and the lowest passing grade

- After you return, you may be asked to furnish your course notes, exams, papers, etc., before credit is granted or a course is certified as meeting a particular graduation requirement.

Who issues the transcript? The U.S. university that sponsors the program? A foreign university? You and your advisor need to know this. The same information will be needed if you are considering a program sponsored by an agency or a foreign university.

Is the program abroad offered by a U.S.-accredited institution? Is the institution accredited to offer academic degrees in its own country? Your home university may require either U.S. or foreign accreditation in order for credit to be accepted. Find out your university's policies BEFORE you apply to a program.

How much credit can I earn? This will depend on your school policies and those of the host institution. Mostly, a full load of courses passed overseas translates into the same number of credits which could be earned at home during the same time period. But not always, so get this clear in advance. Also, find out what minimum grade you need to earn in order to receive credit from your home school—usually, a C or higher is required. If your college requires that you achieve a grade of C or above, you may not be able to take overseas courses on a pass/fail basis because in many systems the lowest passing grade is a D. Therefore, ask if your school will award credit for courses taken pass/fail.

Amount of credit will also depend on whether the study abroad program is on a quarter or semester basis. If your home school offers classes by semester, and the overseas program is on a quarter system, ask your advisor how transfer credit is calculated.

In addition, universities may (or may not) grant credit for independent study, internships and other experiential study, as well as dissertation credit for graduate students who do research abroad. If you are interested in these types of credit, discuss the possibilities and the requirements with your academic advisor and the registrar.

In sum, be sure you know how much credit will be awarded for all overseas study and whether there are any tuition fees that must be paid to your home institution in addition to the fees for the study abroad program.

Grades

Foreign universities may give a number grade rather than a letter, or even give comments in place of a grade. In addition, grading in some overseas universities can be much stricter than in the United States. Transferring of grades to an American system can be complicated. Therefore, some colleges show only the courses and the credits you take, without recording the grades on the transcript. In other cases, grades earned abroad are listed on the home transcript but not included in the grade point average (GPA). Be sure to ask whether your home institution figures grades earned abroad in your grade point average, as this might affect which courses you decided to take.

It's A Fact!

Most graduate schools, medical schools, and law schools will ask to see the original transcript from your international program. These institutions may convert the grades from abroad and include them in your GPA, even if your home institution does not.

Source: From "Study Abroad Student Guide, Part II: Living Abroad," by Bill Hoffa, © 2011 EducationDynamics, LLC. All rights reserved. Reprinted with permission. To view the complete Study Abroad Student Guide, and additional information, visit www.studyabroad.com.

Language Requirements

An important factor when considering a study abroad program is its language of instruction. Do you need to know the local language in order to begin (or complete) the program? If so, how well? In some programs, some courses are offered in the native language, and others in English. For a number of overseas study programs, a specified degree of fluency in the host language is required for entry. Others require that you be willing to study the local language, perhaps at the beginning level. This, of course, is not an issue in English-speaking countries, or with programs in other countries that teach courses for foreigners in English.

You can evaluate your language skills either by taking a language proficiency or placement exam or by taking an appropriate foreign language class. Sometimes testing is done on the home campus, and sometimes programs themselves will test applicants (or accepted students, after arrival, to judge the level of their placement). How well can you understand and communicate in a foreign language? It is wise to be completely realistic about your level of competency. Being able to carry on a simple conversation in another language is no guarantee that you can do academic work in it. On the other hand, opportunities to make quantum leaps forward in your language proficiency are one of the reasons for studying overseas. You might be amazed at how much you will learn once you are surrounded by a language other than English and have ample opportunities to speak, read, and write it.

Many study abroad programs sponsored by American colleges and universities are conducted in cooperation with a foreign university or offer special courses taught by foreign faculty. In such arrangements, courses are typically taught in the language of the host country, and generally require a minimum of two years of college study or the equivalent in that language. Some American colleges and universities offer language immersion programs to prepare their students for this course work.

A second choice is to enroll directly in a foreign university, where courses are usually taught in the host country language—or in an institute set up to meet the needs of foreign and visiting (nonmatriculated) students. In either instance, you will need to be sufficiently fluent in the local language in order to be able to comprehend lectures—including academic and technical terminology—and read scholarly books and other publications. Most foreign universities and institutes require U.S. students to take a language proficiency exam before admission. If your language skills need some brushing up, many foreign universities offer visiting students special courses in the language, and others on the native culture and history. Note: Direct enrollment typically means more effort on your part to ensure your home college/university approval of credit and financial aid transfer.

Consider a program that offers all course work in English, plus a foreign language class (which is typically taught in the language being studied). This is an option within many study abroad programs, including short-term overseas programs, often held in the summer or a winter interim. But review the course offerings carefully, as such programs typically offer only

It's A Fact!

A number of study abroad programs offer some classes in English and some in the local language. With these, you'll be able to understand and participate in classes while you polish your foreign language skills.

a limited selection of courses. Whatever your foreign language skills, you're likely to have a better understanding and appreciation of your host country if you make an effort to learn the local language. Learning a foreign language in a country in which it's spoken is an entirely different experience from learning it at home. Because you are surrounded by the language in everyday life, what you learn in the classroom can be practiced everywhere you go. Even if you acquire only survival language skills, the people you meet will appreciate your efforts. This is likely to open up even more opportunities to practice your proficiency.

It's A Fact!

Knowing a foreign language can be a passport to many different countries beyond the obvious. French, for instance, is spoken not only in France, but Morocco, some West African countries, the Caribbean, and the Canadian province of Quebec. Portuguese is the native tongue of Portugal, but also spoken as the primary language of gigantic Brazil. And Spanish, of course, is spoken in Spain and almost all of Central and South America, and in numerous countries around the world.

Source: From "Study Abroad Student Guide, Part II: Living Abroad," by Bill Hoffa, © 2011 EducationDynamics, LLC. All rights reserved. Reprinted with permission. To view the complete Study Abroad Student Guide, and additional information, visit www.studyabroad.com.

Timing And Duration

When would overseas study be best for you? How much flexibility is there in your academic schedule? How long a sojourn can you afford with your economic resources, even with financial assistance? These are major considerations you need to think about before choosing a program. In the past, most undergraduates who went abroad typically did so during their junior year for the entire year. The majority were foreign language majors, or studied in English-speaking countries. Today, many options exist for study abroad across the curriculum; for participating in programs which vary in duration from a few weeks to a calendar year; and for studying abroad at almost any point during undergraduate degree studies (or after one has graduated). All of these options exist—at least in theory. In practice, your college or university may have rules and requirements which restrict your choices a little or a lot.

Academic Or Semester: About half of all U.S. students currently studying abroad are participating in semester or academic year abroad programs. Such programs, because of their length and opportunities for true immersion in a foreign culture, are likely to make the strongest and most long-lasting impact both academically and in terms of cross-cultural understanding and career preparation. It takes time to adjust to a new living and learning environment, and many would say that the best learning takes place after such adjustment has taken place. But there are other issues to consider. Do you have the discipline to pursue your studies for a semester or year away from home? Can you afford to spend that much time away from your academic program? If the answer to either of these is no, there are still plenty of study abroad options available to you. About half of all U.S. students now studying abroad do so on short-term programs; that is, programs shorter than an academic semester. Shorter programs, if well planned, can offer a more intensive and focused experience—and may be the only realistic alternative in terms of the demands of your degree studies and economic resources.

Summer Study Programs: These programs range in length from two weeks to three months, with the largest number offered for one to two months. You can combine academic course work with program-related travel, or course work can be followed by vacation travel. Sometimes the program is entirely travel (in which case earning credit may not be possible). Such programs are sponsored by American higher educational institutions, as well as by overseas universities, agencies, and organizations. So-called vacation study programs are enormous in number and variety. Such programs are offered all over the world. You can study business law in Australia, fashion design in London, United States–Mexico relations in Mexico, and international finance in Tokyo. Programs range from two- or four-week courses to those that last two or three months. Courses of study vary from those with a strong focus on academics, with the addition of a few field trips, to a study tour, in which travel and learning are combined. Vacation and summer study programs are sponsored by U.S. colleges and universities and foreign higher educational institutions. Many specialized institutes abroad focus on the art, language, and culture of their home countries and offer short-term programs to U.S. nationals.

It's A Fact!

Some language study programs are sponsored by language-teaching institutes, e.g., Alliance Française Goethe Institute.

Also available are study tour programs in which a U.S. professor leads a traveling group of students, alums, or others within one country or to several countries, for credit or just the educational exposure.

Source: From "Study Abroad Student Guide, Part II: Living Abroad," by Bill Hoffa, © 2011 EducationDynamics, LLC. All rights reserved. Reprinted with permission. To view the complete Study Abroad Student Guide, and additional information, visit www.studyabroad.com.

Interim Study Programs: These programs are held in the period between semesters, especially for universities on the four-one-four calendar, or between academic quarters for those operating on the quarter system.

Pre-Freshman Year Programs: These programs are available for students who feel they need a breathing period between completing high school and beginning college.

Follow-Up Or Lab Programs: Led by the instructor, these programs are held to supplement what was learned in class with firsthand, on-site, exposure to what was studied.

Location

Where is the best place for you to study? The answer obviously depends on many different personal, curricular, and institutional considerations. Think this through carefully, as no given place is likely to answer all your needs, and yet each place has something unique to offer. Western Europe is the traditional destination for American students going abroad, and now accounts for about two-thirds of all students. One of the reasons students head for Western European countries is because there are so many well-established program sites. Yet programs now beckon from all over the globe.

But, in increasing numbers, students are also deciding to consider other regions, sometimes based on course work, sometimes on language, cultural, or career interests. Excellent programs are available in the former Soviet Union, Eastern Europe, the Middle East, Africa, Asia, Latin America, South America, the Caribbean, and the islands of the South Pacific. In fact, almost (but not quite) everywhere! You can study volcanology in Costa Rica, political change in South Africa, Buddhism in Tibet, or indigenous music in Zambia. Nothing can compare with learning a foreign language in a country where it's spoken, whether that means learning Spanish in Spain or Wolof in Senegal.

Enrollment Options

Approximately 72% of U.S. undergraduates who end up studying abroad enroll in a study abroad program specially organized for students like them. The sponsor may be a U.S. college or university (the student's own, another, or a consortium) with which it has reached an agreement. Or the sponsor could be a domestic organization other than a college or university, or an overseas university or organization, often as part of its program for other international students. However, depending on your own institution's policies with regard to transfer credit from other domestic or overseas institutions, a host of other options may exist for you. The below list moves from options centered in your own institution to options more centered in overseas institutions.

Enroll in a program designed and overseen by U.S. colleges or universities for American students. The most popular choices of study abroad programs include those sponsored by a student's own institution, by another U.S. college or university, or by a consortium, or group, of U.S. colleges or universities. Such arrangements make possible hundreds of academic year, semester, quarter, and vacation study program opportunities.

Programs sponsored by U.S. colleges allow students to study in a foreign environment while remaining within a U.S. academic framework. Even if the actual course work is taken at a foreign university, academic credit is arranged through the sponsoring U.S. institution. In many cases, special courses in the language and culture of the host country are offered, and the language requirements may be relaxed. The sponsoring college usually also makes housing and round-trip travel arrangements for students, and may arrange cultural excursions.

Programs offered by U.S. institutions basically fall into two main categories, though many variations exist within each:

- **The Island Program:** All courses are arranged for a group of U.S. students and taught by home campus faculty members familiar with the host culture or by foreign faculty hired by the U.S. school. Costs are often about the same as study on the home campus, and financial aid that you receive from your institution or from the government can typically be used. Some of these programs offer intensive language study for language majors. Generally, though, these programs are taught in English, except for foreign language classes, which are taught in the language studied. This is a good option for students who don't speak the local language. It may also be a good choice if this will be your first time overseas. Be aware, however, that no overseas program can provide academic and social services identical to what you are accustomed to at home.

- **Hybrid Programs:** These programs involve study in a foreign institution, combined with courses arranged for the group by the sponsoring U.S. institution. They generally require some knowledge of the host country language. Nonetheless, special university courses for U.S. or other foreign students usually have less demanding language requirements than regular university courses. And some programs offer a choice of foreign institutions, depending on the level of the student's language skills. One benefit of this type of program is that it lets you study at a foreign institution while meeting requirements for your U.S. degree. Many of these programs also offer academic support services similar to those found on a U.S. campus.

Enroll in a program sponsored by an organization other than a U.S. college or university. Some not-for-profit and for-profit organizations in the United States and overseas also sponsor study abroad programs. Of these, some have agreements with colleges and universities allowing students to be registered on their home campuses. Others indicate that academic credit is available or transferable, but students must arrange or verify the credit themselves. If you are considering one of these programs, be sure to investigate your school's credit transfer policy, as well as the policy of the program you are considering.

Enroll in a program for international students at a foreign university. Some universities abroad offer language and culture programs to foreigners. These enable U.S. students (considered international students while overseas) to interact with students from several other countries. Some programs sponsored by foreign universities are specially designed to meet the needs of English-speaking students, with courses offered in English as well as the host country language. In addition, in the 1990s, as academic mobility and exchange in Europe increased, a number of English-language programs were designed for students from other countries. Some of these are available to U.S. students as well.

If you want to enroll in this kind of program, be sure to discuss credit transfer with your advisor. In some cases, foreign schools arrange to transfer credit through an accredited U.S. college. But credit doesn't transfer automatically from foreign universities, and in some cases is not transferable.

Enroll in a foreign university via a U.S. college or university. It is also possible to enroll in foreign universities directly by applying through U.S. programs set up for this purpose— e.g., Arcadia University's Center for Study Abroad or Butler University's Institute for Study Abroad. This intermediation can solve the credit transfer problem, as the overseas course work is placed on an American college transcript. Such a process can increase overall costs, but, in return, may also provide orientation, accommodations, excursions, and on-site support services not otherwise available to occasional or special students.

Enroll directly in a foreign university as a special student. Many universities around the world are open to students from other countries who qualify for admission as special or occasional students. This is similar to taking regular classes in the United States as a non-admitted or part-time student. Credit does not transfer automatically from foreign universities and in some cases is not transferable. Taking classes taught by foreign teachers, alongside students from the host country, can be very exciting and challenging. But it requires an extra measure of enterprise and resourcefulness on your part, since it's up to you to make the arrangements and do the course work without support services from a U.S. institution. You also must be fluent in the language of instruction to consider this option. And there can be difficulty with credit transfer as well with the transferability of your U.S. financial assistance.

Housing Options

Your living situation will have a significant impact on your study abroad experience. Housing can be as grand as a manor house, as rugged as a tent in a rain forest, or as standard issue as a university residence hall.

Many study abroad programs provide student housing. Some arrange home stays, in which you live with a local family. Others provide housing in dormitories or apartments, where your roommates could be students from the host country, from other foreign countries, or from the United States. For short-term programs or those that require extensive travel, students may be housed in hotels, pensions, or student hostels.

Some programs offer a choice of housing arrangements. In most cases, however, the choices are few, as student housing is difficult to find almost everywhere. Dormitory space is often so limited that many foreign universities have strict quotas for the number of rooms allotted to international students.

Financial Aid

If you are currently receiving financial aid for your college education, in many cases you can use it to study abroad. This can be the case with aid from an institution, a foundation, the state or federal government, or other private or public sources. Talk to your study abroad advisor, financial aid officer, or bursar about what can and can't be applied to a program of study abroad.

Quick Tip

Be sure to find out whether programs you are interested in arrange housing for participants; not all do. If it's up to you to find your own housing, ask if the sponsoring institution will assist you. Request an estimate of costs for accommodations, food, travel, and essential living expenses.

Source: From "Study Abroad Student Guide, Part II: Living Abroad," by Bill Hoffa, © 2011 EducationDynamics, LLC. All rights reserved. Reprinted with permission. To view the complete Study Abroad Student Guide, and additional information, visit www.studyabroad.com.

Part Three
Saving For College

Chapter 13

Reasons To Save For College

Why Save For College?

College is an investment for a lifetime—the gift of a college education can open the door to a world of opportunity. Saving, even a little at a time, can make a big difference down the road. With the cost of a college education continuing to increase, the key is to start saving early and regularly.

Rising Cost Of Education

According to the College Board, the average cost for tuition and fees at four-year public institutions has increased nearly 51% over the last 10 years (after adjusting for inflation), and these costs will almost certainly continue to rise. Saving for college can help with the increasing cost of a college education and help you be financially prepared for college.

Education Pays

Saving for your college education is an investment in your future. The savings you make today pay off in an increased earnings potential in the future. According to the U.S. Census Bureau, college graduates earn an average of $1 million more than high school graduates during their careers. The value of your investment in a college education will continue to grow for a lifetime. It will pay for itself both personally and professionally.

About This Chapter: This chapter begins with "Why Save for College?" © 2010 College Savings Plans Network (www.collegesavings.org). All rights reserved. Reprinted with permission. The chapter also includes "Myths about Saving for College," © 2011 FinAid Page, LLC (www.finaid.org). All rights reserved. Reprinted with permission. Additional information from Sallie Mae, Inc. is cited separately within the chapter.

- Among men, median earnings of four-year college graduates were 63% higher than median earnings of high school graduates in 2005.

- Among women, median earnings of four-year college graduates were 70% higher than median earnings of high school graduates in 2005.

Saving Even A Little Can Go A Long Way

Remember—no matter how much you save, even a little can make a difference.

Like any other major investment, the key to saving for college is to start early and save regularly. By saving a set amount at set times, your money can grow as you do.

Set your college savings goals realistically. You may not be able to save enough for all four years of tuition, room and board, and other expenses—but you (and your parents or grandparents) could save enough to get the right start.

Reduce Reliance On Debt

More and more families rely on student loans to pay for college. Though low-interest loans are often available for college financing, paying even small amounts of interest can add up considerably over long periods of time. By saving for college, families can reduce their reliance on loans, earn interest versus paying interest, and help their student leave college debt free.

Myths About Saving For College

There are several myths about saving for college. The most common myths are that there is a penalty for savings, that college savings plans are available only for wealthy families, or that a family will qualify for more need-based aid if they don't save for college. These myths are harmful because they discourage families from saving for college.

Myth Number One: Penalty For Savings

Many families mistakenly believe that they are penalized for saving, and that they would be better off if they didn't save. The Federal Need Analysis Methodology does count a portion of the family's assets in determinations of financial need, so a family with more assets will get less need-based aid. However, the federal government does not count all of the assets, just a fraction, so a family that saves for college will have more money left over than a family that does not save for college.

The federal need analysis formula shelters several types of assets. Money in retirement plan accounts is ignored, as is the net worth of the family's home and any small businesses owned and controlled by the family. A portion of parent assets is also sheltered by an asset protection allowance based on the age of the older parent. This shelters about $50,000 for the typical family with college-age children (median age 48). As a result, less than four percent of dependent children have any contribution from parent assets.

Money in a dependent child's 529 college savings plan (or other qualified tuition plan) is treated as though it were a parent asset on the Free Application for Federal Student Aid (FAFSA). This is a more favorable treatment than for child assets. Child assets are assessed at a 20% rate while parent assets are assessed according to a bracketed scale with a top bracket of 5.64%. While every $10,000 in a 529 college savings plan may reduce need-based aid eligibility by up to $564, that still leaves you with at least $9,436 more available to pay for college than if you hadn't saved.

It's A Fact!

529 college savings plans are a tax-advantaged way of saving for college. Earnings in the plan are tax deferred and, if used to pay for qualified higher education expenses, entirely tax free. These tax benefits were made permanent by the Pension Protection Act of 2006 and will not expire.

Source: From "Myths about Saving for College," © 2011 FinAid Page, LLC (www.finaid.org). All rights reserved. Reprinted with permission.

It's Cheaper To Save Than To Borrow: The more money you save, the more options you'll have and the less you'll need to borrow. It is always cheaper to save now than to borrow later. If you save $200 a month for 10 years at 6.8% interest, you'll accumulate about $34,400. If you were to borrow this money instead of saving, you'd pay $396 a month for 10 years at 6.8% interest, almost twice as much. When you save, the interest is paid to you, while when you borrow, you pay the interest.

Myth Number Two: Student Aid Will Pick Up The Tab

Many parents mistakenly believe that if they don't save for college, they'll be able to shift the costs to their children through loans, or that the federal government and the schools will pick up the tab. Student loans only go so far in covering college costs, and the government and schools consider parents to have the primary responsibility in paying for their children's education. Even if a child gets a lot of need-based aid, it doesn't cover the full costs. The Pell Grant, for example, covers only 10 percent of current private four-year college costs. Work study covers only 10–20 percent of college costs. Failing to start saving now will only hurt you later. The only viable hedge against increases in college costs is to save as much as possible as early as possible.

Myth Number Three: Scholarships Will Cover All The Costs

Families also think that they can rely on scholarships to pay for college. For example, four-fifths of parents expect that their children will receive scholarships, but only about seven percent of students actually receive private sector scholarships. The average amount of the scholarship received by undergraduate students is $2,000. Moreover, due to outside scholarship policies, receiving a private scholarship will often reduce need-based aid packages. It is still worthwhile to search for scholarships, because scholarships often replace loans, but one must be realistic about the chances of winning a scholarship (1 in 15) and the impact of scholarships on paying for college (less than 10 percent).

It's A Fact!

All state 529 college savings plans have low minimum contribution requirements of just $15 to $25 a month. Some states will even match the contributions by low income families to encourage them to save.

Source: From "Myths about Saving for College," © 2011 FinAid Page, LLC (www.finaid.org). All rights reserved. Reprinted with permission.

Myth Number Four: 529 Plans Are Only For The Wealthy

While it may be more difficult for low and moderate income families to save, everybody can benefit from a 529 college savings plan. College savings not only increases access to a college education by spreading the cost over time but it also maximizes choice. It helps families choose the college that is most appropriate for their children, as opposed to just the least expensive college.

Myth Number Five: It's Too Late To Start Saving

It is never too late to start saving for college.

It is best to start saving when the child is young, since your greatest asset is time. If you start saving at birth, about a third of the savings goal will come from earnings on the investment. If you start saving when the child enters high school, less than a tenth of the savings goal will come from earnings on the investment. Some personal finance experts even advise starting to save before birth.

However, there are financial benefits to saving even if the child will enroll in college next year (or even if the child is already in college). Thirty-two states and the District of Columbia offer a state income tax deduction or tax credit for contributions to the state's 529 college savings plan, with four states providing a tax deduction for contributions to any state's 529 college savings plan. This is like getting a small discount on tuition, with the discount equal to your marginal tax rate. That's a 3 percent to 10 percent discount, depending on your state. You might have to keep the money in the plan for a year, since some states base the deduction on contributions net of distributions.

Myth Number Six: The Stock Market Is Too Risky

The stock market is risky, but one can manage the risk through a careful investment strategy.

The S&P 500 dropped 39% in value in 2008, causing some state 529 college savings plans to lose money and many prepaid tuition plans to have actuarial funding shortfalls. This caused about half of families to change how they save for college, according to a 2010 college savings survey.

However, stock market volatility is to be expected. During any 17 year period, the stock market will drop significantly at least two or three times. The severity of the 2008 stock market plunge was unusual, but not the drop itself. When you are saving for a long-term life cycle event like college, you should plan for the volatility by using an age-based asset allocation and by using dollar-cost averaging.

- **Age-Based Asset Allocation:** Age-based asset allocation starts off with an aggressive mix of investments when the child is young and gradually shifts toward a more conservative mix of investments when college approaches. It bottoms out with less than one fifth of the portfolio in risky investments a year before high school graduation. (Risky investments include stocks and other investments where there is a potential risk to principal. Low risk investments include bank certificates of deposit and money market accounts.) When the child is young the amount of any losses will be small and there is a lot of time to recover from the losses. When college is close there is more money at stake.

- **Dollar-Cost Averaging:** Dollar-cost averaging invests a fixed amount of money at a regular interval. When the stock prices go down, the number of shares purchased increases. When stock prices go up, the number of shares purchased decreases. This implements the sage advice to buy low and sell high. Dollar-cost averaging is one of the most effective blind strategies for investing. It works best when the stock market is volatile.

Myth Number Seven: 529 Plans Are Limited To Certain Colleges

Some prepaid tuition plans may be restricted to the tuition and fees at in-state public colleges. But 529 college savings plans are not. They can be used at any accredited public or private college in the United States. This includes vocational and technical schools, two-year colleges, four-year colleges, graduate schools, and professional schools (medical, business, and law schools). 529 college savings plans can be used for Certificates, Associate's degrees, Bachelor's degrees, and Master's degrees, as well as more advanced degrees. They are not restricted to public colleges and can be used at private colleges (nonprofit and for profit), so long as the college's programs are eligible for federal student aid.

American Parents Say Saving For College As Important As Saving For Retirement, According To New Research By Sallie Mae And Gallup

Percentage Saving For College Unchanged Despite Economy, Many Parents Need Education On How To Save, Avoid Costly Mistakes

American families with children who are likely to attend college rank saving for college as high a priority as saving for retirement, with one in five naming it their top saving priority, according to a new national study, conducted by Gallup and Sallie Mae, the nation's leading saving, planning, and paying for college company. Sixty percent of parents have saved for their child's college education, about the same as last year despite the difficult economic environment, and are on track to save $48,367 on average by the time their child turns 18.

Nearly half of those not saving for college do not know how (18%) or are not sure which are the best college savings options (28%).

"The good news is that savers start early and plan to save enough to cover two years at a public university or one year at a private one," said Albert L. Lord, vice chairman and CEO, Sallie Mae. "Sallie Mae is committed to educating parents of all income levels on how they can save responsibly for this important life investment and to providing the tools to get started."

Twenty-four percent of saving-for-college parents risk their financial future by using retirement accounts to save for college and make other costly mistakes by not investing in tax-advantaged options, such as 529 college savings plans. Across all parents saving for college, the average amount saved for college in retirement accounts is $6,503, compared to $3,340 in 529 college savings plans. Although each state offers 529 college savings plans with low fees and tax incentives benefitting all income levels, half of those not currently using one say that they are not at all familiar with 529 plans.

Most savers (60%) use at least two savings vehicles, and the number of options utilized increases with income. General savings accounts and CDs are the most popular (50%) followed by investment accounts (34%). Eight percent save through a college savings rewards program.

Sallie Mae provides a full spectrum of savings solutions, including High-Yield Savings accounts, Certificates of Deposits, 529 college savings plans, and Upromise rewards. The company's Upromise Investments is the largest administrator of college savings plans managing more than $26 billion in 529 assets across 23 plans in 12 states. High-Yield Savings accounts and Certificates of Deposit by Sallie Mae are FDIC insured and have savings interest rates among the highest in the nation. The Upromise rewards program is free to join and through it members have received $575 million for college from everyday spending.

The second annual "How America Saves for College" report, conducted March–May 2010 by Sallie Mae and Gallup, is a nationally representative survey of 2,092 parents with children under the age of 18. The full report is available at www.SallieMae.com/howAmericaSaves.

Chapter 14

Ways To Save For College

[Editor's Note: Although this article is written to parents, the information in it is relevant to teens. Although your parents are often the ones saving for your college education, it is helpful for you to understand the various savings options and the pros and cons of each.]

College Saving While Saving Taxes

In addition to mutual funds, regular brokerage accounts, and bank savings accounts, there are now a number of tax-advantaged alternatives available to help you save for college. Get the facts about each of the options, and decide which type might be right for you:

- 529 plans
- Prepaid tuition plans
- College savings plans
- Coverdell Education Savings Accounts
- Custodial accounts
- Savings bonds

About This Chapter: This chapter contains text excerpted from "Smart Saving For College—Better Buy Degrees," a publication of the Financial Industry Regulatory Authority (www.finra.org). © 2011 FINRA. All rights reserved. FINRA is a registered trademark of the Financial Industry Regulatory Authority, Inc. Reprinted with permission from FINRA. The complete text of this guide is available on the FINRA website, beginning at http://apps.finra.org/investor_Information/Smart/529/000100.asp.

Remember

Remember: The tax rules that apply to college savings options are complicated. Before investing, you may want to check with your tax adviser about the tax consequences of investing in any of these options.

529 Plans

Named after the section of the federal tax code that governs them, 529 plans are tax-advantaged programs that help families save for college. Selecting a plan requires homework. Every state offers at least one 529 plan and now a consortium of private colleges also offers a 529 plan. The tax advantages, investment options, restrictions, and fees can vary a great deal.

Before buying a 529 plan, you should find out about the particular plan you are considering, and be sure you understand the plan's description of fees and expenses. Request an offering circular or official statement from the plan sponsor or your financial professional. Most 529 plans provide this document on their websites, where it may be called the "Disclosure Statement," the "Plan Disclosure Document," or something similar.

Coverdell Education Savings Accounts

Those who want more investment choices may want to consider Coverdell Education Saving Accounts (ESAs).

No Investment Restrictions

Formerly known as Education IRAs, ESAs are another tax-advantaged way to pay for college. Unlike 529 plans, your investment options are virtually limitless. Except for investing in life insurance contracts, you can buy and sell what you want whenever you want. Also, you can set them up at almost any brokerage firm, mutual-fund company, or other financial institution.

Federal Tax Advantages

As with 529 plans, contributions are not deductible, but earnings in ESAs are tax deferred, and withdrawals that are used for qualified education expenses are tax free.

It's A Fact!

You can find links to most 529 plan websites on The National Association of State Treasurers' College Savings Plans Network website, www.collegesavings.org, for information on the 529 plans you are interested in.

Education Expenses Covered

One advantage that ESAs have over other tax-advantaged saving options is that you can make tax-free withdrawals to pay for private elementary and high school expenses, as well as postsecondary school expenses. So if a private school is in the future, one option you might want to consider is saving for that expense in an ESA and using a 529 plan for college.

Contribution Limits

Coverdell Education Saving Accounts (ESAs) have two annual contribution limits for individuals:

1. You can give up to $2,000 to any one beneficiary assuming you meet the ESA income limits.

2. The total of all contributions to all ESAs set up for one beneficiary cannot exceed $2,000. If other family members set up ESAs for your child, you need to check with them to make sure this contribution limit is not exceeded.

If you exceed these contribution limits, there is a six percent excise tax each year on excess contributions.

Custodial Accounts

Custodial accounts—Uniform Gift to Minors Act (UGMA) accounts or Uniform Transfer to Minors Act (UTMA) accounts—are another tax-advantaged way to save for college. A parent, grandparent, or other adult is custodian for the account and makes all the investment decisions until the child for whom the account was opened reaches the age of majority. UGMA accounts are limited to money and securities. UTMA accounts can hold other types of property. You can set up these accounts at almost any brokerage firm, mutual-fund company, or other financial institution.

Advantages

In tax year 2010, for children younger than 18, the first $950 of unearned income is tax free. The next $950 is taxed at the child's federal tax rate. Any earnings over $1,900 are taxed at the custodian's federal tax rate. To learn more about the tax rules for children, you should read IRS Publication 929: *Tax Rules for Children and Dependents*.

As with ESAs, your investing options are virtually limitless. Nor are there any contribution or income limitations. In addition, withdrawals can be used for any purpose, not just qualified education expenses, without penalty.

Disadvantages

When your child reaches the age of majority—18 to 25 depending on the state in which you live—he or she takes control of the account and can use the money in the account for anything. Because you lose control over how the money may be spent, some parents and grandparents may not like this option. Another potential disadvantage is that because the account is considered the child's asset, you can't switch beneficiaries. So if your child decides not go to college or gets a scholarship, you can't switch the money to a brother, sister, or other family member.

Series EE And I Savings Bonds

U.S. Series EE savings bonds issued after 1989 or Series I saving bonds are another tax-advantaged way to save for college.

Advantages

Backed by the full faith and credit of the U.S. government, the interest from these bonds is tax free if used for qualified higher education expenses. Also, interest on Series EE and I savings bonds is usually exempt from state and local taxes.

Disadvantages

The full interest exclusion in tax year 2009 is only available to married couples filing jointly with modified adjusted gross income of less than $104,900, and for single filers with modified adjusted gross income of less than $69,950. The interest exclusion is phased out if your modified adjusted gross income is between $104,900 and $134,900 for joint filers, and between $69,950 and $84,950 for single taxpayers. Regardless of your income, married couples filing separately cannot take advantage of this savings bond program. You can learn more about the Educational Savings Bond Program in IRS Publication 970: *Tax Benefits for Education.*

The rules for using savings bonds for education can be complicated. To learn more about using savings bonds for educational expenses, you should read the Bureau of Public Debt's information on education and savings bonds or you can call the Federal Reserve at (866) 388-1776. You can call the Bureau of Public Debt toll-free at 800-487-2663 for information on the latest rates for Series EE and Series I savings bonds or at 800-722-2678 to learn how to buy savings bonds directly from the federal government. The Bureau of Public Debt's website also provides information on the latest rates for Series EE and Series I savings bonds and how to buy saving bonds directly from the federal government.

Tax-Free Transfer To A 529 Plan

You now can transfer funds from a custodial account to a 529 plan if the plan accepts such transfers. However, you must liquidate any investments you have made in a custodial account because you can only transfer cash and pay taxes, if any, on any gains. Another problem with transferring custodial account funds is that the money is the child's asset, not yours, so you cannot transfer the 529 plan to another beneficiary. There also may be other restrictions and limitations.

Tips For Choosing College Savings Options

Understand The Tax Benefits

A number of college savings options offer tax-advantaged ways to save. Taking advantage of these savings options may greatly affect how much you can accumulate for your child's college education. In addition to the federal tax benefits of many college savings options, there may also be state tax benefits. Savings bonds are usually exempt from state and local taxes. Many states allow you to deduct some or all of your contributions to a 529 plan if you're a resident of the state sponsoring the plan. In addition, states may offer other tax advantages for 529 plans. Because of these state tax benefits, you might want to check out your own state's 529 plan before considering other plans.

Everyone's tax situation is different, and state and federal tax law can be complex. You may want to consult with your tax adviser about which college savings options are best for you.

Savings Bond Online Resource

The Bureau of Public Debt's website, www.treasurydirect.gov, also provides information on the latest rates for Series EE and Series I savings bonds and how to buy savings bonds directly from the federal government.

Examine Fees And Expenses

All of the college savings options discussed above involve various fees and expenses. A college saving option with higher costs must perform better than a low-cost option to generate the same returns for you. Even small differences in fees and expenses can translate into a large difference over time.

Know The Risks As Well As The Rewards Of Your College Savings Options

Compared to saving for retirement, your college saving timeline is relatively short. At most it may be 18 years. And for many people, it's a lot less. This can impact your ability to weather a market decline and increases your risk.

Before investing in any college saving vehicle, carefully evaluate it and its investment options. Investment options with higher rates of return may take risks that are beyond your comfort level and are inconsistent with your goals. To learn more about the investment strategy of investment options you are considering and their risk, you should read the following materials:

- **529 Plans:** Read the offering circular or prospectus. It usually contains the investment strategy and risks of a 529 plan and its investment portfolios. Most 529 plans provide this document on their web sites.

- **Mutual Funds:** Read the prospectus and shareholder reports. Prospectus and shareholders reports are usually available from mutual fund companies or your financial professional. Mutual fund prospectuses also are available in the SEC's EDGAR database.

- **Stocks And Other Securities:** Read a company's registration statement or annual (Form 10-K) and quarterly (Form 10-Q) reports. These are typically available in the SEC's EDGAR database, www.sec.gov/edgar.shtml. For companies that don't file in EDGAR, e-mail the SEC's Office of Investor Education and Advocacy, or call (202) 551-8090, to see whether the company has filed any documents with the SEC.

Quick Tip

If you invest in mutual funds through an ESA or custodial account, you should check the fee table in the prospectus to see how the costs of a mutual fund add up over time. If you invest in stock, make sure you understand how much in commissions you must pay and factor this into any gain you may make.

Understand Your College Savings Plan's Limitations And Restrictions

What happens to your college savings if your child decides not to go to college, you have another child, or you lose your job? These events and many others could dramatically impact your college savings strategy. Unfortunately, most college savings options have various restrictions and limitations that may impact your ability to react to a changing situation. Review carefully any college saving options you're considering to make sure they have the flexibility and control you feel you need.

Chapter 15

Section 529 Plans

An Introduction to 529 Plans

A 529 plan is a tax-advantaged savings plan designed to encourage saving for future college costs. 529 plans, legally known as "qualified tuition plans," are sponsored by states, state agencies, or educational institutions and are authorized by Section 529 of the Internal Revenue Code.

There are two types of 529 plans: prepaid tuition plans and college savings plans. All fifty states and the District of Columbia sponsor at least one type of 529 plan. In addition, a group of private colleges and universities sponsor a prepaid tuition plan.

Prepaid Tuition Plans Versus College Savings Plans

Prepaid tuition plans generally allow college savers to purchase units or credits at participating colleges and universities for future tuition and, in some cases, room and board. Most prepaid tuition plans are sponsored by state governments and have residency requirements. Many state governments guarantee investments in prepaid tuition plans that they sponsor.

College savings plans generally permit a college saver (also called the account holder) to establish an account for a student (the beneficiary) for the purpose of paying the beneficiary's eligible college expenses. An account holder may typically choose among several investment options for his or her contributions, which the college savings plan invests on behalf of the account holder. Investment options often include stock mutual funds, bond mutual funds, and

About This Chapter: This chapter begins with text from "An Introduction to 529 Plans," a publication of the U.S. Securities and Exchange Commission (www.sec.gov), August 2007. The chapter continues with additional information from the College Savings Plans Network (www.collegesavings.org) and Forefield 2011, in Partnership with the American Institute of Certified Public Accountants (www.360financialliteracy.org), which is cited separately within the chapter.

money market funds, as well as age-based portfolios that automatically shift toward more conservative investments as the beneficiary gets closer to college age. Withdrawals from college savings plans can generally be used at any college or university.

Table 15.1 outlines some of the major differences between prepaid tuition plans and college savings plans.

529 Plans And Income Taxes

Investing in a 529 plan may offer college savers special tax benefits. Earnings in 529 plans are not subject to federal tax, and in most cases, state tax, so long as you use withdrawals for eligible college expenses, such as tuition and room and board.

However, if you withdraw money from a 529 plan and do not use it on an eligible college expense, you generally will be subject to income tax and an additional 10% federal tax penalty on earnings. Many states offer state income tax or other benefits, such as matching grants, for investing in a 529 plan. But you may only be eligible for these benefits if you participate in a 529 plan sponsored by your state of residence. Just a few states allow residents to deduct contributions to any 529 plan from state income tax returns.

529 Fees And Expenses

It is important to understand the fees and expenses associated with 529 plans because they lower your returns. Fees and expenses will vary based on the type of plan. Prepaid tuition plans typically charge enrollment and administrative fees. In addition to "loads" for broker-sold plans, college savings plans may charge enrollment fees, annual maintenance fees, and asset management fees. Some of these fees are collected by the state sponsor of the plan, and some are collected by the financial services firms that the state sponsor typically hires to manage its 529 program. Some college savings plans will waive or reduce some of these fees if you maintain a large account balance or participate in an automatic contribution plan, or if you are a resident of the state sponsoring the 529 plan. Your asset management fees will depend on the investment option you select. Each investment option will typically bear a portfolio-weighted average of the fees and expenses of the mutual funds and other investments in which it invests. You should carefully review the fees of the underlying investments because they are likely to be different for each investment option.

Investors that purchase a college savings plan from a broker are typically subject to additional fees. If you invest in a broker-sold plan, you may pay a "load." Broadly speaking, the load is paid to your broker as a commission for selling the college savings plan to you. Broker-sold plans also charge an annual distribution fee (similar to the "12b 1 fee" charged by some mutual funds) of between 0.25% and 1.00% of your investment. Your broker typically receives all or most of these annual distribution fees for selling your 529 plan to you.

Table 15.1. Prepaid Tuition Plans Versus College Savings Plans

Prepaid Tuition Plan	College Savings Plan
Locks in tuition prices at eligible public and private colleges and universities.	No lock on college costs.
All plans cover tuition and mandatory fees only. Some plans allow you to purchase a room and board option or use excess tuition credits for other qualified expenses.	Covers all "qualified higher education expenses," including: tuition, room and board, mandatory fees, books, and computers (if required).
Most plans set lump sum and installment payments prior to purchase based on age of beneficiary and number of years of college tuition purchased.	Many plans have contribution limits in excess of $200,000.
Many state plans guaranteed or backed by state.	No state guarantee. Most investment options are subject to market risk. Your investment may make no profit or even decline in value.
Most plans have age/grade limit for beneficiary.	No age limits. Open to adults and children.
Most state plans require either owner or beneficiary of plan to be a state resident.	No residency requirement. However, nonresidents may only be able to purchase some plans through financial advisers or brokers.
Most plans have limited enrollment period.	Enrollment open all year.

Source: Smart Saving for College, FINRA®

Quick Tip

If you receive state tax benefits for investing in a 529 plan, make sure you review your plan's offering circular before you complete a transaction, such as rolling money out of your home state's plan into another state's plan. Some transactions may have state tax consequences for residents of certain states.

Source: From "An Introduction to 529 Plans," a publication of the U.S. Securities and Exchange Commission, August 2007.

Here are some key characteristics of the most common 529 plan share classes sold by brokers to their customers:

- **Class A shares typically impose a front-end sales load.** Front-end sales loads reduce the amount of your investment. For example, let's say you have $1,000 and want to invest in a college savings plan with a 5% front-end load. The $50 sales load you must pay is deducted from your $1,000, and the remaining $950 is invested in the college savings plan. Class A shares usually have a lower annual distribution fee and lower overall annual expenses than other 529 share classes. In addition, your front-end load may be reduced if you invest above certain threshold amounts—this is known as a breakpoint discount. These discounts do not apply to investments in Class B or Class C shares.

- **Class B shares typically do not have a front-end sales load.** Instead, they may charge a fee when you withdraw money from an investment option, known as a deferred sales charge or "back-end load." A common back-end load is the "contingent deferred sales charge" or "contingent deferred sales load" (also known as a CDSC or CDSL). The amount of this load will depend on how long you hold your investment and typically decreases to zero if you hold your investment long enough. Class B shares typically impose a higher annual distribution fee and higher overall annual expenses than Class A shares. Class B shares usually convert automatically to Class A shares if you hold your shares long enough.

- **Class C shares might have an annual distribution fee, other annual expenses, and either a front- or back-end sales load.** But the front- or back-end load for Class C shares tends to be lower than for Class A or Class B shares, respectively. Class C shares typically impose a higher annual distribution fee and higher overall annual expenses than Class A shares, but, unlike Class B shares, generally do not convert to another class over time. If you are a long-term investor, Class C shares may be more expensive than investing in Class A or Class B shares.

Avoiding Extra Fees

- **Direct-Sold College Savings Plans:** States offer college savings plans through which residents and, in many cases, nonresidents can invest without paying a "load," or sales fee. This type of plan, which you can buy directly from the plan's sponsor or program manager without the assistance of a broker, is generally less expensive because it waives or does not charge sales fees that may apply to broker-sold plans. You can generally find information on a direct-sold plan by contacting the plan's sponsor or program manager or visiting the plan's website. Websites such as the one maintained by the College Savings Plan Network (CSPN), as well as a number of commercial websites, provide links to most 529 plan websites.

- **Broker-Sold College Savings Plans:** If you prefer to purchase a broker-sold plan, you may be able to reduce the front-end load for purchasing Class A shares if you invest or plan to invest above certain threshold amounts. Ask your broker how to qualify for these "breakpoint discounts."

Restrictions

Withdrawal restrictions apply to both college savings plans and prepaid tuition plans. With limited exceptions, you can only withdraw money that you invest in a 529 plan for eligible college expenses without incurring taxes and penalties. In addition, participants in college savings plans have limited investment options and are not permitted to switch freely among available investment options. Under current tax law, an account holder is only permitted to change his or her investment option one time per year. Additional limitations will likely apply to any 529 plan you may be considering.

Quick Tip

Be careful when investing in Class B shares. If the beneficiary uses the money within a few years after purchasing Class B shares, you will almost always pay a contingent deferred sales charge or load in addition to higher annual fees and expenses.

Source: From "An Introduction to 529 Plans," a publication of the U.S. Securities and Exchange Commission, August 2007.

---

529 Plans And Financial Aid Eligibility

While each educational institution may treat assets held in a 529 plan differently, investing in a 529 plan will generally reduce a student's eligibility to participate in need-based financial aid. Beginning July 1, 2006, assets held in prepaid tuition plans and college savings plans will be treated similarly for federal financial aid purposes. Both will be treated as parental assets in the calculation of the expected family contribution toward college costs. Previously, benefits from prepaid tuition plans were not treated as parental assets and typically reduced need-based financial aid on a dollar for dollar basis, while assets held in college savings plans received more favorable financial aid treatment.

Considering A 529 Plan

Before you start saving specifically for college, you should consider your overall financial situation. Remember that you may face penalties or lose benefits if you do not use the money in a 529 account for higher education expenses. If you decide that saving specifically for college is right for you, then the next step is to determine whether investing in a 529 plan is your best college saving option. Investing in a 529 plan is only one of several ways to save for college. Other tax-advantaged ways to save for college include Coverdell education savings accounts, Uniform Gifts to Minors Act (UGMA) accounts, Uniform Transfers to Minors Act (UTMA) accounts, tax-exempt municipal securities, and savings bonds. Saving for college in a taxable account is another option.

It's A Fact!

Each college saving option has advantages and disadvantages, and may have a different impact on your eligibility for financial aid, so you should evaluate each option carefully. If you need help determining which options work best for your circumstances, you should consult with your financial professional or tax advisor before you start saving.

Source: From "An Introduction to 529 Plans," a publication of the U.S. Securities and Exchange Commission, August 2007.

Questions To Ask

Knowing the answers to these questions may help you decide which 529 plan is best for you.

- Is the plan available directly from the state or plan sponsor?

- What fees are charged by the plan? How much of my investment goes to compensating my broker? Under what circumstances does the plan waive or reduce certain fees?

- What are the plan's withdrawal restrictions? What types of college expenses are covered by the plan? Which colleges and universities participate in the plan?

- What types of investment options are offered by the plan? How long are contributions held before being invested?

- Does the plan offer special benefits for state residents? Would I be better off investing in my state's plan or another plan? Does my state's plan offer tax advantages or other benefits for investment in the plan it sponsors? If my state's plan charges higher fees than another state's plan, do the tax advantages or other benefits offered by my state outweigh the benefit of investing in another state's less expensive plan?

- What limitations apply to the plan? When can an account holder change investment options, switch beneficiaries, or transfer ownership of the account to another account holder?

- Who is the program manager? When does the program manager's current management contract expire? How has the plan performed in the past?

Finding More Information

Offering Circulars For 529 Plans: You can find out more about a particular 529 plan by reading its offering circular. Often called a disclosure statement, disclosure document, or program description, the offering circular will have detailed information about investment options, tax benefits and consequences, fees and expenses, financial aid, limitations, risks, and other specific information relating to the 529 plan. Most 529 plans post their offering circulars on publicly available websites. The National Association of State Treasurers created the College Savings Plan Network which provides links to most 529 plan websites.

Additional Information About Underlying Mutual Funds: You may want to find more about a mutual fund included in a college savings plan investment option. Additional information about a mutual fund is available in its prospectus, statement of additional information, and semiannual and annual report. Offering circulars for college savings plans often indicate how you can obtain these documents from the plan manager for no charge. You can also review these documents on the Securities and Exchange Commission (SEC)'s EDGAR database.

Investment Adviser Public Disclosure Website: Many college savings plans' program managers are registered investment advisers. You can find more about investment advisers through the Investment Adviser Public Disclosure website. On the website, you can search for an investment adviser and view the Form ADV of the adviser. Form ADV contains information about an investment adviser and its business operations as well as disclosure about certain disciplinary events involving the adviser and its key personnel.

Broker–Dealer Public Disclosure Website: You can find more about a broker through FINRA's BrokerCheck website. On the website, you can search for any disciplinary sanctions against your broker, as well as information about his or her professional background and registration and licensing status.

Other Online Resources: You can learn more about 529 plans and other college saving options on FINRA's Smart Saving for College website. The website contains links to other helpful sites, including the College Savings Plan Network and the Internal Revenue Service's Publication 970 (*Tax Benefits for Higher Education*). FINRA's investor alert on 529 plans also provides valuable information for investors.

Top Ten Myths About 529 Plans

"Top 10 Myths About 529 Plans," © 2010 College Savings Plans Network (www.collegesavings.org). All rights reserved.

1. Myth: 529 plans are only for wealthy investors.

Fact: 529 plans have much lower required minimum contribution amounts than many other investments, making them accessible and convenient for families of any income level. Families can usually start a plan with as little as $15 to $25 per month.

2. Myth: Parents can just take out loans to pay for college, or children will get financial aid.

Fact: Approximately 60 percent of federal financial aid comes in the form of student loans, and all loans represent debt that a family must incur. Any savings, even in small increments, that a family can put away will offset the final amount of debt it must take on to pay for college.

3. Myth: Due to the recession and state budget gaps, investors in prepaid 529 plans have lost all of their investment.

Fact: There are currently 13 states that offer a Prepaid Tuition or Guaranteed Savings Plan that allow for the prepurchase of tuition based on today's rates to be paid out at the future cost when the beneficiary is in college. While some states needed to rectify budget gaps created by the recent financial crisis, to date, a prepaid tuition plan has never run out of money to pay back investors.

4. Myth: 529 plans are only for young children.

Fact: There is no maximum age for a 529 plan. Assets may be used at eligible schools offering adult career training or advanced degrees, including part-time programs.

5. Myth: If parents save now, a child won't be eligible to receive as much financial aid later.

Fact: The Deficit Reduction Act of 2005 specifies that funds saved in 529 plans are generally considered to be parental assets, which means that only about six percent of these assets are currently counted towards the family's expected contribution in federal need-based financial aid calculations.

6. Myth: A 529 plan can only be used at schools in my home state.

Fact: Assets from 529 plans may be used at any school that is accredited and eligible to accept federal financial aid. This includes nearly all public and private colleges in the United States and many trade and technical schools as well. It even includes some colleges located outside of the United States.

7. Myth: The tax advantages of 529 plans will expire.

Fact: The Pension Protection Act of 2006 repealed the 2010 sunset of the federal tax exemption for Section 529 plans and ensures that money saved for higher education in 529 plans can continue to be used tax-free to help pay for college.

8. Myth: A 529 plan can only be used for a four-year college.

Fact: Assets from 529 plans may be used at any eligible school, including two- and four-year colleges, graduate schools, and vocational and technical schools. Funds may be used for tuition, fees, certain room and board costs, and in 2010, computers and course-related software.

9. Myth: If a child doesn't go to college, parents will lose their money.

Fact: A 529 account holder can change the plan's beneficiary to another eligible member of the family, such as siblings or even oneself with no tax penalty.

10. Myth: Opening a 529 plan is complicated.

Fact: Most 529 plans allow account holders to open an account online, and a wealth of information is available online for families seeking more information about 529 plans. CSPN's website, www.CollegeSavings.org, offers convenient tools and valuable information to help families make wise decisions about saving for college.

The Private College 529 Plan

"Private College 529 Plans," © Forefield 2011 in Partnership with the American Institute of Certified Public Accountants (www.360financial literacy.org). Reprinted with permission.

How Does It Work?

The Private College 529 Plan operates like a typical prepaid tuition plan by allowing parents or grandparents to prepay tuition today that their child or grandchild can use in the future at any member college. But instead of the state carrying the risk that contributions won't meet future tuition increases, the colleges carry that risk. Specifically, the member colleges guarantee that the amount of tuition purchased today will satisfy the proportionate amount at the time the child or grandchild enrolls.

For example, let's say a parent or grandparent purchases tuition certificates today that are worth two years of tuition at College ABC. The child or grandchild would then be covered for two years of tuition in the future at College ABC, no matter how much tuition rises or what happens in the markets.

Member Colleges And Tuition Certificates

Currently, there are over 270 participating member colleges in the Private College 529 Plan (for a complete list, call 1-888-718-7878 or visit www.privatecollege529.org). When you open an account, you purchase a certificate in the child's name. You don't choose a college ahead of time. The certificate you purchase will represent a different value at each member college because each college has a different tuition rate. For example, a $20,000 certificate purchased today may be worth one year of tuition at College ABC but only half a year of tuition at College XYZ.

Each year, new tuition rates are set for each member college. As an added bonus for plan participants, member colleges must discount their tuition between 0.5% and 2% from their official "sticker price" rates. Any certificate you purchase is valued at the plan's current year's tuition rates. Each certificate must be held for at least three years before it can be used. If a member college ever withdraws from the plan, it is obligated to honor all certificates that were purchased prior to its withdrawal.

One last point: keep in mind that opening an account in the plan doesn't guarantee that a child or grandchild will be accepted at a member college—the application process is separate and unrelated.

Other Benefits

The Private College 529 Plan has no joining fees, maintenance fees, or annual fees—all administration and management costs are paid by the member colleges. And like state-sponsored prepaid tuition plans, the increase in value between the amount you prepay and the amount of tuition for which the certificate is redeemed is free from federal income tax. Anyone can open an account, and you can contribute as little as $25 per month or larger lump sums up to $190,000—the 2009/2010 contribution limit.

Chapter 16

Coverdell Education Savings Accounts

Among the various tax-favored college payment plans is the Coverdell Education Savings Account, previously known as an education IRA. Revamped as well as renamed, Coverdell accounts are earning a better grade from taxpayers who are looking to stash cash for a child's schooling.

Up to $2,000 can be contributed annually to a Coverdell account (it was $500 in its earlier IRA incarnation). Plus, you have longer to put the money in, you can pay for more types of education expenses with the money, and you can combine Coverdell cash with other education tax breaks.

As of January 2004, if the plan is owned by a parent, it's considered a parental asset and therefore has a minimal effect on the amount of aid available. This was an important change: Prior to that date Coverdells were considered as a student's asset and as such could significantly increase the expected family contribution.

The basic account setup remains. While adults contribute to the savings plan, a child age 17 or younger is named as the account's beneficiary. The contributions aren't tax deductible, but they do grow tax free and the funds can be withdrawn tax free as long as they are used to pay eligible schooling costs.

New Name, Better Benefits

But that's where the similarity between the old education IRA and the new Coverdell plan (renamed in honor of the late U.S. Sen. Paul Coverdell of Georgia) ends.

About This Chapter: "Coverdell accounts," © 2011 Bankrate.com, N. Palm Beach, FL. Reprinted with permission. For additional information, visit www.bankrate.com.

In addition to the increased $2,000 contribution limit, the Internal Revenue Service now allows:

- Money to be added to the plan up until the April tax-filing deadline.

- Contributions for a child 18 or older if the youngster has special needs.

- Any adult—parents, grandparents, godparents or friends—to put money in a child's education IRA, but the total put in the account from all sources cannot exceed $2,000. There's a six percent annual excess contribution tax if more than that is contributed for the same child, even when the money comes from different people.

- Higher income limits for contributors. To contribute fully, a person must make no more than $95,000 if filing as a single taxpayer, $190,000 if married filing jointly. Limited contributions are allowed for single taxpayers earning up to $110,000 and married couples making up to $220,000. Beyond those higher incomes, a person cannot contribute. And remember, the contributions are simply for the future education of the child. The contributor gets no tax break for adding to the account.

- Money to be used for some precollege expenses, including tuition, room and board, books, and computers for public, private, or parochial elementary and secondary schools.

- Money to be simultaneously contributed for the same child to a Coverdell account and a state college tuition program.

- A distribution from the account in the same year that the Hope (renamed American Opportunity) and Lifetime Learning credits are claimed as long as the money is not used to pay for the same expenses.

Selecting An Account Home

Okay, you've determined that a Coverdell Education Savings Account is a worthwhile component of your overall educational savings plan. So where do you put the money?

Any financial institution (a bank, investment company, brokerage, etc.) that handles traditional IRAs can help you set up and manage a Coverdell account. You can put contributions into any qualifying investment vehicle—stocks, bonds, mutual funds, certificates of deposit—offered at the institution that will serve as the account's custodian.

If you want to diversify, you can split the money up into several investments. There's no limit on the number of Coverdell accounts that you can establish for a child. The only limit is on the total contributions: You can't put more than $2,000 a year away for the student, regardless of how many accounts he or she has. Just be sure that management fees for multiple accounts don't eat into your overall savings return.

Unused Coverdell Money

If a child decides college is not really for him, what happens to any unused education IRA money diligently contributed all these years? Then the student pays at age 30, withdrawing any balance in the account within 30 days of the 30th birthday, and owing tax on the earnings plus a 10 percent penalty.

The IRS, however, offers a way out of this taxable situation. The student can roll over the full balance to another Coverdell plan for another family member. This could be a younger sibling, niece, nephew, or even his own son or daughter.

Table 16.1. Coverdell At A Glance

Pros	Cons
$2,000 contribution from numerous sources	$2,000 limit to contributions in a single year from all sources
Considered parental asset, not child's	Contributions are not tax deductible
Contributions grow tax free	Annual income limits for contributors
Contributions withdrawn tax free as long as they are spent on accepted school expenses	Unused money must be withdrawn by beneficiary within 30 days of 30th birthday and tax and penalty must be paid
Money can be used for elementary or secondary school	
Contributions allowed to Coverdell and state savings plan simultaneously	
You control the investment vehicle	

Chapter 17

Custodial Accounts And Trusts

In most states, minors do not have the right to contract, and so cannot own stocks, bonds, mutual funds, annuities, and life insurance policies. In particular, parents cannot simply transfer assets to their minor children, but instead must transfer the assets to a trust. The most common trust for a minor is known as a custodial account (an UGMA or UTMA account).

The Uniform Gift to Minors Act (UGMA) established a simple way for a minor to own securities without requiring the services of an attorney to prepare trust documents or the court appointment of a trustee. The terms of this trust are established by a state statute instead of a trust document. The Uniform Transfer to Minors Act (UTMA) is similar, but also allows minors to own other types of property, such as real estate, fine art, patents and royalties, and for the transfers to occur through inheritance. UTMA is slightly more flexible than UGMA.

To establish a custodial account, the donor must appoint a custodian (trustee) and provide the name and social security number of the minor. The donor irrevocably gifts the money to the trust. The money then belongs to the minor but is controlled by the custodian until the minor reaches the age of trust termination. (The age of trust termination is 18 to 21, depending on the state and whether it is an UGMA or an UTMA. Most UGMAs end at 18 and most UTMAs at 21, but it does depend on the state.) The custodian has the fiduciary responsibility to manage the money in a prudent fashion for the benefit of the minor. Custodial accounts are most often established at banks and brokerages.

It is important to title the account correctly. An "In Trust For" account, also known as a Totten Trust or guardian account, is not an UGMA/UTMA account. It is a revocable transfer that passes to the beneficiary without probate upon the death of the donor. (Totten Trusts are assets of the account owner, not the beneficiary, for financial aid purposes.) The proper way of titling a custodial account is "[Custodian's Name] as custodian for [Minor's Name] under the [Name of Minor's State of Residence] Uniform Gift to Minors Act." Substitute the word "Transfer" for the word "Gift" if you intend to establish an UTMA account instead of an UGMA account. Note that this method of titling is only correct for the United States. In Canada, for example, one would title the account "[Custodian's Name] as trustee for [Minor's Name], a minor."

It's A Fact!

Any money in custodial accounts for which a parent is the custodian will be counted as part of the parent's taxable estate if the parent is the legal guardian of the child and the child has not yet reached the age of trust termination.

Table 17.1. Types Of Accounts

Account Title	Account Type	Whose Asset On The Free Application for Federal Student Aid (FAFSA)
Parent in trust for child	Totten Trust	Parent
Child in trust for parent	Totten Trust	Child
Parent and child	Joint account	Split evenly
Child and parent	Joint account	Split evenly
Parent as custodian for child	Custodial account	Child
Parent as trustee for child	Custodial account	Child

The income from a custodial account must be reported on the child's tax return and is taxed at the child's rate, subject to the Kiddie Tax rules. The parent is responsible for filing an income tax return on behalf of the child. There is no special tax treatment for UGMA accounts. Children aged 14 and older must sign their own tax returns.

Neither the donor nor the custodian can place any restrictions on the use of the money when the minor becomes an adult. At that time the child can use the money for any purpose whatsoever without requiring permission of the custodian, so there's no guarantee that the child will use the money for his or her education. Also, since UGMA and UTMA accounts are in the name of a single child, the funds are not transferrable to another beneficiary.

Impact On Student Aid Eligibility

For financial aid purposes, custodial accounts are considered assets of the student. This means that custodial bank and brokerage accounts have a high impact on financial aid eligibility.

However, since 2009–10 the treatment of custodial 529 college savings plans has been more favorable. A custodial 529 plan of a dependent student is treated as an asset of the parent on the Free Application for Federal Student Aid (FAFSA). (A custodial 529 plan of an independent student is still treated as a student asset. Also, the CSS/Financial Aid PROFILE form treats 529 plans that name a student as a beneficiary as an asset of the student regardless of who owns the 529 plan account.) This means that a custodial 529 college savings plan for a dependent student has a low impact on financial aid eligibility.

If money is transferred from an UGMA/UTMA account to a section 529 plan, the section 529 plan should be titled the same as the UGMA/UTMA account. When the child reaches the age of trust termination, the child will become the account owner for the section 529 plan. The custodian is not permitted to change the beneficiary of the section 529 plan, because the responsibility of the custodian to use the assets of the UGMA/UTMA account for the benefit of the child does not terminate when the funds are withdrawn from the account.

(Prior to 2006–07, funds in a custodial 529 college savings plan were treated as a child asset on the FAFSA because they derived from an irrevocable gift to the child. Congress attempted in the Higher Education Reconciliation Act of 2005 to change the treatment from a child asset to a parent asset. However, a legislative drafting error causes custodial 529 plan accounts to not be reported as an asset on the FAFSA. Congress corrected this error in the College Cost Reduction and Access Act of 2007, but with a year delay in the effective date to July 1, 2009, the 2009–10 award year. The correction treats qualified education benefits as an asset of the student if the student is an independent student and an asset of the parent if the student is a dependent student, regardless of whether the student or parent owns the account.)

Undoing A Transfer/Gift

It is not possible to transfer money back to the parent from a child's custodial account because the original transfer was an irrevocable gift. Once the money has been given to the child, it is

---

It's A Fact!

One method of dealing with the financial aid impact of an custodial bank or brokerage account is to liquidate the account and transfer the proceeds into a custodial 529 plan account. (Investments in a 529 plan must be made in cash.)

---

owned by the child. The child does not have the capacity to gift the money back to the parent, and the custodian would be violating his or her fiduciary responsibility if he or she transferred the money back into his or her own name or used it for his or her own personal benefit. (If a custodian does this, or otherwise behaves in a fashion that the IRS interprets as indicating that no gift was actually ever made, the custodian would owe back taxes at his or her rate, plus penalties. Also, the child could sue to recover the funds.)

However, nothing prevents the custodian from spending the money for the benefit of the child, so long as the expenses aren't parental obligations or otherwise benefit the custodian. Parental obligations are expenses a parent is normally expected to provide for his or her child, such as food, clothing, medical care, and shelter. But if the child wants a computer or to go to summer camp, it is usually acceptable to spend the child's money on those expenses. Likewise, you can spend the child's money for the child's college education. The parent can then set aside some of his or her own money in a college savings account owned by the parent. Obviously, this only works if there are nonparental obligation expenses that the parent would otherwise have provided for his or her children. Attempts to undo an UGMA transfer in this fashion should only be done in consultation with a qualified accountant.

(The model UTMA legislation included a paragraph that would permit the money in a custodial account to be spent for the use and benefit of the minor "without regard to (i) the duty or ability of the custodian personally or of any other person to support the minor, or (ii) any other income or property of the minor which may be applicable or available for that purpose." Although one might argue that this would allow one to spend the money even on parental obligations, it is important to note that this paragraph was not generally included in state UTMA legislation, nor UGMA legislation. Often, when this language was included, an additional clause stating "A delivery, payment, or expenditure under this section is in addition to, not in substitution for, and shall not affect any obligation of a person to support the minor" was added as well as a requirement to "keep custodial property separate and distinct from all other property." In addition, there are tricky tax consequences to spending the money on parental obligations. It is clear that if you spend the money for the benefit of the child on nonparental obligations, you're ok. Anything else, check first with an accountant who is familiar with the laws of your state.)

Quick Tip

The Deficit Reduction Act of 2005 added another method of eliminating the negative financial aid impact of a custodial account. Effective July 1, 2006, the custodial versions of 529 college savings plans, prepaid tuition plans, and Coverdell Education Savings Accounts are treated as the asset of the parent for federal student aid purposes when the student is a dependent student. So if you roll over a custodial account into one of these three types of accounts you will shift its financial aid treatment from a student asset to a parent asset.

Chapter 18

Working During College

Going To College Part Time Has Perks And Perils

Some Part-Time College Students Share Their Tips For Success

Dawn Kolb started college like most students: high school diploma hot off the presses and bags packed for a four-year degree. She was a full-time civil engineering student at the University of Pittsburgh ready to do it all. But after her father died, Kolb found herself wading in an unexpected pool of hardships and took two years off from the rigors of the classroom to figure out what she "actually wanted to do with [her] life." After struggling to keep her grades up in a full load of classes while also working full time, Kolb made another big decision: Go to school part time.

"My grades were not handling it, and I needed to find a way to pass and still make money," says Kolb, 29, who graduated with a bachelor's degree last year after eight years of study in computer science. "Most people who go to school part time are going for a reason—they can only handle so much."

The number of students going to college part time is on the rise. But is it worth it? While being a part-time rather than full-time student certainly has its' perks, unexpected challenges can lurk in the fine print.

About This Chapter: This chapter begins with "Going to College Part Time Has Perks and Perils," by Jackie Mantey. Copyright 2007 *U.S. News & World Report*. Reproduced by permission from www.usnews.com. It also includes "7 Reasons to Work Your Way Through College," by Kim Clark. Copyright 2009 *U.S. News & World Report*. Reproduced by permission from www.usnews.com. The chapter ends with "Financial Literacy," a publication of the U.S. Department of Education, December 2009.

Students choose to go to school part time for a number of reasons—to pursue internships, raise a family—but it usually comes down to money, says Salme Harju Steinberg, president emeritus of Northeastern Illinois University. "It's the only choice some students have," she says. "It's the only way these students have access to higher education."

To take on the brunt of the ever-rising costs of higher education, part timers typically work full time (47 percent work 35 or more hours a week) and take half the credit hours of full-time students. In 2005, 85 percent of college part timers were employed while cracking the books, compared with just half of full-time students.

But those who go to school part time can often land themselves in a tough spot. The majority of part-time students have a higher-than-average college debt than full-time students, according to the National Center for Education Statistics (NCES). Part-time students are also more likely to leave school without a diploma. And while students sometimes interrupt their enrollment for financial reasons, when they return they often receive less financial aid because their temporarily increased earnings hinder eligibility. That on-again-off-again relationship with school can also hurt their chances of receiving financial aid they don't have to pay back. "The proportion of loans is growing by leaps and bounds, while grants are diminishing," says Youlonda Copeland-Morgan of the College Board (and a former admissions dean for Harvey Mudd College).

Most part-time students end up taking two more years than full-time students to earn a bachelor's degree. But for some, graduation can take up to 10 years, leaving many students more discouraged and ready to drop out: There's a 19 percent gap in bachelor's degree completion, with part-time students trailing. Part-time enrollment has a negative effect on those students' postsecondary outcomes, NCES reports.

This isn't a coincidence. A larger percentage of part-time undergrads are from low-income backgrounds and often have to place a priority on work over study.

But part-time studies can work and have its advantages. Kristi Galakas, a part-time student at the University of Virginia, says she has been able to take classes with other part-time students, such as a war history class with Iraq war veterans and nursing classes with nurses already on the job. By spending less time in the classroom, she's been able to add the title of Miss Virginia and founder of the campus prelaw magazine to her résumé. "Being a part-time student shouldn't hold you back," says Galakas, 26. "More and more grad programs and employers want years of work experience. I now have a little more to offer."

Indeed, says Kolb. "Time management became a lot easier to handle, and I wasn't as stressed out," she says. Kolb averaged 12 credit hours a semester and 25 work hours a week. Copeland-Morgan says getting a mentor before and during college is one of the best decisions part-time students can make. "Going to school part time can mean losing critical peer and professional relationships and support," she says. "If they don't have mentors, it can be hard to stay focused and address issues."

"The student needs very good advising on courses he or she will need. They don't want to end up taking courses they can't use for graduation because it could put them back a year or even two," Steinberg says, adding that full-time students have more leeway in that regard. "And knowing that financial aid is limited is crucial for overall planning."

It's also important to honestly ask yourself a number of questions, such as, "Am I willing to go to school for a longer period of time?" and "How will this benefit me specifically? Will I be challenged enough academically?"

"You have to be happy," Kolb says. "I would have much rather taken a long time with school than feel overwhelmed and kill myself to still finish. It's a very personal decision."

Seven Reasons To Work Your Way Through College

Many students say they don't want to take part-time jobs when they start college because they'll need all their time to study (or party).

But new research confirms what parents and counselors have been saying for years: Part-time campus jobs not only raise cash but can help raise students' grade-point averages.

After interviewing and examining data on hundreds of undergraduates from 1996 through 2004, researchers found that the average GPA of freshmen at four-year universities who worked between one and 20 hours a week was 3.13. Those who didn't work at all had GPAs averaging just 3.04.

A warning: Charlene Marie Kalenkoski of Ohio University and Sabrina Wulff Pabilonia of the U.S. Bureau of Labor Statistics did find that while a little work is good, too much is bad for students. Freshmen who worked more than 20 hours a week had GPAs of just 2.95.

A similar pattern, though with slightly different numbers, was seen among community college students.

Counselors say there are seven reasons students should take part-time and, if possible, on-campus work-study jobs to earn at least their pocket money:

1. **Earn Bucks:** Working just 10 hours a week typically generates at least $75 a week, which should be plenty to fund weekend entertainment and incidental costs. Frugal students working 15 hours a week or so can cover books and supplies as well. Those typically run about $500 a semester.

2. **Learn To Budget:** Students who have to earn their own pocket and entertainment money learn budgeting and are less likely to overspend than those who can charge a Cancún spring break or pizza party to a parental credit card, counselors say.

3. **Time Manage:** Part-time jobs force students to learn time-management skills they'll need the rest of their lives.

4. **Improve Learning:** Part-time jobs seem to improve academic performance. Research shows students who work no more than 20 hours a week have higher grades and are more likely to graduate college than both those who don't work at all and those who put in too many hours.

5. **Career Experiment:** Part-time jobs give students chances to learn what kind of work they like and, perhaps more important, don't like. That can help them avoid costly mistakes such as majoring in something they later learn they hate.

6. **Build Résumé:** Working during school helps students build their résumés, which gives advantages to graduates looking for career-oriented jobs.

7. **Connect With Professors And Students:** Some work-study jobs give students opportunities to do research or work with professors. But even those who don't get plum work-study assignments say on-campus jobs help them make friends with other students and network with university staff. Some studies show that those with on-campus jobs are more successful students, perhaps because of the connections they forge on the job.

Financial Literacy

Financial literacy (education on the management of personal finances) is an essential part of planning and paying for postsecondary education. Everyone needs to understand the options with respect to the vast array of financial products, services, and providers to make sound financial decisions.

Quick Tip
Learn fiscal fitness now for a lifetime of financial well-being.

Source: From "Financial Literacy," a publication of the U.S. Department of Education, December 2009.

Fiscal fitness means practicing smart money management techniques. Decisions you make about handling your money before and during college can have a huge impact on your future. Before making major financial decisions, educate yourself about options and be consistent in making informed financial decisions. Learning good personal finance skills now can help you reach your goals and find success sooner. Your life goals are important, and we want to make sure you have the money to make them a reality.

Financial Planning

When you want something in life, it's best to have a plan for how you will get it. Everyone wants a life of financial security—the ability to save and invest so that your money is working for you in a way that enables you to fulfill your life's goals. To achieve financial security, you need to create a financial plan.

A financial plan is simply a roadmap for how you will manage your money on an ongoing basis. At its most basic, a financial plan involves defining your money goals, identifying the steps it will take to reach those goals, and then following through with those steps. The sooner you develop and implement a financial plan, the sooner you can be financially secure, so get started now.

Practice Good Credit Habits

Even if you don't need loans to pay for college, sooner or later you will probably need to borrow money. Your borrowing and repayment history is tracked by the financial industry to create your credit score, which helps lenders gauge whether you are a good credit risk. The better your credit score, the easier it will be for you to borrow money and the better terms you will be offered. A good credit score can save you thousands of dollars over your lifetime. Here are some ways to build and maintain a good credit score (typically a score of 700 or higher) and avoid financial headaches:

- **Always pay your bills and loan installments on time.** To avoid late fees, note the due dates for bills and installments as soon as you receive them. Keep a copy of all bills and loan payments you make.

- **Don't bounce checks.** Bouncing a check means writing a check for more money than you have available in your account. Aside from hurting your credit score, banks usually charge you a fee for every bounced check. The fees are automatically charged to your account, which can cause subsequent checks to bounce, leading to more fees, more bounced checks, etc. Bounced checks can lead to real money problems and even get you into legal trouble. The good news is that with a little caution and diligence, you can prevent bounced checks altogether by being aware of the amount of money in your bank account and spending only what you can afford.

- **Avoid credit cards.** In college, you'll get tons of credit card offers. Your best move? Shred them. Don't sign up for a credit card just to get something for free. As attractive as easy credit might seem, credit card interest can put you in a very deep financial hole that can take years to dig out of. If you feel you need a credit card or you want to start building your credit history, apply for one credit card with the lowest interest rate available then charge only what you can afford to repay. Also, pay the balance in full to avoid interest charges.

- **Don't ignore credit problems, get help as soon as possible.** In spite of your best intentions, you may get in over your head. Credit problems include missed payments, bounced checks, and credit card debt; these problems lead to a lower credit score and a more difficult time when borrowing money in the future. Sometimes, people mistakenly believe that if they ignore their credit problems, these problems will go away. Instead, their credit problems will only get worse. If it happens to you, don't waste time feeling foolish and ashamed, because you will be in good company; even celebrities have credit problems. So get help immediately, nip credit problems in the bud, and save yourself lots of stress.

A Few Basic Financial Tips For College Students

- **Organize your files.** Creating a paper and/or electronic filing system will make paying your bills on time and meeting deadlines easier. Record keeping also helps avoid potential disputes—disagreements regarding whether the terms you agreed to with banks, stores, or friends have been upheld including timing of payment and amounts. You'll also want to keep records for tax purposes.

- **Make a budget and stick to it.** A budget is just a self-imposed guideline for how much money you can spend and what you can spend it on. You will be amazed at how much farther your money goes when you have a budget. Life is unpredictable, so don't forget to allocate money for unexpected expenses in your budget.

Quick Tip

If you have credit problems and need advice, your college financial aid office may be a valuable free resource to help you get back on track.

Source: From "Financial Literacy," a publication of the U.S. Department of Education, December 2009.

- **Buy used books.** Many students and their parents are shocked to learn how much textbooks cost. They can average $1,000 a year. Most campus bookstores sell used books that can help reduce this cost. You might also save money by buying or renting textbooks online.

- **Leave your car at home.** Cars cost more than just gas money. Don't forget about insurance, parking (and parking tickets!) and repair expenses. Walk, use public transportation, and/or ride a bike. You may also want to arrange a carpool with friends if public transportation isn't available.

- **Watch the Automated Teller Machine (ATM) fees.** They can add up quickly. Look for a bank with free ATMs near your school.

- **Choose the right meal plan.** An unlimited plan may be tempting, but you might be satisfied with a less expensive plan. Also, if you've paid for a meal plan, be sure to use it! You're just paying twice if you eat out somewhere else.

- **Save on snacks.** If you can, avoid buying snacks at vending machines or convenience stores. Stock up at your local grocery store and keep them with you during the day to avoid more expensive and less healthy on-the-go options.

- **Consider all the costs of living off campus.** Many students like the idea of trading dorm life for their own off campus apartment, only to realize that there are more costs involved than they realized. Aside from rent, you will probably have utility bills and grocery expenses, at a minimum. You may also need to pay rental insurance and property maintenance fees. So before you decide to move off campus, learn what other expenses you'll be responsible for, in addition to rent.

- **Use student discounts to your advantage.** It's common for movie theaters, concert halls, restaurants, insurance companies, and travel companies to offer steep discounts with a student I.D. Just ask!

- **Start saving.** A few dollars here and there can make a big difference later in life. Saving and investing your money puts your money to work for you. If you have a job, pay yourself first. Have your bank automatically deposit a set amount from your paycheck into a savings account.

- **Keep life in balance.** Money management is important, but it's only a means to get you where you want to be in life. Strong values, good friends, and a solid education should all be part of your plan for success.

Chapter 19

Other Ways To Save For College

Credit Card Rebate And Loyalty Programs

Loyalty programs, also known as affinity programs, provide a rebate to the consumer in exchange for shopping at particular retailers or purchasing particular products or services. This chapter provides information about loyalty programs that provide a reward in the form of tuition benefits, such as credits to a section 529 plan. They are similar in nature to airline frequent flyer programs.

Typically, such programs do not require you to show a membership card to get the rebates. Instead, you register your credit cards with them and they track the purchases you make at participating merchants using the cards. You can also earn rebates by shopping online through the company websites. This makes the programs a painless way to earn a little extra money for college.

Affinity programs with a college savings emphasis include:

- BabyCenter (free)

- BabyMint (free)

- Fidelity 529 College Rewards MasterCard (free)

- FutureTrust (free)

- MyKidsCollege (free)

About This Chapter: Information in this chapter is from "Credit Card Rebate and Loyalty Programs" and "Savings Social Networking Programs," © 2011 FinAid Page, LLC (www.finaid.org). All rights reserved. Reprinted with permission. Additional text under the heading "Savings Bonds" is from "Introduction to Savings Bonds" and "Education Planning," publications of the U.S. Department of the Treasury, 2010.

- SAGE Tuition Rewards Program (free)

- Upromise (free)

Of these, Upromise has the largest retailer network, followed by BabyMint.

A key benefit of all of these programs is that you do not need to change your purchasing habits to earn rebates for college savings. The retailer networks associated with these programs are large enough that most families will earn some rebates without altering their spending patterns. Of course, by carefully targeting your purchases, you can maximize your rebates.

It's A Fact!

Some of the loyalty programs allow one to redeem the rebates as cash instead of investing them in a section 529 college savings plan. Some also allow one to transfer the rebates to repay student loans.

Source: From "Credit Card Rebate and Loyalty Programs," © 2011 FinAid Page, LLC (www.finaid.org). All rights reserved. Reprinted with permission.

The rebates received from a loyalty program are not subject to income tax or sales tax. (Many states charge sales taxes on all gross receipts from sales, including rebates for which the retailer is reimbursed. However, the consumer already paid sales tax on the amount of the rebate when they purchased the product or service that generated the loyalty program rebate, so no additional sales tax is due when the rebate is received.)

Other online rebating programs, albeit without a saving for college theme, include Ebates (800 retailers), FatWallet (500 retailers), and BondRewards (500 retailers, rebates in the form of U.S. Savings Bonds). There are also more traditional rebate cards, like Discover Card, and roundup savings programs like Bank of America's Keep the Change (debit card) and American Express's One Card (credit card).

Quick Tip

If two products provide equivalent value, but the more expensive item offers a rebate, sometimes it is better to buy the less expensive item. Compare net prices after subtracting the amount of the rebate. The average rebate is between four percent and five percent.

Source: From "Credit Card Rebate and Loyalty Programs," © 2011 FinAid Page, LLC (www.finaid.org). All rights reserved. Reprinted with permission.

It's A Fact!

The sites restrict access to a child's portfolio to just those friends and family and businesses authorized by the parent. A key focus is on protecting the student from the untamed wilds of the web.

Savings Social Networking Programs

Savings social network sites try to encourage friends, family, and businesses to contribute to a child's college education. These facilitator or "college registry" sites make it less awkward to ask for support. They also provide a benefit to the donor, such as updates on the child's academic progress. The donor can use their contributions to encourage the student to get good grades and succeed in school. The sites may automatically solicit contributions before important events, such as birthdays and graduations. This helps the contributors avoid the embarrassment of forgetting a special occasion. They may also include a rebate component similar to those of the credit card loyalty programs.

These sites leverage several recent trends in higher education:

- College students create secure online portfolios of their work that can be viewed by friends and family.

- Organizations like The "I Have a Dream" Foundation (IHAD) allow businesses to adopt a class of low-income students and promise to sponsor their college education.

- Social networking sites that are popular among students like Facebook and MySpace.

Savings facilitator sites include:

- College Piggy ($4.99 monthly fee)

- Earn Your Future ($2.50 processing fee per report card, 3.5% fee per contribution)

- Freshman Fund (free for recipients, 5% fee per contribution)

- GradeFund (5% fee upon distribution with a $5 minimum)

- SchoolRaise (5% fee per contribution upon distribution)

- Tuition Gifters ($39.95 per year)

Some of the college savings loyalty programs also have social networking features. For example, Upromise allows friends and family to set up Upromise accounts that funnel their rebates into your account and also offers a "Guest Shopping" URL for people who are not Upromise members to use to direct college savings rebates to your account.

Caveats

It remains to be seen whether these registry sites are effective tools for building a college savings fund. While they avoid the awkwardness of personally asking for money, personal contact is often essential to successfully raising money. These sites are already at a disadvantage due to the impersonal nature of e-mail. Will they be able to overcome the limitations of the medium? Will they become as commonplace as wedding registries are today?

Another open question is whether these services are worth the cost. Forty dollars a year at 4% interest for 17 years is the equivalent of nearly $1,000, with two-thirds coming from fees and the rest from interest.

Savings Bonds

Savings Bonds have been called the all-American investment. They are an easy way to save money safely and get a good market return. Rates change every May and November based on either current market rates or inflation. Current rates can be found at the Savings Bond website (http://www.treasurydirect.gov/instit/savbond/savbond.htm).

There are two main types of bonds offered. The Inflation Indexed—or I Bond—is designed to offer all Americans a way to save that protects the purchasing power of their investment by assuring them a real rate of return over and above inflation. I Bonds have features that make them attractive to many investors. They are sold at face value in denominations of $50, $75, $100, $200, $500, $1,000, $5,000, and $10,000 and earn interest for as long as 30 years. I Bond earnings are added every month and interest is compounded semiannually. They are state and local income tax exempt. In addition, federal income tax on I Bond earnings can be deferred until the bonds are cashed or stop earning interest after 30 years. Investors cashing I Bonds before five years are subject to a three-month earnings penalty.

The Series EE Savings Bonds pay interest equal to 90 percent of the average five-year Treasury securities yield for the preceding six months. This means that the rates on EE bonds are based on rates set by participants in the large government bond trading market. The Series I Bond, on the other hand, carries a fixed base rate plus a semiannual calculation based on the rate of inflation as measured by the Consumer Price Index.

Education Tax Exclusion

The savings bond education tax exclusion permits qualified taxpayers to exclude from their gross income all or part of the interest paid upon the redemption of eligible Series EE and I Bonds issued after 1989, when the bond owner pays qualified higher education expenses at an eligible institution.

Additional Requirements To Qualify

- Qualified higher education expenses must be incurred during the same tax year in which the bonds are redeemed.

- You must be at least 24 years old on the first day of the month in which you bought the bond(s).

- When using bonds for a child's education, the bonds must be registered in the parent's name(s). The child can be listed as a beneficiary on the bond, but not as a co-owner.

- When using bonds for your own education, the bonds must be registered in your name.

- If you're married, you must file a joint return to qualify for the exclusion.

- You must meet certain income requirements.

- Your postsecondary institution must qualify for the program by being a college, university, or vocational school that meets the standards for federal assistance (such as guaranteed student loan programs).

Qualified Expenses

Qualified educational expenses include:

- Tuition and fees (such as lab fees and other required course expenses).

- Expenses that benefit you, your spouse, or a dependent for whom you claim an exemption.

- Expenses paid for any course required as part of a degree or certificate-granting program.

- Expenses paid for sports, games, or hobbies qualify only if part of a degree or certificate program.

It's A Fact!

The costs of books or room and board are not qualified expenses.

Source: From "Education Planning," a publication of the U.S. Department of the Treasury, 2010.

The amount of qualified expenses is reduced by the amount of any scholarships, fellowships, employer-provided educational assistance, and other forms of tuition reduction.

You must use both the principal and interest from the bonds to pay qualified expenses to exclude the interest from your gross income. If the amount of eligible bonds you've cashed during the year exceeds the amount of qualified educational expenses paid during the year, the amount of excludable interest is reduced pro rata.

Example: Assuming bond proceeds equal $10,000 ($8,000 principal and $2,000 interest) and the qualified educational expenses are $8,000, you could exclude 80 percent of the interest earned, which would equal $1,600. (.8 x 2000 = $1,600)

Income Limitations

The full interest exclusion is only available to married couples filing joint returns and to single filers. Modified adjusted gross income includes the interest earned under a certain limit in each case. These income limits apply in the year you use bonds for educational purposes, not the year you buy the bonds. Exclusion benefits are phased out for joint or single filers with modified adjusted gross income that exceeds the limit. Full instructions and limits are outlined on IRS Form 8815.

Tax Year 2010 Income Limits

For single taxpayers, the tax exclusion begins to be reduced with a $70,100 modified adjusted gross income and is eliminated for adjusted gross incomes of $85,100 and above. For married taxpayers filing jointly, the tax exclusion begins to be reduced with a $105,100 modified adjusted gross income and is eliminated for adjusted gross incomes of $135,100 and above. Married couples must file jointly to be eligible for the exclusion.

Tax Year 2009 Income Limits

For single taxpayers, the tax exclusion begins to be reduced with a $69,950 modified adjusted gross income and is eliminated for adjusted gross incomes of $84,950 and above. For married taxpayers filing jointly, the tax exclusion begins to be reduced with a $104,900 modified adjusted gross income and is eliminated for adjusted gross incomes of $134,900 and above. Married couples must file jointly to be eligible for the exclusion.

Another Education Savings Option

Aside from the Education Tax Exclusion, there is another way to use savings bonds to pay for children's education expenses. Interest income on bonds purchased in a child's name alone or with a parent as beneficiary (not co-owner), can be included in the child's income each year as it accrues, or can be deferred until the bonds are redeemed. In either case, the child will be subject to any federal income tax on the interest.

Parents may file a federal income tax return in the child's name (the child will need to have a Social Security Number), reporting the total accrued interest on all bonds registered to the child. The intention to report savings bond interest annually, i.e., on an accrual basis, must be noted on the return.

The decision to report accrued interest income annually applies to all future years, and can be changed only by filing IRS Form 3115 with the IRS. Full details of this option and its requirements are outlined in IRS Publication 550, *Investment Income and Expenses*.

No tax will be due unless the child has total income in a single year equal to the threshold amount that requires a return to be filed, and no further returns need to be filed until that annual income level has been reached. Starting with tax year 2006, for children under the age of 18, unearned income over a specified threshold amount for that age group will be taxed at the parent's rate. If the child is age 18 or older, income will be taxed at the child's rate.

With this approach, the tax liability on the bond interest is determined on an annual basis so that when the bonds are redeemed, only the current year's accrual will be subject to federal income tax. Make sure you keep complete records when using this system.

Part Four
Financial Aid And
The Federal Government

Chapter 20

An Overview Of Federal Aid For Students

What It Costs: See The Big Picture

Many students worry that tuition and the other costs of continuing their education will be out of reach. But don't let the price tag stop you. It's only part of the picture. Keep in mind the major benefits of investing in your education.

Most students receive some kind of financial aid to help pay for the cost of their education. A few students even get a free ride, where all their costs are paid for.

With your determination and assistance from financial aid, you can make the education you dream about a reality. Use this chapter to learn how.

Who Gives Aid: Find The Figures

The U.S. Department of Education should be your first source to access financial aid. They award about $100 billion a year in grants, work-study assistance, and low-interest loans.

Aid also comes from scholarships from state governments, schools, employers, individuals, private companies, nonprofits, religious groups, and professional organizations.

There's money out there. You can find it.

Applying For Federal Aid: Meet The FAFSA

At some point, you need to fill out the Free Application for Federal Student Aid (FAFSA). For information about the FAFSA, see Chapter 21 of this book. You can also get information from your school counselor. Most colleges also have a financial aid office you can contact for information.

About This Chapter: Information in this chapter is from "Financial Aid 101" and "Learn What's Available," publications of the U.S. Department of Education, 2010.

What You Pay: Understand The EFC

The aid you qualify for depends on your Expected Family Contribution, or EFC. The EFC is a number that schools use to determine how much federal aid you would receive if you attended that school.

When you apply for federal student aid, you will be asked to provide information about your or your family's finances, such as income, assets, and family size. After you submit the application, you will receive an EFC based on this information.

Your contribution may come from a combination of savings, current income, and loans.

What Aid Covers: Add It Up

There are five basic costs associated with going to college. Financial aid may be used for:

- Tuition and fees
- Room and board
- Books and supplies
- Personal expenses
- Travel

Quick tip

For even more help, read the U.S. Department of Education's "Steps to Federal Student Aid" fact sheet, or use "Completing the FAFSA," a detailed online tutorial at http://studentaid.ed.gov/students/publications/completing_fafsa/index.html. You can also call the Federal Student Aid Information Center at 1-800-4-FED-AID (1-800-433-3243), or click the "Live Help" link on the Contact Us page of the FAFSA website, then click the "CUSTOMER SERVICE LIVE" button.

Source: From "Financial Aid 101," a publication of the U.S. Department of Education, 2010.

Learn What's Available: Scholarships, Grants, Loans, And More

Scholarships: Earn To Learn

Scholarships are gifts. They don't need to be repaid. There are thousands of them, offered by schools, employers, individuals, private companies, nonprofits, religious groups, and professional and social organizations.

Some scholarships are merit based. You earn them by meeting or exceeding certain standards set by the scholarship giver. They might be awarded based on academic achievement, or a combination of academics and a special talent, trait, or interest. Other scholarships are based on financial need. Here are some tools to help find yours:

It's A Fact!

One of the best ways to learn about all the available federal loans, grants, and work-study opportunities is in *Funding Education Beyond High School: The Guide to Federal Student Aid*. You can find this publication at http://studentaid.ed.gov/students/publications/student_guide/index.html.

Source: From "Learn What's Available," a publication of the U.S. Department of Education, 2010.

- **Federal Student Aid Scholarship Search:** https://studentaid2.ed.gov/getmoney/scholarship/v3browse.asp

- **State Higher Education Agency Listings:** http://wdcrobcolp01.ed.gov/Programs/EROD/org_list.cfm?category_ID=SHE

University Grants: Need And Receive

Grants are also gifts, but they're usually based on financial need.

Most often, grant aid comes from federal and state governments and individual colleges. Available federal grants include:

- **Pell Grant:** These are federal grants awarded to undergraduate students.

- **Academic Competitiveness Grant (ACG):** The ACG is for college freshmen and sophomores who are eligible for Pell Grants and who took rigorous classes in high school.

- **Federal Supplemental Educational Opportunity Grant (FSEOG):** The FSEOG is awarded to undergraduate students with exceptional financial need.

- **National Science And Mathematics Access To Retain Talent (SMART) Grant:** The National SMART Grant is awarded to college juniors and seniors who are eligible for Pell Grants and are majoring in mathematics, technology, engineering, a foreign language critical to national security, or physical, life, or computer sciences. Students must also have grade point averages of at least 3.0 in their majors to be eligible.

- **Teacher Education Assistance For College And Higher Education (TEACH) Grant:** The TEACH Grant is for students who plan to teach in schools that serve low-income students.

It's A Fact!

There's more grant money available now than 10 years ago.

Source: From "Learn What's Available," a publication of the U.S. Department of Education, 2010.

Loans: Borrow For The Future

Loans are a contract to borrow money and repay it over time, with interest. In the case of most federal student loans, you do not need to begin repaying them until several months after you leave college or are no longer enrolled at least half time.

Every year, more than $70 billion in federal student aid is given out in the form of low-interest loans. These are delivered through the William D. Ford Federal Direct Loan Program (Direct Loan Program).

Some banks and financial institutions offer private student loans. These loans often have variable interest rates, require a credit check, and may not provide the benefits of federal student loans.

If taking out loans makes you feel a little nervous, you are in good company. Many students feel the same way. But looking at loans as an investment in your future can help you get past your fear.

To learn more about federal student loans, read Federal Aid First, an online brochure from the U.S. Department of Education available at http://federalstudentaid.ed.gov/federalaidfirst/index.html. Chapter 24 of this book also contains information about federal loans.

Work-Study: Get A Job

The Federal Work-Study (FWS) program provides part-time jobs for students with financial need to help them pay for their education.

The program is administered by participating schools. It's designed to put you to work in the community, or in a job related to your studies, whenever possible.

Service Members And Veterans: Understand The Benefits

The U.S. Military offers several ways to help pay for your education. See todaysmilitary.com for more information. Chapter 41 of this book also discusses education benefits and the military.

If you are a veteran, the Department of Veterans Affairs offers a variety of education benefits. Read about them online, or call 1-888-GI-BILL-1 (1-888-442-4551).

It's A Fact!

More than 3,400 schools participate in the Federal Work-Study program. In 2009, over 900,000 students received work-study aid.

Source: From "Learn What's Available," a publication of the U.S. Department of Education, 2010.

Other Sources Of Aid: Find More Funding

Funding Education Beyond High School: The Guide to Federal Student Aid from the U.S. Department of Education features a section called Other Financial Aid Sources. It includes many other ideas to pay for your education, such as the AmeriCorps community service organization. AmeriCorps is also discussed in Chapter 39 of this book.

Tools And Tips: Find And Save Money

A little homework can earn you a lot of cash for college. A little common sense can help you use your money wisely. Here are a few tips to get started:

- **Use the financial aid and scholarship wizards on the Federal Student Aid website, available at https://studentaid2.ed.gov/getmoney/scholarship/scholarship_search_select.asp?13817/.** You can search for scholarships based on talents, interests, background, and more.

- **Check the colleges you're considering for merit- or non-need-based scholarships for academically talented students.**

- **Check with your state education agency to find out if you're eligible for state assistance based on merit.**

- **See if you are eligible for an athletic scholarship, if you are athletically inclined.** Chapter 35 of this book discusses opportunities for college-bound athletes.

- **Stick close to home.** Most state colleges and universities offer lower tuition to in-state residents.

- **Go to a lower-cost community college for one or two years, then transfer to a four-year school.**

- **Live at home.** You could save thousands of dollars.

Chapter 21

Applying For Federal Student Aid

Introduction

The official Free Application for Federal Student Aid (FAFSA) form is at www.FAFSA.gov—not at a ".com" website. If you go to a .com site, you will probably be asked to pay to submit the FAFSA. Remember, the first F in FAFSA stands for free—so use the official government site to submit your application. Also remember, if you want to apply for federal student aid, you must complete a FAFSA. It's easy and there is plenty of help along the way, if you have questions.

If you have additional questions about federal student aid or how to complete an electronic or paper application after you review this chapter, you can call the Federal Student Aid Information Center (FSAIC) at 1-800-4-FED-AID (1-800-433-3243) or contact your financial aid administrator (FAA). You can also go to the U.S. Federal Student Aid's *Student Aid on the Web* site at www.studentaid.ed.gov. *Student Aid on the Web* is your source for free, in-depth information on preparing for and funding education beyond high school.

You also may want to check out FAFSA4caster[SM]. This product is an online tool designed to help provide awareness of federal student aid eligibility before officially applying for federal student aid. It helps estimate the cost of an education after high school. FAFSA4caster will serve to estimate the user's eligibility for federal aid and allows users to factor in other aid sources. For more information, go to www.fafsa4caster.ed.gov.

How To Complete The Application

There are three ways to complete a FAFSA:

About This Chapter: Information in this chapter is from "Completing the FAFSA[SM] 2011–12," a publication of the U.S. Department of Education, January 2011.

- Online (*FAFSA on the Web*) at www.fafsa.gov (recommended)

- PDF FAFSA (download file) at www.studentaid.ed.gov/PDFfafsa

- Paper FAFSA (request a copy by calling 1-800-4-FED-AID [1-800-433-3243])

In some cases, you might be able to apply directly through your school. You should check with the financial aid administrator at the school you are interested in attending to see if the school can assist you with your application. If you are using *FAFSA on the Web*, the PDF, or the paper FAFSA (sometimes referred to as the paper form), you can use the instructions in this chapter as a guide to help you complete the application process.

Applying online is generally faster and easier for three reasons:

- *FAFSA on the Web* has built-in help to guide you through the application process.

- Skip logic in *FAFSA on the Web* guides you to answer key questions and may allow you to skip other questions and complete the application faster.

- The schools you list on your application will receive your processed information faster.

If you do not have a computer with internet access at home, you can usually find internet access at your local library, high school, or a financial aid office at a nearby campus. Over 98 percent of applications are submitted electronically.

Using A Federal Student Aid PIN To Sign Your Application

You and your parents are encouraged to apply for a Federal Student Aid PIN (personal identification number) to sign your online application. For a student who provides parental information on the FAFSA, at least one parent whose information is provided on the application must sign.

Your PIN will serve as an identifier and as your electronic signature. It works much like the personal identification number you get from your bank. You can apply for a PIN from within *FAFSA on the Web* or at the Federal Student Aid PIN website at www.pin.ed.gov. After completing the PIN application, you must choose how you want your PIN delivered to you. You have the following choices:

- Create your own PIN

- Have a system-generated PIN instantly displayed online

- Have a system-generated PIN instantly sent in a secure link to your e-mail address

- Have a system-generated PIN mailed to your mailing address

You or your parent (if you are a dependent student) may use the new PIN immediately to sign your FAFSA. Then within one to three days of the PIN being issued, your name, date of birth, and Social Security Number (SSN) are verified with the Social Security Administration (SSA). If the SSA confirms your information, your PIN is then valid for all its uses, which include the following:

- Access to your *Student Aid Report* online

- Access to your data to make corrections

- The option to complete a FAFSA Renewal with most of your information retained from the previous year

- Access to your information on other Federal Student Aid websites, such as the *National Student Loan Data System*[SM]

If there is a problem with the SSA match, your PIN will be deactivated and you will be notified.

You are not required to have a PIN to complete and submit an original application; however, using a PIN is the fastest way to sign your application.

Both web and paper FAFSA filers may provide their e-mail addresses by completing Question 13. If you provide your e-mail address you will receive your student financial aid correspondence by e-mail. Otherwise, leave Question 13 blank and you will receive all of your correspondence by postal mail.

As previously stated, *FAFSA on the Web* applicants are not required to have a PIN to apply. If you do not have a PIN to electronically sign your application, you can print, sign, and mail in a signature page. If you choose to submit your application and mail in a signature page, a PIN will automatically be sent to you, by e-mail or by postal mail, if we determine that you do not already have a PIN assigned to you. If you already have a PIN and need a copy of it sent to you, you can go to www.pin.ed.gov to request a duplicate copy.

Quick Tip

If you have any questions about the PIN process, you should either visit the PIN website at www.pin.ed.gov or call the Federal Student Aid Information Center at 1-800-4-FED-AID (1-800-433-3243).

If You Filed A FAFSA Previously

If you have a previous application on file, when you start to complete your 2011–12 application you will be asked if you want the information from that application to prefill the new application. You will be given this option if you filed a 2010–11 FAFSA. This process will allow you to complete the 2011–12 FAFSA in less time.

General Information

Reasons For Completing A FAFSA

Federal Student Aid uses the data on your FAFSA to calculate an Expected Family Contribution (EFC). The EFC is an indicator of your family's financial strength to pay for education after high school. Your school will subtract your EFC from your total cost of attendance. The result is your financial need.

The EFC is not the amount of money that your family must provide. Rather, you should think of the EFC as an index that colleges use to determine how much financial aid (grants, loans, or work-study) you would receive if you were to attend their school.

Your application results are transmitted to the school(s) listed on your FAFSA, and the school(s) uses the EFC amount to determine the amount of financial aid that you are eligible to receive. Many states and schools also use the FAFSA data to award aid from their programs. Some states and schools also may require you to complete additional applications.

It's A Fact!

Completing and submitting a FAFSA is free, whether you file electronically or on paper. In fact, charging students and/or parents a fee for completing and/or submitting the FAFSA is prohibited by law.

Eligibility

In general, to receive aid from the federal student aid programs, you must meet the following requirements:

- Be a U.S. citizen or eligible noncitizen.

- Have a high school diploma or General Educational Development (GED) certificate, pass an approved ability to benefit test, successfully complete six credit hours or the equivalent course work toward a degree or certificate, or have completed a high school education in a home school setting that is recognized as a home school or private school under state law.

- Enroll or be accepted for enrollment in an eligible program as a regular student seeking a degree or certificate.

- Be registered with Selective Service if required (in general, if you are a male age 18 through 25).

- Meet satisfactory academic progress standards set by your school.

- Certify that you are not in default on a federal loan or owe money on a federal grant.

- Certify that you will use federal student aid only for educational purposes.

- If you have previously received federal student aid, you must certify that you were not convicted for a drug offense that occurred while you were enrolled in school and receiving aid.

If you have previously received federal student aid, you may not be eligible to receive additional federal aid if, while you were enrolled in school and receiving federal student aid, you had a drug offense for selling or possessing illegal drugs and that offense led to a conviction under federal or state law.

If you have previously received federal student aid and have concerns about your eligibility for 2011–12 because of a drug offense, you may call the Federal Student Aid Information Center at 1-800-4-FED-AID (1-800-433-3243) for assistance. If you are applying online, you will be walked through the process with a series of screening questions. If you are applying on paper, you will receive a worksheet through the mail to determine whether the conviction affects your eligibility for federal student aid in the upcoming award year.

The Application Process

Getting Started

You have three options to complete the application:

- Online (*FAFSA on the Web*) at www.fafsa.gov (recommended)

- PDF FAFSA (Download file) at www.studentaid.ed.gov/PDFfafsa

- Paper FAFSA (request a copy by calling 1-800-4-FED-AID)

To complete *FAFSA on the Web*, you begin by going to www.fafsa.gov and clicking on Start Here. Next, you will provide your name, date of birth, and Social Security number. You will be guided step by step through the preliminary application process by following the time-saving suggestions below:

- Gather the documents you need.

- Print and complete the *FAFSA on the Web Worksheet* (optional).

- Apply for a Federal Student Aid PIN if you do not have one.

- Parents of dependent students apply for a PIN if they do not have one.

- Plan how to sign your FAFSA (using a PIN or a signature page).

- Note eligibility requirements.

- Note important deadline dates.

Quick Tip

Do not leave any questions blank either on the web version or paper version unless told to do so.

If you do not sign your *FAFSA on the Web* application electronically with a PIN, you, and your parents, if you are a dependent student, will need to print out, sign, and mail in a signature page with the proper signatures within 14 days. Submitting a signature page will increase the time it takes to process your application or transmit your application data to the schools you listed on your application.

To complete a PDF FAFSA, you can download the file from www.studentaid.ed.gov/PDFfafsa. You may type in your responses on the form and print it, or you may simply print the form and write in your answers. Remember, you must sign, date, and mail the form to the address provided. If you want to complete a paper FAFSA, you must call the Federal Student Aid Information Center at 1-800-4-FED-AID (1-800-433-3243) to have a form mailed to you. If you choose to fill out a PDF or paper FAFSA, use a pen with black ink. Also, dollar amounts should be rounded to the nearest whole dollar. Dates must be reported in numbers in the boxes provided, and numbers below 10 should have a zero in front. (For instance, April would be reported as 04.) Print clearly in capital letters and skip a space between words.

As you complete the FAFSA, you—and your parents, if applicable—should have the following records available to help you answer questions on the application:

- Social Security card

- Driver's license (if any)

- Permanent Resident Receipt Card (if applicable)

- W-2 forms and other 2010 records of money earned

- 2010 income tax return (see the instructions on the FAFSA if the tax return has not been completed)

- Records of child support paid

- Records of taxable earnings from Federal Work-Study or other need-based work programs

- Records of student grant, scholarship, and fellowship aid, including AmeriCorps awards, that was included in your (or your parents') adjusted gross income (AGI)

- Current stock, bond, and other investment records

- Current business and farm records

- Current bank statements

A dependent student (as determined in Questions 45–57) should have all the records listed above from his or her parents except for their driver's licenses.

Submitting Your Completed Application

Double-check your answers to make sure they are complete and accurate. Be sure you have provided the necessary signatures electronically or on paper.

If you are applying electronically, follow the online instructions to print a copy of your application for your records. Be sure to submit your application and receive your confirmation page. If you are applying on paper, make copies of your completed application for your files before you mail it. Do not put letters, tax forms, or any extra materials in the envelope provided. They will be destroyed. Make sure that you put any important documents such as tax forms or letters in a secure file so you can refer to them in the future if you need them. When you get ready to mail in your completed application, put the form (pages three through eight) in an envelope and mail the completed application to the appropriate address, which is listed on the front page of the FAFSA under "Mailing Your FAFSA."

What Happens After You Apply

After receiving your completed application, the FAFSA processor will analyze your FAFSA information and, using a formula established into law by Congress, calculate an Expected Family Contribution (EFC) for you. The results of your application will be sent to the schools

Quick Tip

When filling out the FAFSA, be sure to read the information on the Privacy Act and use of your Social Security number.

you list on your application and to you in the form of a Student Aid Report (SAR) or a SAR Acknowledgement. If you have a valid e-mail address on file, you will receive an e-mail that provides you with a link to view and print your SAR data online. You will receive this e-mail if the following conditions are true:

- Your name, date of birth, and Social Security number match Social Security Administration records

- You and your parents have signed the application or SAR

If you do not meet both of the conditions above, you will receive your application results in the mail: *A Student Aid Report* (SAR).

When To Expect The Results

You can always check the status of your application by calling 1-800-4-FED-AID (1-800-433-3243) or by accessing www.fafsa.gov, clicking on Start Here, and going to the Log In page. Enter your name, Social Security number, and date of birth. Clicking on Next will take you to the My FAFSA page where you can click on View Processed Information. Wait at least 24 hours after you submit your FAFSA electronically before checking its status. By applying electronically and providing your e-mail address, you will receive information about your application within three to five days. If you applied electronically but did not provide an e-mail address, you will receive a SAR Acknowledgement in the mail within two to three weeks of processing. If you applied on paper and did not provide an e-mail address, you will receive a SAR in the mail within two to three weeks of processing.

If you need to make changes to your application information, follow the procedures in the previous paragraph. You will then be given the option to make any necessary changes or corrections. Note, however, that you must not make any changes to income or asset information if that information was correct at the time you submitted your original application. Such information represents a snapshot of your family's financial strength and should not be updated.

Key Application Dates And Deadlines

The application processor must receive your completed application no later than June 30, 2012. Your school must have your correct and complete application information by your last day of enrollment during the 2011–12 year or by mid-September 2012, whichever comes first. There are no exceptions to these dates.

Note also that various state and school deadlines may apply to you. These deadlines are often early in the calendar year (2011 for the 2011–12 award year). Check with your school's financial aid office to make sure you are aware of—and are able to meet—all student financial aid deadlines. Therefore, you should apply as soon after January 1, 2011 as possible. State deadlines are listed under Deadlines on the *FAFSA on the Web* site, on the front of the *FAFSA on the Web Worksheet*, and on the front of the PDF and paper FAFSA.

Receiving Student Aid

Aid from the federal student aid programs will be paid to you through your school. The school will notify you of your aid package. Your aid awards will likely be disbursed each payment period (semester, quarter, trimester, etc.). Typically, your school will first use the aid to pay tuition and fee charges and room and board, if provided by the school. Any remainder will be paid to you for your other education-related expenses.

To meet your financial need, each school you list on the FAFSA will send you a notice of the types and amounts of aid you're eligible to receive. Financial need is the difference between your school's cost of attendance (including living expenses), as calculated by your school, and your EFC.

It's A Fact!

The amount of your financial aid award will be affected by whether you're a full-time or part-time student and whether you attend school for a full academic year or less.

If you believe that you have unusual circumstances that should be taken into account in determining your financial need, contact the financial aid administrator at the school awarding your aid. Unusual circumstances might include extremely high medical or dental expenses or a significant change in income from one year to the next. Please note that the financial aid administrator's decision is final and cannot be appealed to the U.S. Department of Education.

Common Issues

Getting Assistance While Completing The FAFSA

On the home page, www.fafsa.gov, go to Contact Us at the top of the page. This page lists all of the available options for getting additional assistance. You can get live help through a secure online chat session with a customer service representative. You can call 1-800-4-FED-AID (1-800-433-3243). TTY users can call 1-800-730-8913. Lastly, you can send an e-mail with any technical issues you may have while you are completing the application. The address is FederalStudentAid/CustomerService@ed.gov.

Income Information From The Previous Year

The law requires that the Department of Education ask for income information from the year before you go to school. Studies have consistently shown that verifiable income tax information from the most recently completed tax year (2010 for the 2011–12 award year) is more accurate than projected (2011) information and provides a reasonable basis for determining family financial strength in calculating the Expected Family Contribution (EFC).

Unusual Circumstances

If you or your family has unusual circumstances (such as loss of employment, loss of benefits, death, or divorce), complete the FAFSA to the extent that you can and submit it as instructed. Then talk to the financial aid administrator (FAA) at the school you plan to attend. If your family's circumstances have changed from the tax year 2010, the FAA may decide on a case-by-case basis to adjust data elements used to calculate your EFC. Any adjustment the FAA makes must relate only to your individual circumstances and not to any conditions that exist for a whole class of students. The FAA's decision is final and cannot be appealed to the U.S. Department of Education.

Special Circumstance For Parents' Data

If you are considered a dependent student and have no contact with your parents and are unable to provide your parents' data on the FAFSA, you may have a special circumstance. If you are completing *FAFSA on the Web*, answer the questions regarding special circumstances and the remaining student questions. Sign and submit the form for processing. If you are completing a paper application, complete as much of the form as you can, sign it, and submit it for processing. Your application will be incomplete and no EFC will be calculated; however, the financial aid offices at the schools listed on your FAFSA will still receive your data. Contact those schools listed on your FAFSA for further assistance to complete your application.

It's A Fact!

When filling out the FAFSA, it is important to note that special circumstances do not include living separately from your parents or your parents' refusal to provide their information. Examples of special circumstances include parental incarceration and leaving home because of an abusive situation.

Reporting A Live-In Relative's Income

Generally, if you live with an aunt, uncle, or grandparent, you do not need to report that relative's income on your FAFSA. You can only report your birth parents' or adoptive parents' income on your FAFSA. Only if a relative has adopted you and is now your adoptive parent can you report that person's information on your FAFSA. However, you must report for question 45(j) any cash support given by relatives except food and housing.

Questions About Student Loans And Work Study Opportunities

Some schools use the answers about loans and work-study on the FAFSA to construct a financial aid package for you. Answering Yes to being interested in either or both types of aid does not obligate you to take out a loan or accept a work-study position. It usually just means that the school will consider offering you a loan(s) or work-study as part of your financial aid package. If you do indicate on the application that you are interested in either or both loans and work-study, you can change your mind and not accept the loan(s) or work-study later. Keep in mind that if you answer No to the work-study question when you apply—and subsequently change your mind—a work-study job may not be available if all of the work-study funds at the school have been awarded to other students.

Living With A Girlfriend Or Boyfriend Who Pays The Rent

You should not report any information for a friend or roommate unless the two of you are actually married or are considered to have a common-law marriage under state law. You must report in Question 44(j) any cash support given by the friend, except food and housing. You would have to report the rent the roommate paid on your behalf.

Cash Support Versus In-Kind Support

Cash support is support given either in the form of money or money that is paid on your (the student's) behalf. You must report cash support as untaxed income. Thus, if a friend or relative gives you grocery money, it must be reported as untaxed income in Question 44(j). If the friend or relative pays your electric bill or part of your rent, you must also report those payments.

Examples of in-kind support are free food or housing that a family receives, usually in exchange for work or services. You usually don't report such support.

However, the application does require you to report the value of housing a family receives as compensation for a job. The most common example is free housing or a housing allowance provided to military personnel or members of the clergy, which is required to be reported in Question 44(g).

Student Aid As Income

Generally, grants and scholarships that do not exceed tuition, fees, books, and required supplies are not considered to be taxed or untaxed income. If you have a Reserve Officers' Training Corps (ROTC) scholarship, a private scholarship, or any other kind of grant or scholarship, that grant or scholarship will be considered as an available resource by the financial aid office when packaging aid.

You should report grants and scholarships you reported on your tax return. You should then report these items as exclusions from income in Question 43(d): Student's 2010 Additional Financial Information. These amounts will be treated as exclusions from your income.

U.S. Citizens With Alien Registration Numbers (A-Numbers)

If you are a U.S. citizen but have an Alien Registration Number (A-Number), indicate that you are a U.S. citizen on your application; do not provide your A-Number.

Pending Marriage

You must answer Question 46 based on your marital status on the day you complete and sign your FAFSA. Answer Yes if you are married on the day you complete and sign your FAFSA; otherwise, answer No. If you answer No and then marry after you originally file your FAFSA, you cannot change your answer. When you apply in a subsequent year and remain married, you will file as a married student at that time.

Emancipated Minors

If you can provide a copy of a court's decision that you are or were an emancipated minor as determined by a court in your state of legal residence, you may meet the definition of an independent student. You would answer Yes to question 53 if you are currently an emancipated minor. You would also answer Yes if you were an emancipated minor immediately before you reached the age of being an adult in your state. The court must be located in your state of legal residence at the time the court's decision was issued. You may be asked to provide a copy of the court's decision.

Legal Guardianship

If you can provide a copy of a court's decision that you are or were in a legal guardianship as determined by a court in your state of legal residence, you may meet the definition of an independent student. You would answer Yes to question 54 if you are currently in legal guardianship. You would also answer Yes if you were in legal guardianship immediately before you reached the age of being an adult in your state. The court must be located in your state of legal residence at the time the court's decision was issued. You may be asked to provide a copy of the court's decision.

Veterans

If you were a National Guard or Reserve enlistee and were called to active duty or were an active duty military member, you are considered a veteran for purposes of completing the FAFSA. If you were a member of the National Guard or a Reserve enlistee called to active duty for other than state or training purposes, and were released under a condition other than dishonorable, you are considered a veteran for FAFSA purposes.

Active Duty And Independent Student Status

If you are currently serving in the National Guard or as a Reserve enlistee and are called to active duty for other than state or training purposes, you would answer Yes to Question 49 and would then be considered an independent student.

Filing Taxes Before Filling Out The FAFSA

Ideally, you should complete a FAFSA after you've done your tax return, but don't wait until April. Many schools award aid on a first-come, first-served basis. Also, you may not be eligible for state aid if you wait until April to submit your FAFSA. Many state aid deadlines are early in the calendar year (calendar year 2011 for the 2011–12 award year). If you haven't completed your tax return, you should calculate your adjusted gross income (AGI) and taxes paid using the instructions for IRS Form 1040. You can get the instructions and the form at a public library or download them in Portable Document Format (PDF) from www.irs.gov/formspubs/index.html.

Quick Tip

Keep in mind that if you submit your FAFSA application before you complete an annual tax return, you may need to make corrections later if your income or tax information isn't accurate. You will also need to return any federal student aid you received based upon incorrect information.

You might have to provide your college with a copy of your completed tax return (assuming you're required to file one) before you receive federal student aid.

Divorced Parents

If your parents are divorced, report the information of the parent with whom you lived the most during the 12 months preceding the date you completed the FAFSA. It does not make a difference which parent claims you as a dependent for tax purposes. If you did not live with either parent or lived equally with each parent, the parental information must be provided for the parent from whom you received the most financial support during the preceding 12 months or the parent from whom you received the most support the last time support was given.

Stepparents

You should provide the Social Security number (SSN) and last name of the same person or people for whom you are reporting financial information. For example, if you are entering financial information for your mother and stepfather on the FAFSA, provide the SSNs and names of your mother and stepfather (you would not need to provide your father's SSN, since you are not entering his financial information).

It's A Fact!

If you are a dependent student and your parent is remarried, the stepparent's information must be included or you will not be considered for federal student financial aid. If your stepparent refuses to supply information, and you believe that your situation is unique or unusual, you should discuss the matter further with your financial aid administrator.

Household Size

Anyone in the immediate family who receives more than 50 percent support from a dependent student's parents or an independent student and spouse may be counted in the household size even if that person does not reside in the house. For example, a sibling who is over 24 but still receives the majority of his/her support from the parents can be included. Siblings who are dependent (as defined by the FAFSA) as of the date you apply for aid are also included, regardless of whether they receive more than 50 percent of their support from the parents. Any other person who resides in the household and receives more than 50 percent support from the parents may also be counted, as long as they will continue to reside with your parents and the support is expected to continue through June 30, 2012. An unborn child who will be born during the 2011–12 award year may also be counted in the household size if the parents, or independent student and spouse, will provide more than half of the child's support through the end of the 2011–12 award year (June 30, 2012).

Household size and tax exemptions are not necessarily the same. Exemptions look at the previous year or tax year and household size refers to the school year for which the student is applying for aid.

Separated Parents

If your parents have been separated for several months, you should report only the income and asset information of the parent you have lived with the most during the past 12 months, even if your parents filed a joint tax return and claimed you as a dependent. Use a W-2 Form or other record(s) to determine that parent's share of the income reported and taxes paid on the tax return.

Separated Student With A Joint Tax Return

If you (the student) are separated but filed a joint tax return, you should report only your portion of the exemptions, income, and taxes paid.

Number Of People In Household Attending College

Any person (other than your parents) who is counted in the household and will be attending any term of the academic year at least half time qualifies to be counted in the number of people who are attending college. The person must be working toward a degree or certificate leading to a recognized education credential at a postsecondary school eligible to participate in the federal student aid programs. You (the student) need not be enrolled half time to be counted in the number in college.

Reporting Results To Your School

Your school must have your information by your last day of enrollment in 2011–12, or by mid-September 2012, whichever is earlier. If your school has not received your application information electronically, you must submit your paper SAR to the school by the deadline. But do not wait until the deadline date so you have plenty of time to submit your information and make any necessary corrections. Either the electronic record, the Institutional Student Information Record (ISIR), or the paper SAR that has been processed by the Department must have an official EFC. Once the school receives your information, it will use your EFC to determine the amount of your federal grant, loan, or work-study award, if you are eligible. The FAA will send you a financial aid award letter explaining the aid the school is offering.

Missing Student Aid Report (SAR)

If you do not receive an e-mail with a link to your SAR (if you provided an e-mail address on your FAFSA), or your paper SAR or *SAR Acknowledgement* in the mail within two to three weeks after submitting your application, call the Federal Student Aid Information Center at 1-800-4-FED-AID (1-800-433-3243). If you have a touchtone phone, you can use the automated system to find out whether your application has been processed or to request duplicate copies of your report. You will need to provide your Social Security number and the first two letters of your last name. You can also check the status of your FAFSA and print a copy of your SAR at www.fafsa.gov.

If you apply using *FAFSA on the Web*, you will receive a confirmation page with a confirmation number after you select "Submit My FAFSA Now." This confirmation guarantees that your application has been received by the U.S. Department of Education, and the confirmation number can be used by the Federal Student Aid Information Center to track your application if necessary.

Misuse Of Federal Student Aid

If you have reason to suspect fraud, waste, or abuse involving federal student aid funds, you should call the U.S. Department of Education's Inspector General's toll-free hotline at: 1-800-MIS-USED (1-800-647-8733).

Chapter 22

Understanding The Expected Family Contribution

What is the EFC?

The Expected Family Contribution (EFC) is a number that is used to determine a student's eligibility for federal student aid. This number results from the financial information the student provides on his or her Free Application for Federal Student Aid (FAFSA). The EFC is reported on the Student Aid Report (SAR). Financial aid administrators (FAAs) determine an applicant's need for federal student aid from the U.S. Department of Education (the Department) and other sources of assistance by subtracting the EFC from the student's cost of attendance (COA). The EFC formula is used to determine the EFC and ultimately determine the need for aid from the following types of federal student financial assistance programs:

- Federal Pell Grant

- Teacher Education Assistance for College and Higher Education Grant (TEACH Grant)

- Subsidized Stafford Loan through the William D. Ford Federal Direct Loan Program

- Campus-based aid programs:

  - Federal Supplemental Educational Opportunity Grant (FSEOG)

  - Federal Perkins Loan

  - Federal Work-Study (FWS)

About This Chapter: Information in this chapter is from "The EFC Formula, 2011–2012," a publication of the U.S. Department of Education, 2010.

The methodology for determining the EFC is found in Part F of Title IV of the Higher Education Act of 1965, as amended (HEA). Updated tables used in the computation of the EFC for the 2011–2012 Award Year were published in the *Federal Register* on May 27, 2010 (ifap.ed.gov/fregisters/FR052710NeedAnalysis.html) (75 FR 29744).

What is the source of data used in EFC calculations?

All data used to calculate a student's EFC comes from the information the student provides on the FAFSA. A student may submit a FAFSA in one of the following ways:

1. Through the internet by using *FAFSA on the Web*

2. By filing an application electronically through a school

3. By mailing a FAFSA to the Central Processing System (CPS)

Students who applied for federal student aid in the previous award year may be eligible to reapply using a renewal FAFSA online. Applying for federal aid is free. However, to be considered for nonfederal aid (such as institutional aid), a student may have to fill out additional forms.

We encourage applicants to complete the appropriate electronic version of the FAFSA because the electronic version has built-in edits that customize the questions that are presented to the applicant based on answers to prior questions and reduce applicant errors. The electronic version also contains additional instructions and help features and allows the Department to send application results to the applicant and schools more quickly.

Who processes the application, and how is a student notified of his or her EFC?

The CPS receives the student's application data, either electronically or on the paper application, and uses it to calculate an EFC. After the FAFSA has been processed, the CPS sends the student an output document containing information about his or her application results. This document, which can be paper or electronic, is called a SAR. The SAR lists all the information from the student's application and indicates whether or not the application was complete and signed. If the application is complete and signed and no data conflicts, the SAR also includes the student's EFC. Students are instructed to carefully check the information on the SAR to ensure its accuracy. All schools listed on the student's FAFSA receive application information and processing results in an electronic file called an Institutional Student Information Record (ISIR).

Which EFC Formula Worksheet should be used?

There are three regular (full-data) formulas—(A) for the dependent student, (B) for the independent student without dependents other than a spouse, and (C) for the independent student with dependents other than a spouse. Also, there is a simplified version of each formula with fewer data elements. Instructions for applicants who are eligible for the automatic zero EFC calculation are included in each worksheet.

What is the definition of an independent student?

Because the EFC formula for a dependent student uses parental data, and the two formulas for independent students do not, the first step in calculating a student's EFC is to determine his or her dependency status. For the 2011–2012 Award Year, a student is automatically determined to be an independent applicant for federal student aid if he or she meets one or more of the following criteria:

- Student was born before January 1, 1988.

- Student is married or separated (but not divorced) as of the date of the application.

- At the beginning of the 2011–2012 school year, the student will be enrolled in a master's or doctoral degree program (such as MA, MBA, MD, JD, PhD, EdD, or graduate certificate, etc.).

- Student is currently serving on active duty in the U.S. Armed Forces, or is a National Guard or Reserves enlistee called into federal active duty for other than training purposes.

- Student is a veteran of the U.S. Armed Forces.

- Student has one or more children who receive more than half of their support from him or her between July 1, 2011 and June 30, 2012.

- Student has dependent(s) (other than children or spouse) who live with him or her and who receive more than half of their support from the student, now and through June 30, 2012.

- At any time since the student turned age 13, both of the student's parents were deceased, the student was in foster care, or the student was a dependent/ward of the court.

- As determined by a court in the student's state of legal residence, the student is now or was upon reaching the age of majority, an emancipated minor (released from control by his or her parent or guardian).

- As determined by a court in the student's state of legal residence, the student is now or was upon reaching the age of majority, in legal guardianship.

179

> **It's A Fact!**
> A financial aid administrator (FAA) can make a determination of independence with documentation of special circumstances, even if the student initially filed as a dependent student.

- On or after July 1, 2010, student was determined by a high school or school district homeless liaison to be an unaccompanied youth who was homeless.

- On or after July 1, 2010, student was determined by the director of an emergency shelter or transitional housing program funded by the U.S. Department of Housing and Urban Development to be an unaccompanied youth who was homeless.

- On or after July 1, 2010, student was determined by a director of a runaway or homeless youth basic center or transitional living program to be an unaccompanied youth who was homeless or was self-supporting and at risk of being homeless.

- Student was determined by the college financial aid administrator to be an unaccompanied youth who is homeless or is self-supporting and at risk of being homeless.

Which students qualify for the simplified EFC formulas?

The following criteria determine which students have their EFCs calculated by a simplified formula. Assets are not considered in the simplified EFC formulas. For the 2011–2012 Award Year, a dependent student qualifies for the simplified EFC formula under the following conditions:

> **What's It Mean?**
> **Legal Dependent:** Any child of the student who receives more than half of their support from the student (the child does not have to live with the student), including a biological or adopted child. Also, any person, other than a spouse, who lives with the student and receives more than half of his or her support from the student now and will continue to receive more than half of his or her support from the student through June 30, 2012.
>
> **Veteran:** A student who (1) has engaged in active service in the U.S. Armed Forces (Army, Navy, Air Force, Marines, or Coast Guard), or has been a member of the National Guard or Reserves who was called to active duty for purposes other than training, or was a cadet or midshipman at one of the service academies, or attended a U.S. military academy preparatory school, and (2) was released under a condition other than dishonorable. A veteran is also a student who does not meet this definition now but will by June 30, 2012.

1. One of the following must be true:

   - Anyone included in the parents' household size (as defined on the FAFSA) received benefits during 2009 or 2010 from any of the designated means-tested Federal benefit programs: the Supplemental Security Income (SSI) Program, the Food Stamp Program, the Free and Reduced Price School Lunch Program, the Temporary Assistance for Needy Families (TANF) Program, and the Special Supplemental Nutrition Program for Women, Infants, and Children (WIC); OR

   - The student's parents filed or were eligible to file a 2010 IRS Form 1040A or 1040EZ3, they filed a 2010 IRS Form 1040 but were not required to do so, or the parents were not required to file any income tax return; OR

   - The student's parent is a dislocated worker.

2. In addition, the 2010 income of the student's parents must be $49,999 or less.

   - For tax filers, use the parents' adjusted gross income from 2010 Form 1040A or 1040EZ5 to determine if income is $49,999 or less.

   - For non-tax filers, use the income shown on the 2010 W-2 forms of both parents (plus any other earnings from work not included on the W-2s) to determine if income is $49,999 or less.

For the 2011–2012 Award Year, an independent student qualifies for the simplified EFC formula if both (1) and (2) below are true:

1. One of the following must be true:

   - Anyone included in the student's household size (as defined on the FAFSA) received benefits during 2009 or 2010 from any of the designated means-tested Federal benefit programs: the SSI Program, the Food Stamp Program, the Free and Reduced Price School Lunch Program, the TANF Program, and WIC; OR

   - The student and student's spouse (if the student is married) each meet one of the following conditions: filed or was eligible to file a 2010 IRS Form 1040A or 1040EZ8, filed a 2010 IRS Form 1040 but was not required to do so, or was not required to file any income tax return; OR

   - The student (or the student's spouse, if any) is a dislocated worker.

2. In addition, the student's (and spouse's) 2010 income must be $49,999 or less.

- For tax filers, use the student's (and spouse's) adjusted gross income from 2010 Form 1040A or 1040EZ10 to determine if income is $49,999 or less.

- For non-tax filers, use the income shown on the student's (and spouse's) 2010 W-2 forms (plus any other earnings from work not included on the W-2s) to determine if income is $49,999 or less.

Which students qualify for an automatic zero EFC calculation?

Certain students are automatically eligible for a zero EFC. New for 2011–2012: Recent legislative changes mandate an increase in the income threshold for an automatic zero EFC from $30,000 to $31,000 for the 2011–2012 Award Year.

For the 2011–2012 Award Year, a dependent student automatically qualifies for a zero EFC if the following conditions are true:

1. One of the following must be true:

   - Anyone included in the parents' household size (as defined on the FAFSA) received benefits during 2009 or 2010 from any of the designated means-tested Federal benefit programs: the SSI Program, the Food Stamp Program, the Free and Reduced Price School Lunch Program, the TANF Program, and WIC; OR

   - The student's parents filed or were eligible to file a 2010 IRS Form 1040A or 1040EZ13, they filed a 2010 Form 1040 but were not required to do so, or the parents were not required to file any income tax return; OR

   - The student's parent is a dislocated worker.

2. In addition, the 2010 income of the student's parents must be $31,000 or less.

   - For tax filers, use the parents' adjusted gross income from 2010 Form 1040A or 1040EZ15 to determine if income is $31,000 or less.

   - For non-tax filers, use the income shown on the 2010 W-2 forms of both parents (plus any other earnings from work not included on the W-2s) to determine if income is $31,000 or less.

An independent student with dependents other than a spouse automatically qualifies for a zero EFC if both (1) and (2) below are true:

1. One of the following must be true:

- Anyone included in the student's household size (as defined on the FAFSA) received benefits during 2009 or 2010 from any of the designated means-tested Federal benefit programs: the SSI Program, the Food Stamp Program, the Free and Reduced Price School Lunch Program, the TANF Program, and WIC; OR

- The student and student's spouse (if the student is married) each meet one of the following conditions: filed or was eligible to file a 2010 IRS Form 1040A or 1040EZ18, filed a 2010 IRS Form 1040 but was not required to do so, or is not required to file any income tax return; OR

- The student (or the student's spouse, if any) is a dislocated worker.

2. In addition, the student's (and spouse's) 2010 income is $31,000 or less.

- For tax filers, use the student's (and spouse's) adjusted gross income from 2010 Form 1040A or 1040EZ20 to determine if income is $31,000 or less.

- For non-tax filers, use the income shown on the student's (and spouse's) 2010 W-2 forms (plus any other earnings from work not included on the W-2s) to determine if income is $31,000 or less.

It's A Fact!

An independent student without dependents other than a spouse is not eligible for an automatic zero EFC.

Why might a calculation of an EFC using the EFC worksheets differ from the EFC reported on a student's SAR?

When it appears that an applicant has reported inconsistent data, the CPS may make certain assumptions to resolve the inconsistency. These assumed values, which are reported on the student's SAR, are used to calculate the student's EFC. Therefore, in some cases, the EFC produced by the EFC worksheets may differ from the EFC produced by the CPS if the assumed values are not used.

In addition, to help reconcile EFC Formula Worksheet calculations with those of the CPS, all calculations should be carried to three decimal places and then rounded to the nearest whole numbers—round upward for results of .500 to .999, round downward for results of .001

to .499. Rounding should be performed so that the intermediate value that is the result of each step does not have any decimal digits.

> **Quick Tip**
>
> To obtain a copy of "The EFC Formula, 2011–2012," go to http://ifap.ed.gov/efcformulaguide/ attachments/101310EFCFormulaGuide1112.pdf. This PDF contains all of the necessary worksheets for calculating your EFC.

Chapter 23

Federal Education Grants

The Teacher Education Assistance For College And Higher Education (TEACH) Grant Program

The TEACH Grant Program provides grants of up to $4,000 per year to students who intend to teach in a public or private elementary or secondary school that serves students from low-income families.

Conditions

In exchange for receiving a TEACH Grant, you must agree to serve as a full-time teacher in a high-need field in a public or private elementary or secondary school that serves low-income students. As a recipient of a TEACH Grant, you must teach for at least four academic years within eight calendar years of completing the program of study for which you received a TEACH Grant.

Student Eligibility Requirements

To receive a TEACH Grant you must meet the following criteria:

- Complete the Free Application for Federal Student Aid (FAFSA^{SM}), although you do not have to demonstrate financial need.

About This Chapter: Information in this chapter is from the following publications by the U.S. Department of Education: "TEACH Grant Program," 2010; "Federal Pell Grant," 2011; "Federal Supplemental Educational Opportunity Grant (FSEOG)," 2006; "Academic Competitiveness Grant (ACG)," 2009; "The National Science and Mathematics Access to Retain Talent Grant (National SMART Grant)," 2010; and "Iraq and Afghanistan Service Grant," 2010.

- Be a U.S. citizen or eligible noncitizen.

- Be enrolled as an undergraduate, postbaccalaureate, or graduate student in a postsecondary institution that has chosen to participate in the TEACH Grant Program.

- Be enrolled in course work that is necessary to begin a career in teaching or plan to complete such course work. Such course work may include subject area courses (e.g., math courses for a student who intends to be a math teacher).

- Meet certain academic achievement requirements (generally, scoring above the 75th percentile on a college admissions test or maintaining a cumulative GPA of at least 3.25).

- Sign a TEACH Grant Agreement to Serve.

It's A Fact!

If you fail to complete the service obligation required by the TEACH grant, all amounts of TEACH Grants that you received will be converted to a Federal Direct Unsubsidized Stafford Loan. You must then repay this loan to the U.S. Department of Education (ED). You will be charged interest from the date the grant was disbursed.

Source: From "TEACH Grant Program," a publication of the U.S. Department of Education, 2010.

High-Need Field

High-need fields are Bilingual Education and English Language Acquisition, Foreign Language, Mathematics, Reading Specialist, Science, Special Education, and other identified teacher shortage areas as of the time you receive the grant or as of the time you begin teaching in that field. Teacher subject shortage areas (not geographic areas) are listed in ED's annual Teacher Shortage Area Nationwide Listing. To access the listing, visit www.ed.gov/about/offices/list/ope/pol/tsa.doc.

Schools Serving Low-Income Students

Schools serving low-income students include any elementary or secondary school that is listed in ED's annual directory of designated low-income schools for teacher cancellation benefits. To access the directory, visit www.tcli.ed.gov and click on the Search button.

TEACH Grant Agreement To Serve

Each year you receive a TEACH Grant, you must sign a TEACH Grant Agreement to Serve that will be available on an ED website. The Agreement to Serve specifies the conditions under which the grant will be awarded and the teaching service requirements. It also includes an acknowledgment by you that you understand that if you do not meet the teaching service requirements you must repay the grant as a Federal Direct Unsubsidized Stafford Loan, with interest accrued from the date the grant funds were disbursed. The TEACH Grant Agreement to Serve will require the following:

- For each eligible program for which you received TEACH Grant funds, you must serve as a full-time teacher for a total of at least four academic years within eight calendar years after you completed or withdrew from the academic program for which you received the TEACH Grant.

- You must perform the teaching service as a highly qualified teacher at a low-income school. The term "highly qualified teacher" is defined in Section 9101(23) of the Elementary and Secondary Education Act of 1965 or in Section 602(10) of the Individuals with Disabilities Education Act.

- Your teaching service must be in a high-need field.

- You must comply with any other requirements that ED determines to be necessary.

- If you do not complete the required teaching service obligation, TEACH Grant funds you received will be converted to a Federal Direct Unsubsidized Stafford Loan that you must repay, with interest charged from the date of each TEACH Grant disbursement.

Next Steps

If you are interested in learning more about the TEACH Grant Program, you should contact the financial aid office at the college where you will be enrolled to find out whether it participates in the TEACH Grant Program.

Federal Pell Grant

A Federal Pell Grant, unlike a loan, does not have to be repaid. Pell Grants are awarded usually only to undergraduate students who have not earned a bachelor's or a professional degree. (In some cases, however, a student enrolled in a postbaccalaureate teacher certification program might receive a Pell Grant.) Pell Grants are considered a foundation of federal financial aid, to which aid from other federal and nonfederal sources might be added.

Grant Amount

The maximum Pell Grant award for the 2010–11 award year (July 1, 2010 to June 30, 2011) and the 2011–12 award year (July 1, 2011 to June 30, 2012) is $5,550. The amount you get, though, will depend not only on your financial need, but also on your costs to attend school, your status as a full-time or part-time student, and your plans to attend school for a full academic year or less.

It's A Fact!

The maximum award amount is given for any Pell Grant eligible student whose parent or guardian died as a result of military service in Iraq or Afghanistan after Sept.11, 2001. You must be under 24 years old or enrolled at least part time in college at the time of your parent's or guardian's death.

Source: From "Federal Pell Grant," a publication of the U.S. Department of Education, 2011.

You may receive up to two consecutive Pell Grant awards during a single award year to accelerate your program toward your degree. You must be enrolled at least half time and in a program that leads to an associate or bachelor's degree or certificate.

If you received a Pell Grant for the first time on or after July 1, 2008, you can only receive the Pell Grant for up to 18 semesters or the equivalent.

Fund Disbursement

Your school can apply Pell Grant funds to your school costs, pay you directly (usually by check), or combine these methods. The school must tell you in writing how much your award will be and how and when you'll be paid. Schools must disburse funds at least once per term (semester, trimester, or quarter). Schools that do not use semesters, trimesters, or quarters must disburse funds at least twice per academic year.

Federal Supplemental Educational Opportunity Grant (FSEOG)

The Federal Supplemental Educational Opportunity Grant (FSEOG) program is for undergraduates with exceptional financial need. Pell Grant recipients with the lowest expected family contributions (EFCs) will be considered first for a FSEOG. Just like Pell Grants, the FSEOG does not have to be repaid.

Grant Amount

You can receive between $100 and $4,000 a year, depending on when you apply, your financial need, the funding at the school you're attending, and the policies of the financial aid office at your school.

Fund Disbursement

If you're eligible, your school will credit your account, pay you directly (usually by check), or combine these methods. Your school must pay you at least once per term (semester, trimester, or quarter). Schools that do not use semesters, trimesters, or quarters must disburse funds at least twice per academic year.

Academic Competitiveness Grant (ACG)

The Academic Competitiveness Grant was made available for the first time for the 2006–2007 school year for first-year college students who graduated from high school after January 1, 2006, and for second-year college students who graduated from high school after January 1, 2005.

Grant Amount

An Academic Competitiveness Grant provides $750 for the first year of study and $1,300 for the second year.

Eligibility Requirements

To be eligible for each academic year, a student must meet the following criteria:

*   Be a U.S. citizen or eligible noncitizen
*   Be a Federal Pell Grant recipient

It's A Fact!

The amount of the Academic Competiveness Grant, when combined with a Pell Grant, may not exceed the student's cost of attendance. In addition, if the number of eligible students is large enough that payment of the full grant amounts would exceed the program appropriation in any fiscal year, the amount of the grant to each eligible student may be ratably reduced.

Source: From "Academic Competitiveness Grant (ACG)," a publication of the U.S. Department of Education, June 2009.

- Be enrolled at least half time in a degree program

- Be a first- or second-year undergraduate student or a student in a certificate program of at least one year in a degree program at a two-year or four-year degree-granting institution

- Have completed a rigorous secondary school program of study (after January 1, 2006, if a first-year student, and after January 1, 2005, if a second-year student)

- If a first-year student—not have been previously enrolled in an ACG-eligible program while at or below age of compulsory school attendance

- If a second-year student—have at least a cumulative 3.0 grade point average (GPA) on a 4.0 scale as of the end of the first year of undergraduate study

Recognized Rigorous Secondary School Programs Of Study

For qualifying for an ACG, any one of the following programs meet the "rigorous secondary school program of study" requirement:

1. Rigorous secondary school programs designated by state education agencies (SEAs) and state-authorized local education agencies (LEAs) and recognized by the Secretary of Education.

2. Advanced or honors secondary school programs established by states.

3. Secondary school programs identified by a state-level partnership recognized by the State Scholars Initiative of the Western Interstate Commission for Higher Education (WICHE) of Boulder, Colorado.

4. A program for a student who completes at least two courses in the International Baccalaureate (IB) Diploma Program with a score of four or higher on the course examinations or at least two Advanced Placement (AP) courses with a score of three or higher on the College Board's exams for those courses.

5. A secondary school program in which a student completes, at minimum, the following courses:

   - Four years of English

   - Three years of math, including algebra I and a higher level class such as algebra II, geometry, or data analysis and statistics

   - Three years of science, including one year each of at least two of the following courses: biology, chemistry, and physics

• Three years of social studies

• One year of a language other than English

The National Science And Mathematics Access To Retain Talent Grant (National SMART Grant)

The National SMART Grant is available during the third and fourth years of undergraduate study (or fifth year of a five-year program) to at least half-time students who are eligible for the Federal Pell Grant and who are majoring in physical, life, or computer sciences; mathematics, technology, or engineering; a critical foreign language; or nonmajor single liberal arts programs. The student must also maintain a cumulative grade point average (GPA) of at least 3.0 in course work required for the major. The National SMART Grant award is in addition to the student's Pell Grant award.

Grant Amount

A National SMART Grant will provide up to $4,000 for each of the third and fourth years of undergraduate study. The amount of the SMART Grant, when combined with a Pell Grant, may not exceed the student's cost of attendance. In addition, if the number of eligible students is large enough that payment of the full grant amounts would exceed the program appropriation in any fiscal year, the amount of the grant to each eligible student may be ratably reduced.

Quick Tip

For each calendar year, the U.S. Secretary of Education publishes a list of all rigorous secondary school programs of study. You can find the list at http://www2.ed.gov/admins/finaid/about/ac-smart/state-programs.html.

Source: From "Academic Competitiveness Grant (ACG)," a publication of the U.S. Department of Education, June 2009.

Eligible Students

To be eligible for a SMART grant, a student must meet the following criteria:

• Be a U.S. citizen or eligible noncitizen

• Be eligible for a Pell Grant during the same award year

• Be enrolled at least half time

- Be in the third or fourth year of an undergraduate degree program (or fifth year of a five-year program)

- Be pursuing a major in physical, life, or computer sciences; mathematics, technology, or engineering; a critical foreign language; or nonmajor single liberal arts programs

- Have at least a 3.0 GPA on a 4.0 scale as of the end of the second award year and continue to maintain a 3.0 GPA that must be checked prior to the beginning of each payment period (e.g., semester)

Iraq And Afghanistan Service Grant

Beginning with the 2010–11 award year, a student who is not eligible for a Pell Grant but whose parent or guardian was a member of the U.S. Armed Forces and died as a result of service performed in Iraq or Afghanistan after September 11, 2001 may be eligible to receive the Iraq and Afghanistan Service Grant. To be eligible for the grant, a student must be under 24 years old or enrolled in college at least part time at the time of the parent's or guardian's death.

The grant award is equal to the amount of a maximum Pell Grant for the award year—not to exceed the cost of attendance for that award year.

Chapter 24

Federal Student Loans

Federal Perkins Loans

A Federal Perkins Loan is a low-interest (5%) loan for both undergraduate and graduate students with exceptional financial need. Federal Perkins Loans are made through a school's financial aid office. Your school is your lender, and the loan is made with government funds. You must repay this loan to your school.

Your school will either pay you directly (usually by check) or apply your loan to your school charges. You'll receive the loan in at least two payments during the academic year.

Amount

You can borrow up to $5,500 for each year of undergraduate study (the total you can borrow as an undergraduate is $27,500). For graduate studies, you can borrow up to $8,000 per year (the total you can borrow as a graduate is $60,000, which includes amounts borrowed as an undergraduate). The amount you receive depends on when you apply, your financial need, and the funding level at the school.

Loan Charges

Other than interest, there are no other charges for a Perkins Loan. However, if you skip a payment, if it's late, or if you make less than a full payment, you might have to pay a late charge plus any collection costs.

About This Chapter: This chapter includes information from the following publications by the U.S. Department of Education: "Campus-Based Aid: Federal Perkins Loans," November 2009; "Direct Stafford Loans," June 2010; "Direct PLUS Loans for Parents," February 2011; "Direct PLUS Loans for Graduate and Professional Degree Students," February 2011; and "Loan Consolidation," June 2010.

Repayment

If you're attending school at least half time, you have nine months after you graduate, leave school, or drop below half-time status before you must begin repayment. This time is called the grace period. If you're attending less than half time, check with your college or career school to find out how long your grace period will be. For more information on repaying and your obligations as a borrower, see Chapter 25, "Repaying Federal Student Loans."

Direct Stafford Loans

Direct Stafford Loans, from the William D. Ford Federal Direct Loan (Direct Loan) Program, are low-interest loans for eligible students to help cover the cost of higher education at a four-year college or university, community college, or trade, career, or technical school. Eligible students borrow directly from the U.S. Department of Education (the Department) at participating schools.

Direct Stafford Loans include the following types of loans:

- **Direct Subsidized Loans**: Direct Subsidized Loans are for students with financial need. Your school will review the results of your Free Application for Federal Student Aid (FAFSA^{SM}) and determine the amount you can borrow. You are not charged interest while you're in school at least half time and during grace periods and deferment periods.

- **Direct Unsubsidized Loans**: You are not required to demonstrate financial need to receive a Direct Unsubsidized Loan. Like subsidized loans, your school will determine the amount you can borrow. Interest accrues (accumulates) on an unsubsidized loan from the time it's first paid out. You can pay the interest while you are in school and during grace periods and deferment or forbearance periods, or you can allow it to accrue and be capitalized (that is, added to the principal amount of your loan). If you choose not to pay the interest as it accrues, the total amount you have to repay will increase because you will be charged interest on a higher principal amount.

It's A Fact!

Before July 1, 2010, Stafford, PLUS, and Consolidation Loans were also made by private lenders under the Federal Family Education Loan (FFEL^{SM}) Program. As a result of recent legislation, no further loans will be made under the FFEL Program beginning July 1, 2010. All new Stafford, PLUS, and Consolidation Loans will come directly from the Department under the Direct Loan Program.

Source: From "Direct Stafford Loans," a publication of the U.S. Department of Education, June 2010.

It's A Fact!

Depending on your financial need, you may be eligible to receive a subsidized loan for an amount up to the annual subsidized loan borrowing limit for your level of study. If you have education expenses that have not been met by subsidized loans and other aid, you may also receive an unsubsidized loan so long as you don't exceed the combined subsidized and unsubsidized annual loan limits.

Source: From "Direct Stafford Loans," a publication of the U.S. Department of Education, June 2010.

Additional loan types provided under the Direct Loan Program include Direct PLUS Loans (for parents and graduate and professional degree students) and Direct Consolidation Loans (to combine federal education loan debts into a single loan).

Applying For A Stafford Loan

As with all federal student aid, you must complete the Free Application for Federal Student Aid (FAFSA). Most students use *FAFSA on the Web* to complete their application. Schools use the information from your FAFSA to determine how much student aid you will receive. Stafford Loans are generally included as part of your award package, which may contain other types of aid to help meet the costs of going to college or career school.

Master Promissory Note (MPN): When you receive a Stafford Loan for the first time, you must complete a Master Promissory Note (MPN). The MPN is a legal document in which you promise to repay your loan and any accrued interest and fees to the Department. It also explains the terms and conditions of your loan. In most cases, one MPN can be used for loans that you receive over several years of study. If you previously signed an MPN to receive a FFEL Program loan, you will need to sign a new MPN for a Direct Loan. Your school will either give you a copy of the MPN or offer you the option of completing the MPN online at www.studentloans.gov.

Loan Limits

There are limits on the maximum amount you are eligible to receive each academic year (annual loan limit) and in total (aggregate loan limits). The actual amount you can borrow each year depends on your year in school, whether you are a dependent or independent student, and other factors, and may be less than the maximum amounts shown in Table 24.1. Your school will determine what types of loans and how much you may borrow.

The following table provides maximum annual and aggregate (total) loan limits for subsidized and unsubsidized Direct Stafford Loans.

These annual loan limit amounts are the maximum yearly amounts you can borrow in both subsidized and unsubsidized loans. You can have one type of loan or a combination of both. Because you can't borrow more than your cost of attendance minus any other financial aid you'll get, you may receive less than the annual maximum amounts. Also, the annual loan limits assume that your program of study is at least a full academic year.

The maximum annual and total loan limits include any Stafford Loans you may have received under the FFEL Program.

Graduate and professional students enrolled in certain health profession programs may receive additional unsubsidized Stafford Loan amounts each academic year beyond those shown in Table 24.1. For these students, there is also an increased aggregate loan limit of $224,000 (maximum $65,500 subsidized).

Table 24.1. Annual And Aggregate Loan Limits

Year	Dependent Undergraduate Student (except students whose parents are unable to obtain PLUS Loans)	Independent Undergraduate Student (and dependent students whose parents are unable to obtain PLUS Loans)	Graduate and Professional Degree Student
First Year	$5,500: No more than $3,500 of this amount may be in subsidized loans.	$9,500: No more than $3,500 of this amount may be in subsidized loans.	$20,500: No more than $8,500 of this amount may be in subsidized loans.
Second Year	$6,500: No more than $4,500 of this amount may be in subsidized loans.	$10,500: No more than $4,500 of this amount may be in subsidized loans.	$20,500: No more than $8,500 of this amount may be in subsidized loans.
Third And Beyond (each year)	$7,500: No more than $5,500 of this amount may be in subsidized loans.	$12,500: No more than $5,500 of this amount may be in subsidized loans.	$20,500: No more than $8,500 of this amount may be in subsidized loans.
Maximum Total Debt From Stafford Loans When You Graduate (aggregate loan limits)	$31,000: No more than $23,000 of this amount may be in subsidized loans.	$57,500: No more than $23,000 of this amount may be in subsidized loans.	$138,500: No more than $65,500 of this amount may be in subsidized loans. The graduate debt limit includes Stafford Loans received for undergraduate study.

Funds Disbursement

You'll be paid through your school, generally in at least two installments. No installment may exceed one-half of your loan amount. Your school will use your loan money first to pay for tuition and fees, room and board, and other school charges. If any loan money remains, you'll receive the funds by check or other means, unless you give the school written authorization to hold the funds until later in the enrollment period.

Generally, if you're a first-year undergraduate student and a first-time borrower, your school cannot disburse your first payment until 30 days after the first day of your enrollment period.

Current Interest Rates

Direct Subsidized Loans: The following interest rates apply to Direct Subsidized Loans:

- **Undergraduate Students**: If the first disbursement of your subsidized loan is between July 1, 2010 and June 30, 2011, the interest rate on your loan is fixed at 4.5%. The interest rate on subsidized loans first disbursed to undergraduate students between July 1, 2011 and June 30, 2012 will be fixed at 3.4%.

- **Graduate And Professional Degree Students:** The interest rate is fixed at 6.8%.

Direct Unsubsidized Loans: The interest rate is fixed at 6.8% for all borrowers (undergraduate and graduate).

Prior Federal Loans And Financial Aid History: If you currently have a Stafford Loan and would like to check the interest rate, servicer information, and other financial aid history, go to the National Student Loan Data System at http://www.nslds.ed.gov/nslds_SA/.

Interest Rate Cap For Military Members: If you qualify under the Service Members Civil Relief Act, the interest rate on loans you obtained before entering military service may be capped at 6% during your military service. You must contact your loan servicer to request this benefit. In addition, the federal government does not charge interest (for a period of no more than 60 months) on Direct Loans first disbursed on or after October 1, 2008, while a borrower is serving on active duty or performing qualifying National Guard duty during a war or other military operation or other emergency, and serving in an area of hostilities qualifying for special pay.

Other Charges

There is a loan fee on all Direct Subsidized and Unsubsidized Loans. The loan fee is a percentage of the amount of each loan you receive. For loans first disbursed between July 1, 2010 and June 30, 2011 the loan fee is 1.0%. We will deduct the loan fee proportionately from each loan disbursement. The specific loan fee that you are charged will be reflected in a disclosure statement that the federal government sends to you.

Loan Repayment

When you receive your first Direct Loan, you will be contacted by the servicer for that loan (you repay your loan to the loan servicer). Your loan servicer will provide regular updates on the status of your Direct Loan and any additional Direct Loans that you receive. If you're not sure who your loan servicer is, you can look it up on www.nslds.ed.gov.

After you graduate, leave school, or drop below half-time enrollment, you will have a six-month grace period before you begin repayment. During this period, you'll receive repayment information from your loan servicer, and you'll be notified of your first payment due date. Payments are usually due monthly.

Repayment Plans: The Direct Loan Program offers several repayment plans that are designed to meet the different needs of individual borrowers. Generally, you'll have 10 to 25 years to repay your loan, depending on the repayment plan that you choose. You will receive more detailed information on your repayment options during entrance and exit counseling sessions at your school. To learn more about Direct Loan repayment plans, see Chapter 25.

Loan Cancellation

Under a few circumstances, your loan may be cancelled, or discharged. You may qualify for forgiveness of some or all of your loan balance in the following situations:

- If you teach full time for five years at a school or educational service agency serving low-income families and meet other requirements

- After you have made 120 payments on a Direct Loan while employed in certain public service jobs (additional conditions apply)

For more information, see Chapter 27.

Quick Tip

Under certain circumstances, you can receive a deferment or forbearance that allows you to temporarily stop or lower the payments on your loan. For more information, see Chapter 25, "Deferring (Postponing) Repayment Of Federal Student Loans."

Source: From "Direct Stafford Loans," a publication of the U.S. Department of Education, June 2010.

Direct PLUS Loans For Parents

Parents of dependent students may apply for a Direct PLUS Loan to help pay their child's education expenses as long as certain eligibility requirements are met. Graduate and professional students may apply for PLUS Loans for their own expenses—see the information later in this chapter about PLUS Loans for graduate and professional students.

To be eligible for a Direct PLUS Loan for Parents:

- The parent borrower must be the student's biological or adoptive parent. In some cases, the student's stepparent may be eligible.

- The student must be a dependent student who is enrolled at least half time at a school that participates in the Direct Loan Program℠. Generally, a student is considered dependent if he or she is under 24 years of age, has no dependents, and is not married, a veteran, a graduate or professional degree student, or a ward of the court.

- The parent borrower must not have an adverse credit history (a credit check will be done). If the parent does not pass the credit check, the parent may still receive a loan if someone (such as a relative or friend who is able to pass the credit check) agrees to endorse the loan. The endorser promises to repay the loan if the parent fails to do so. The parent may also still receive a loan if he or she can demonstrate extenuating circumstances.

- The student and parent must be U.S. citizens or eligible noncitizens, must not be in default on any federal education loans or owe an overpayment on a federal education grant, and must meet other general eligibility requirements for the federal student aid programs.

Additional loan types provided under the Direct Loan Program include Direct Stafford Loans (for undergraduate and graduate students), Direct PLUS Loans (for graduate and professional degree students), and Direct Consolidation Loans (to combine federal education loan debts into a single loan).

Getting A Loan As A Parent

For a Direct PLUS Loan, the parent must complete a Direct PLUS Loan Application and Master Promissory Note (MPN). The MPN is a legal document in which the borrower promises to repay the loan and any accrued interest and fees to the Department. It also explains the terms and conditions of the loan. In most cases, one MPN can be used for loans that a parent receives over multiple academic years although a separate Loan Request must be filed for each school year. If the parent previously signed an MPN to receive an FFEL PLUS loan, he or she will need to sign a new MPN for a Direct PLUS Loan.

The school's financial aid office can provide instructions on applying for a PLUS Loan and may offer the option of completing the PLUS application and MPN online at www.student loans.gov.

Loan Amount

The annual limit on a PLUS Loan is equal to the student's cost of attendance minus any other financial aid the student receives. For example, if the cost of attendance is $6,000 and the student receives $4,000 in other financial aid, the student's parent can request up to $2,000.

Fund Disbursement

ED will send the loan funds to the student's school. In most cases, the loan will be disbursed in at least two installments, and no installment will be more than half the loan amount. The school will use the loan money first to pay the student's tuition, fees, room and board, and other school charges. If any loan funds remain, the parent will receive the amount as a check or other means, unless he or she authorizes the amount to be released to the student or transferred into the student's account at the school. Any remaining loan funds must be used for the student's education expenses.

Interest Rate

The interest rate is fixed at 7.9%. Interest is charged from the date of the first disbursement until the loan is paid in full.

Prior Federal Loans And Financial Aid History: Students and parents may check the interest rate, servicer information, and other financial aid history at the National Student Loan Data System (http://www.nslds.ed.gov/nslds_SA/).

Interest Rate Cap For Military Members: If a parent qualifies under the Service Members Civil Relief Act, the interest rate on loans obtained before entering military service may be capped at 6% during the parent's military service. Parents must contact their loan servicer to request this benefit. In addition, we do not charge interest (for a period of no more than 60 months) on Direct Loans first disbursed on or after October 1, 2008, while a borrower is serving on active duty or performing qualifying National Guard duty during a war or other military operation or other emergency, and serving in an area of hostilities qualifying for special pay.

Other Charges

The parent will pay a fee of 4% of the loan amount, deducted proportionately each time a loan disbursement is made.

It's A Fact!

A parent's PLUS Loan cannot be transferred to the student so that it becomes the student's responsibility to repay. The parent is responsible for repaying the PLUS Loan.

Source: From "Direct PLUS Loans for Parents," a publication of the U.S. Department of Education, February 2011.

Loan Repayment

The repayment period for a Direct PLUS Loan begins at the time the PLUS loan is fully disbursed, and the first payment is due within 60 days after the final disbursement. However, for Direct PLUS Loans with a first disbursement date on or after July 1, 2008, the parent may defer repayment while the student on whose behalf the parent borrowed the loan is enrolled on at least a half-time basis, and for an additional six months after the student ceases to be enrolled at least half time.

The parent will repay the servicer listed on the disclosure statement provided when he or she received the loan. The loan servicer will provide regular updates on the status of the PLUS Loan, and any additional PLUS Loans that a parent receives. The loan servicer also will be listed in the parent's account at www.nslds.ed.gov.

Repayment Plans: The Direct PLUS Loan Program for parents offers three repayment plans—standard, extended, and graduated—that are designed to meet the different needs of individual borrowers. The terms differ between the repayment programs, but generally borrowers will have 10 to 25 years to repay a loan. For more information, see Chapter 25.

Loan Forgiveness (Discharge)

Under certain conditions, a PLUS Loan can be cancelled, or discharged. A cancellation releases the parent from all obligations to repay the loan. For more information, see Chapter 27, "Loan Cancellation (Forgiveness) Of Federal Student Loans."

It's A Fact

Under the Loan Forgiveness for Public Service Employees Program, PLUS Loan borrowers may have the balance of their loans forgiven if they are employed full time in a public service job and make 120 payments on their loans during that period.

Source: From "Direct PLUS Loans for Parents," a publication of the U.S. Department of Education, February 2011.

Direct PLUS Loans For Graduate And Professional Degree Students

Graduate and professional degree students can borrow a Direct PLUS Loan to help cover education expenses.

The terms and conditions applicable to PLUS Loans for parents also apply to PLUS Loans for graduate and professional students. These terms and conditions include the following:

- A determination that you (the applicant) do not have an adverse credit history
- A fixed interest rate of 7.9% for Direct PLUS Loans

Unlike parent PLUS applicants, you (the student applicant) are required to complete the Free Application for Federal Student Aid (FAFSA[SM]). In addition, before you can receive a PLUS Loan, your school must have determined your maximum eligibility for Direct Subsidized and Unsubsidized Stafford Loans.

Additional loan types provided under the Direct Loan Program[sm] include Direct Stafford Loans (for undergraduate and graduate students), Direct PLUS Loans (for parents), and Direct Consolidation Loans (to combine federal education loan debts into a single loan).

Applying For A PLUS Loan

For a PLUS Loan, you must complete a Direct PLUS Loan Application and Master Promissory Note (MPN). The MPN is a legal document in which you promise to repay the loan and any accrued interest and fees to the Department. It also explains the terms and conditions of the loan. In most cases, one MPN can be used for loans that you receive over several years of study, although a separate Loan Request must be filed for each school year. If you previously signed an MPN to receive an FFEL PLUS Loan, you will need to sign a new MPN for a Direct PLUS Loan.

Your school's financial aid office can provide instructions on how to apply for a PLUS Loan and may offer the option of completing the PLUS application and MPN online at www. studentloans.gov.

Loan Amount

The maximum PLUS Loan amount you can borrow is your cost of attendance (determined by the school) minus any other financial assistance you will receive.

Current Interest Rate

The interest rate for Direct PLUS Loans is a fixed rate of 7.9%.

Prior Federal Loans And Financial Aid History: If you currently have a federal loan and would like to check the interest rate, servicer information, and other financial aid history, go to the National Student Loan Data System at http://www.nslds.ed.gov/nslds_SA/.

Interest Rate Cap For Military Members: If you qualify under the Service Members Civil Relief Act, the interest rate on loans you obtained before entering military service may be capped at 6% during your military service. You must contact your loan servicer to request this benefit. In addition, we do not charge interest (for a period of no more than 60 months) on Direct Loans first disbursed on or after October 1, 2008, while a borrower is serving on active duty or performing qualifying National Guard duty during a war or other military operation or other emergency, and serving in an area of hostilities qualifying for special pay.

Other Charges

There is a fee of 4% of the loan amount, deducted proportionately each time a loan disbursement is made.

Loan Repayment

When you receive your first PLUS Loan, you will be contacted by the servicer for that loan (you repay your loan to the loan servicer). Your loan servicer will provide regular updates on the status of your PLUS Loan, and any additional loans that you receive. If you're not sure who your loan servicer is, you can look it up on www.nslds.ed.gov.

The repayment period for a Direct PLUS Loan begins at the time the PLUS loan is fully disbursed, and the first payment is due within 60 days after the final disbursement. However, you may defer repayment while you are enrolled at least half time. If your Direct PLUS Loan was first disbursed on or after July 1, 2008, you may also defer repayment for an additional six months after you cease to be enrolled at least half time.

Repayment Plans: There are several repayment plans that are designed to meet the different needs of individual borrowers. Generally, you'll have 10 to 25 years to repay your loan, depending on the repayment plan that you choose. You will receive more detailed information on your repayment options during entrance and exit counseling sessions at your school. To learn more about repayment plans, see Chapter 25.

Loan Consolidation

A Direct Consolidation Loan allows a borrower to consolidate (combine) multiple federal student loans into one loan. The result is a single monthly payment instead of multiple monthly payments.

Make sure to carefully consider whether loan consolidation is the best option for you. While loan consolidation can simplify loan repayment and lower your monthly payment, it also can significantly increase the total cost of repaying your loans. Consolidation offers lower monthly payments by giving you up to 30 years to repay your loans. But, if you increase the length of your repayment period, you'll also make more payments and pay more in interest than you would otherwise. In fact, in some situations, consolidation can double your total interest expense. If you don't need monthly payment relief, you should compare the cost of repaying your unconsolidated loans against the cost of repaying a consolidation loan.

You also should take into account the impact of losing any borrower benefits offered under repayment plans for the original loans. Borrower benefits from your original loan, which may include interest rate discounts, principal rebates, or some loan cancellation benefits, can significantly reduce the cost of repaying your loans. You may lose those benefits if you consolidate.

Quick Tip

Once your loans are combined into a Direct Consolidation Loan, they cannot be removed. That's because the loans that were consolidated have been paid off and no longer exist. Take the time to study the pros and cons of consolidation before you submit your application. For additional information, visit www.loanconsolidation.ed.gov.

Source: From "Loan Consolidation," a publication of the U.S. Department of Education, June 2010.

Types Of Loans

Most federal student loans are eligible for consolidation, including subsidized and unsubsidized Direct and FFEL Stafford Loans, Direct and FFEL PLUS Loans, Supplemental Loans for Students (SLS), Federal Perkins Loans, Federal Nursing Loans, Health Education Assistance Loans, and some existing consolidation loans. Private education loans are not eligible for consolidation. If you are in default, you must meet certain requirements before you can consolidate your loans.

For a complete list of the federal student loans that can be consolidated, contact the Direct Loan Origination Center's Consolidation Department by calling 1-800-557-7392 or visit www.loanconsolidation.ed.gov. TTY users may call 1-800-557-7395.

Eligibility

Generally, you are eligible to consolidate after you graduate, leave school, or drop below half-time enrollment.

To qualify for a Direct Consolidation Loan, you must meet the following requirements:

- You must have at least one Direct Loan or Federal Family Education Loan (FFEL) that is in grace or repayment.

- You can consolidate most defaulted education loans if you make satisfactory repayment arrangements with the current loan servicer(s) or agree to repay your new Direct Consolidation Loan under the Income Contingent Repayment Plan or the Income Based Repayment Plan.

- If you have a Direct Consolidation Loan, you cannot consolidate again unless you include an additional FFEL or Direct Loan. If you have a FFEL Consolidation Loan you also may be able to consolidate again under certain circumstances. For additional details, go to www.loanconsolidation.ed.gov.

If you consolidate your loans, you do not need to pay any application fees and you will not be charged any prepayment penalties.

Interest Rate

A Direct Consolidation Loan has a fixed interest rate for the life of the loan. The fixed rate is based on the weighted average of the interest rates on the loans being consolidated, rounded up to the nearest one-eighth of 1%, and cannot exceed 8.25%.

Applying For A Loan

There are several ways that you can apply for a Direct Consolidation Loan:

- Apply online at www.loanconsolidation.ed.gov

- Download a paper copy of the application and promissory note at www.loanconsolidation.ed.gov

- Apply over the phone if you have all Direct Loans—1-800-557-7392

- Request an application package be mailed to you by calling 1-800-557-7392 (TDD 1-800-557-7395) or 334-206-7400 (outside the United States) or by e-mailing consolidation@mail.eds.com

> ## It's A Fact!
>
> A PLUS Loan made to the parent of a dependent student cannot be transferred to the student. Therefore, a student who is applying for loan consolidation cannot include his or her parent's PLUS Loan.
>
> Source: From "Loan Consolidation," a publication of the U.S. Department of Education, June 2010.

Repayment

Repayment of a Direct Consolidation Loan begins immediately upon disbursement of the loan. (Your first payment will be due within 60 days.) The payback term ranges from 10 to 30 years, depending on the amount of education debt being repaid and the repayment plan you select. Direct Consolidation Loans that include parent PLUS loans are not eligible for the Income-Based Repayment Plan. For additional details on repayment plans available for Direct Consolidation Loans, go to the Loan Consolidation website at http://loanconsolidation.ed .gov/borrower/brights.html or check with your loan servicer.

Repayment Plans: There are several repayment plans that are designed to meet the different needs of individual borrowers. You will receive more detailed information on your repayment options when you consolidate your loan.

Loan Deferment Or Cancellation

Under certain circumstances, you can receive a deferment or forbearance that allows you to temporarily stop or lower the payments on your loan. For more information, see the chapter on deferring (postponing) repayment of federal student loans.

Under a few circumstances, your loan can be cancelled (discharged). For more information, see the chapter on cancellation of federal student loans.

Chapter 25

Repaying Federal Student Loans

If you're a federal student loan recipient, there are two key points to remember. First, the interest rate you pay is lower than commercial rates because the federal government subsidizes the loan. Second, if you are a student borrower, you don't have to begin to repay your Perkins or Stafford Loans until you leave school or drop below half time.

As generous as these terms are, you shouldn't forget that you do have to repay your loan. Failure to do so could result in your loan(s) being declared delinquent or in default. This could have a negative impact on your financial status and creditworthiness in the future. This chapter outlines repayment requirements and describes the rare circumstances under which your obligation to repay can be reduced or forgiven.

Borrower's Responsibilities

When you obtain a federal student loan you have certain responsibilities. Some important ones are listed below.

Repayment Obligations

- Think about what your repayment obligation means before you take out a student loan.

- If you don't repay your student loan on time or according to the terms in your promissory note, you could default on this legal obligation, which has serious consequences and will adversely affect your credit rating.

About This Chapter: Information in this chapter is from the following publications by the U.S. Department of Education: Excerpts from Section C of *The Guide to Federal Student Aid* ("Repaying Your Student Loan"), March 2010, compiled summer 2009; "Repayment Information," February 2011; and "Repayment Plans and Calculators," December 2010.

The Promissory Note

- When you sign a promissory note, you're agreeing to repay the loan according to the terms of the note.

- The note states that unless you meet the requirements for loan discharge (cancellation), you must repay the loan, even if you don't complete your education.

- Also, you must repay your loan even if you can't get a job after you complete the program or you didn't like the education you received. The U.S. Department of Education does not guarantee the quality of education you receive or that you will find a job in your field of study.

Always Make Payments

- You must make payments on your loan even if you don't receive a bill or repayment notice.

- Billing statements (or coupon books) are sent to you as a convenience. You're obligated to make payments even if you don't receive any reminders.

- You must also make monthly payments in the full amount required by your repayment plan. Partial payments do not fulfill your obligation to repay your student loan on time.

Paying While Waiting For Deferment Or Forbearance

- If you apply for a deferment or forbearance, you must continue to make payments until you have been notified that your request has been approved.

- If you don't, you might end up in default.

- Keep a copy of any request form you submit, and document all contact you have with the holder of your loan.

Notification Of Changes

Notify your lender or loan servicing agency when you do any of the following:

- Graduate

- Withdraw from school

- Drop below half-time status

- Change your name, address, or Social Security number

- Transfer to another school

Entrance And Exit Counseling

- If you are a first-time borrower you must complete an entrance counseling session before you're given your first loan disbursement. This session provides you with useful tips and tools to help you develop a budget for managing your educational expenses and helps you to understand your loan responsibilities. Parent PLUS Loan borrowers do not participate in entrance counseling.

- You must receive exit counseling before you leave school to make sure you understand your rights and responsibilities as a borrower. You will receive information about repayment and your loan provider will notify you of the date loan repayment begins (usually six months after you graduate, leave school, or drop below half-time enrollment). Parent PLUS Loan borrowers do not participate in exit counseling.

Borrower's Rights

Loan Facts

You have a right to know the details of your loan (depending on your loan, some of the following might be included as part of your entrance counseling). Below is what you need to know and must receive from your school, lender, or the Direct Loan Servicing Center:

- The full amount of the loan and the current interest rate
- The date you must start repayment
- A complete list of any charges you must pay (loan fees) and information on how those charges are collected
- Information about the yearly and total amounts you can borrow
- Information about the maximum repayment periods and the minimum repayment amount
- An explanation of default and its consequences
- An explanation of available options for consolidating your loans and a statement that you can prepay your student loan(s) at any time without a penalty

---

It's A Fact!

New Social Security numbers are issued only in very rare circumstances.
See www.ssa.gov/ssnumber/ for rules on changing them.

Source: From Section C of *The Guide to Federal Student Aid* ("Repaying Your Student Loan"), March 2010, compiled summer 2009.

It's A Fact!

The U.S. Department of Education's National Student Loan Data System[SM] (NSLDS[SM]) provides information on your federal loans including loan types, disbursed amounts, outstanding principal and interest, and the total amount of all your loans. To access NSLDS, go to www.nslds.ed.gov.

Source: From "Repayment Information," a publication of the U.S. Department of Education, February 2011.

Before Leaving School

Before you leave school, you will receive the following information about your loan (as part of exit counseling) from your school, lender, or the Direct Loan Servicing Center:

- A current description of your loans, including average anticipated monthly payments

- The amount of your total debt (principal and estimated interest), your current interest rate, and the total interest charges on your loan

- If you have FFEL[SM] Loans, the name of the lender or agency that holds your loans, where to send your payments, and where to write or call if you have questions

- If you have Direct Loans, the address and telephone number of the U.S. Department of Education's Direct Loan Servicing Center

- An explanation of the fees you might be charged during the repayment period, such as late charges and collection or litigation costs if you're delinquent or in default

- A reminder of available options for loan consolidation and a reminder that you can pre-pay your loan without penalty at any time

- A description of applicable deferment, forbearance, and discharge (cancellation) provisions

- Repayment options and advice about debt management that will help you in making your payments

- Notification that you must provide your expected permanent address and the name and address of your expected employer

- Notification that you must also provide any corrections to your school's records concerning your name, Social Security number, references, and driver's license number (if you have one)

Grace Period

If you are attending school at least half time, you have a set period of time after you graduate, leave school, or drop below half-time status before you must begin repayment on a Stafford or Perkins Loan. This period of time is called a grace period.

- You will receive a grace period before your repayment period begins on a Stafford or Perkins Loan.

- Your grace period will be six or nine months depending on the type of loan.

- PLUS Loans do not have a grace period.

- If you are called to active military duty for more than 30 days, the grace period will be delayed.

It's A Fact!

Parent PLUS Loan borrowers whose loans were first disbursed on or after July 1, 2008, may choose to have repayment deferred while the student for whom the parent borrowed is enrolled at least half time and for an additional six months after that student is no longer enrolled at least half time. Interest that accrues during these periods will be capitalized if not paid by the parent during the deferment.

Source: From "Repayment Information," a publication of the U.S. Department of Education, February 2011.

Loan Repayment Schedule

Your school, lender, or the Direct Loan Servicing Center, as appropriate, must give you a loan repayment schedule that states the following:

- When your first payment is due

- The number and frequency of payments

- The amount of each payment

Sale Of Loan

If you or your parents borrow under the FFEL Program, you (or your parents, or graduate and professional degree students for PLUS Loans) must be notified when the loan is sold if the sale results in making payments to a new lender or agency. Both the old and new lender must provide this notification. You must be given:

It's A Fact!

The repayment period for a Direct PLUS Loan begins at the time the PLUS loan is fully disbursed, and the first payment is due within 60 days after the final disbursement. However, a graduate student PLUS Loan borrower (as well as a parent PLUS borrower who is also a student) can defer repayment while the borrower is enrolled at least half time, and, for PLUS loans first disbursed on or after July 1, 2008, for an additional six months after the borrower is no longer enrolled at least half time. Interest that accrues during these periods will be capitalized if not paid by the borrower during the deferment.

Source: From "Repayment Information," a publication of the U.S. Department of Education, February 2011.

- The identity of the new lender or agency holding the loan

- The address where you or your parents must send payments, and the telephone numbers of both the old and new lender or agency

Repayment Plans

You have a choice of several repayment plans that are designed to meet the different needs of individual borrowers. The amount you pay and the length of time to repay your loans will vary depending on the repayment plan you choose. Generally, you'll have from 10 to 25 years to repay your loan, depending on which repayment plan you choose.

Standard Repayment

With the standard plan, you'll pay a fixed amount each month until your loans are paid in full. Your monthly payments will be at least $50, and you'll have up to 10 years to repay your loans.

Your monthly payment under the standard plan may be higher than it would be under the other plans because your loans will be repaid in the shortest time. For that reason, having a 10-year limit on repayment, you may pay the least interest.

Quick Tip

To calculate your estimated loan payments, go to the Standard Repayment plan calculator at http://www2.ed.gov/offices/OSFAP/DirectLoan/RepayCalc/dlentry1.html.

Source: From "Repayment Plans and Calculators," a publication of the U.S. Department of Education, December 2010.

Extended Repayment

Under the extended plan, you'll pay a fixed annual or graduated repayment amount over a period not to exceed 25 years. If you're a FFEL borrower, you must have more than $30,000 in outstanding FFEL Program loans. If you're a Direct Loan borrower, you must have more than $30,000 in outstanding Direct Loans. This means, for example, that if you have $35,000 in outstanding FFEL Program loans and $10,000 in outstanding Direct Loans, you can choose the extended repayment plan for your FFEL Program loans, but not for your Direct Loans. Your fixed monthly payment is lower than it would be under the Standard Plan, but you'll ultimately pay more for your loan because of the interest that accumulates during the longer repayment period.

This is a good plan if you will need to make smaller monthly payments. Because the repayment period will be 25 years, your monthly payments will be less than with the standard plan. However, you may pay more in interest because you're taking longer to repay the loans. Remember that the longer your loans are in repayment, the more interest you will pay.

Graduated Repayment

With this plan, your payments start out low and increase every two years. The length of your repayment period will be up to 10 years. If you expect your income to increase steadily over time, this plan may be right for you. Your monthly payment will never be less than the amount of interest that accrues between payments. Although your monthly payment will gradually increase, no single payment under this plan will be more than three times greater than any other payment.

Income Based Repayment (IBR) Effective July 1, 2009

Income Based Repayment is a new repayment plan for the major types of federal loans made to students. Under IBR, the required monthly payment is capped at an amount that is intended to be affordable based on income and family size. You are eligible for IBR if the monthly repayment amount under IBR will be less than the monthly amount calculated under a 10-year standard repayment plan. If you repay under the IBR plan for 25 years and meet other requirements you may have any remaining balance of your loan(s) cancelled. Additionally, if you work in public service and have reduced loan payments through IBR, the remaining balance after 10 years in a public service job could be cancelled. For more important information about IBR go to IBR Plan Information at http://studentaid.ed.gov/PORTALSWebApp/students/english/IBRPlan.jsp.

Income Contingent Repayment (ICR) (Direct Loans Only)

This plan gives you the flexibility to meet your Direct Loans[SM] obligations without causing undue financial hardship. Each year, your monthly payments will be calculated on the basis of your adjusted gross income (AGI, plus your spouse's income if you're married), family size, and the total amount of your Direct Loans. Under the ICR plan you will pay each month the lesser of the following options:

1. The amount you would pay if you repaid your loan in 12 years multiplied by an income percentage factor that varies with your annual income

2. Twenty percent of your monthly discretionary income

If your payments are not large enough to cover the interest that has accumulated on your loans, the unpaid amount will be capitalized once each year. However, capitalization will not exceed 10 percent of the original amount you owed when you entered repayment. Interest will continue to accumulate but will no longer be capitalized (added to the loan principal).

The maximum repayment period is 25 years. If you haven't fully repaid your loans after 25 years (time spent in deferment or forbearance does not count) under this plan, the unpaid portion will be discharged. You may, however, have to pay taxes on the amount that is discharged.

It's A Fact!

As of July 1, 2009, graduate and professional student Direct PLUS Loan borrowers are eligible to use the ICR plan. Parent Direct PLUS Loan borrowers are not eligible for the ICR repayment plan.

Source: From "Repayment Plans and Calculators," a publication of the U.S. Department of Education, December 2010.

Income-Sensitive Repayment Plan (FFEL[SM] Loans Only)

With an income-sensitive plan, your monthly loan payment is based on your annual income. As your income increases or decreases, so do your payments. The maximum repayment period is 10 years. Ask your lender for more information on FFEL Income-Sensitive Repayment Plans.

> ## Quick Tip
>
> If you have specific questions about repaying FFEL, Direct, or Perkins Loans, contact your loan servicer. In the case of Perkins Loans, your servicer will be the school that made the loan. If you don't know who your loan servicer is, go to www.nslds.ed.gov to find out.
>
> Source: From "Repayment Information," a publication of the U.S. Department of Education, February 2011.

Additional Information

The publications *Funding Education Beyond High School: The Guide to Federal Student Aid* and *Your Federal Student Loans: Learn the Basics and Manage Your Debt*, available from http://studentaid.ed.gov, provide additional information on repayment options. For additional information on the Income Based Repayment plan, see the IBR Fact Sheet at http://studentaid.ed.gov/students/publications/factsheets/factsheet_IncomeBasedRepayment.pdf.

Loan Interest Rates

The Table 25.1 (on the next page) provides interest rates for Direct and FFEL Program Loans.

Variable Monthly Interest Payments

Interest accrues on a daily basis on your loans. Factors such as the number of days between your last payment, the interest rate, and the amount of your loan balance determine the amount of interest that accrues each month.

> ## Interest Rate Tips
>
> To access information on your federal loans including interest rates, go to www.nslds.ed.gov. For additional details on Direct Loan and FFEL interest rates effective July 1, 2010, go to: http://studentaid.ed.gov/PORTALSWebApp/students/english/FFEL_DL_InterestRates.jsp.
>
> In some cases, you might be able to reduce your interest rate if you sign up for electronic debiting. To learn more, go to: http://studentaid.ed.gov/PORTALSWebApp/students/english/edebit.jsp?tab=repaying.
>
> Source: From "Repayment Information," a publication of the U.S. Department of Education, February 2011.

Table 25.1. Direct And FFEL Loan Interest Rates

	Loan Interest Rates By Disbursement Dates		
Loan Type	First disbursed between July 1, 2010 and June 30, 2011 (Direct Loans only)	First disbursed between July 1, 2006 and June 30, 2010	First disbursed between July 1, 1998 and June 30, 2006
Direct and FFEL Subsidized Loans (undergraduate students)	Fixed at 4.5%	7/1/2006–6/30/2008: Fixed at 6.8%; 7/1/2008–6/30/2009: Fixed at 6.0%; 7/1/2009–6/30/2010: Fixed at 5.6%	The interest rate is variable (adjusted annually on July 1st) and will not exceed 8.25%. Between 7/1/2010 and 6/30/2011, loans in repayment or forbearance have an interest rate of 2.47%, and loans in an in-school, grace, or deferment period have a lower rate of 1.87%.
Direct and FFEL Subsidized Loans (graduate students)/Direct and FFEL Unsubsidized Loans	Fixed at 6.8%	Fixed at 6.8%	The interest rate is variable (adjusted annually on July 1st) and will not exceed 8.25%. Between 7/1/2010 and 6/30/2011, loans in repayment or forbearance have an interest rate of 2.47%, and loans in an in-school, grace, or deferment period have a lower rate of 1.87%.
Direct PLUS Loans (Parent, graduate, and professional students)	Fixed at 7.9%	Fixed at 7.9%	The interest rate is variable (adjusted annually on July 1st) and will not exceed 9.0%. Between 7/1/2010 and 6/30/2011, the interest rate is 3.27%.
FFEL PLUS Loans (parent, graduate, and professional students)	Not Applicable	Fixed at 8.5%	The interest rate is variable (adjusted annually on July 1st) and will not exceed 9.0%. Between 7/1/2010 and 6/30/2011, the interest rate is 3.27%.

Trouble Making Payments

If you're having trouble making payments on your loans, contact your loan servicer as soon as possible. Your servicer will work with you to determine the best option for you. Options include the following:

- Changing repayment plans.

- Requesting a deferment. If you meet certain requirements, a deferment allows you to temporarily stop making payments on your loan.

- Requesting a forbearance. If you don't meet the eligibility requirements for a deferment but are temporarily unable to make your loan payments, then (in limited circumstances) a forbearance allows you to temporarily stop making payments on your loan, temporarily make smaller payments, or extend the time for making payments.

Default

If you default, it means you failed to make payments on your student loan according to the terms of your promissory note, the binding legal document you signed at the time you took out your loan. In other words, you failed to make your loan payments as scheduled. Your school, the financial institution that made or owns your loan, your loan guarantor, and the federal government all can take action to recover the money you owe. Some consequences of default include the following:

- National credit bureaus can be notified of your default, which will harm your credit rating, making it hard to buy a car or a house.

- You will be ineligible for additional federal student aid if you decide to return to school.

- Loan payments can be deducted from your paycheck.

- State and federal income tax refunds can be withheld and applied toward the amount you owe.

- You will have to pay late fees and collection costs on top of what you already owe.

- You can be sued.

For more information and to learn what actions to take if you default on your loans, see the Department of Education's Default Resolution Group website at http://www2.ed.gov/offices/OSFAP/DCS/index.html.

It's A Fact!

If you stop making payments on a federal loan and don't get a deferment or forbearance, your loan could go into default, which has serious consequences.

Source: From "Repayment Information," a publication of the U.S. Department of Education, February 2011.

Loan Cancellation (Discharge)

In certain circumstances, your loan can be cancelled/discharged. See Chapter 27, "Loan Cancellation (Forgiveness) Of Federal Student Loans," for more information.

Cancellation And Deferment Options For Teachers

If you're a teacher serving in a low-income or subject-matter shortage area, it may be possible for you to cancel or defer your student loans. See the Chapters 26 and 27 to see if you qualify.

Loan Forgiveness For Public Service Employees

Under the Public Service Loan Forgiveness Program, if you are employed in a public service job, you may have the balance of your loans forgiven if you make 120 on-time monthly payments under certain repayment plans after October 1, 2007. You must be employed full time in a public service job during the same period in which the qualifying payments are made and at the time that the cancellation is granted. The amount forgiven is the remaining outstanding balance of principal and accrued interest on eligible Direct Loans that are not in default. For additional details, see Chapter 27.

Civil Legal Assistance Attorney Student Loan Repayment Program (CLAARP)

The Civil Legal Assistance Attorney Student Loan Repayment Program was established to encourage qualified individuals to enter and continue employment as civil legal assistance attorneys. See http://studentaid.ed.gov/PORTALSWebApp/students/english/CLAARP.jsp for more information.

Loan Consolidation

A Consolidation Loan allows you to combine your federal student loans into a single loan. See the chapter on federal aid for students for more information.

Chapter 26

Deferring (Postponing) Repayment Of Federal Student Loans

If you have trouble making your education loan payments, immediately contact the organization that services your loan. You might qualify for a deferment, forbearance, or other form of payment relief. It's important to take action before you are charged late fees. For Federal Perkins Loans, contact your loan servicer or the school that made you the loan. For Direct and FFEL[SM] Stafford Loans, contact your loan servicer. If you do not know who your servicer is, you can look it up in the U.S. Department of Education's National Student Loan Data System[SM] (NSLDS[SM]) at http://www.nslds.ed.gov/nslds_SA/.

Deferment

You can receive a deferment for certain defined periods. A deferment is a temporary suspension of loan payments for specific situations such as reenrollment in school, unemployment, or economic hardship. For a list of deferments, see Table 26.1.

You don't have to pay interest on the loan during deferment if you have a subsidized Direct or FFEL Stafford Loan or Federal Perkins Loan. If you have an unsubsidized Direct or FFEL Stafford Loan, you're responsible for the interest during deferment. If you don't pay the interest as it accrues (accumulates), it will be capitalized (added to the loan principal), and the amount you have to pay in the future will be higher. You have to apply for a deferment to your loan servicer (the organization that handles your loan), and you must continue to make payments until you've been notified your deferment has been granted. Otherwise, you could become delinquent or go into default.

About This Chapter: Information in this chapter is from the following documents from the U.S. Department of Education: "Postponing Repayment," December 2010; "Loan Deferment Summary Chart," October 2009; "Stafford Loan Teacher Deferments," March 2006.

Military Service Deferment

An active duty military deferment is available to borrowers in the Direct, FFEL, and Perkins Loan programs who are called to active duty during a war or other military operation or national emergency. This deferment is available while the borrower is serving on active duty during a war or other military operation or national emergency or performing qualifying National Guard duty during a war or other military operation or national emergency. If the borrower was serving on or after Oct. 1, 2007, the deferment is available for an additional 180-day period following the demobilization date for the qualifying service.

Post-Active Duty Student Deferment

A Direct, FFEL, or Perkins Loan borrower who is a member of the National Guard or other reserve component of the U.S. Armed Forces (current or retired) and is called or ordered to active duty while enrolled at least half time at an eligible school (or within six months of having been enrolled at least half time) is eligible for a deferment during the 13 months following the conclusion of the active duty service, or until the borrower returns to enrolled student status on at least a half-time basis, whichever is earlier.

Economic Hardship Deferment

A Direct, FFEL, or Federal Perkins Loan borrower may qualify for an economic hardship deferment for a maximum of three years if the borrower is experiencing economic hardship according to federal regulations. Table 26.1 shows Stafford and Perkins Loan deferments for loans disbursed on or after July 1, 1993. For information on deferments for loans received before that date, Direct Stafford Loan, FFEL, and PLUS Loan borrowers should contact their loan servicer.

Table 26.1. Loan Deferment

Deferment Condition	Stafford Loans		Perkins Loans
	Direct Loans	FFEL Loans	
At least half-time study at a postsecondary school	Yes	Yes	Yes
Study in an approved graduate fellowship program or in an approved rehabilitation training program for the disabled	Yes	Yes	Yes
Unable to find full-time employment	Up to three years	Up to three years	Up to three years
Economic hardship (includes Peace Corps Service)	Up to three years	Up to three years	Up to three years
Engages in service listed under discharge/cancellation conditions	No	No	Yes
Active Military Duty while borrower is on active duty during a war or other military operation or national emergency and if the borrower was serving on or after Oct. 1, 2007, for an additional 180-day period following the demobilization date for the qualifying service	Yes	Yes	Yes

It's A Fact!

The following facts apply to loan deferments:

- For PLUS Loans and unsubsidized Stafford Loans, only principal is deferred. Interest continues to accrue.

- A Direct Loan borrower who had an outstanding balance on a FFEL Loan first disbursed before July 1, 1993, when the borrower received his or her first Direct Loan, is eligible for additional deferments.

- Information in Table 26.1 about FFEL Loans applies to loans first disbursed on or after July 1, 1993, to a borrower who has no outstanding FFEL or Federal Supplemental Loans for Students (Federal SLS) loan on the date he or she signed the promissory note. (Note that the Federal SLS Program was repealed beginning with the 1994–95 award year.) Different deferments are available for borrowers with pre-July 1, 1993, loans.

Source: From "Loan deferment summary chart," a publication of the U.S. Department of Education, October 2009.

Stafford Loan Teacher Deferments

Repayment of loans from the FFEL or Direct Loan programs may be deferred for full-time teaching in a federally designated teacher shortage area for a maximum of three years if you received a FFEL for enrollment in classes that started between July 1, 1987, and June 30, 1993, and you had no outstanding FFEL on the date you signed the promissory note for the loan.

If you qualify for teacher service deferment of a FFEL for enrollment between July 1, 1987, and June 30, 1993, you may also defer any additional FFEL or Direct Loan that you received after June 30, 1993. If your loan is unsubsidized, you must still pay the interest that accumulates on the loan during eligible periods of deferment. You would pay this interest either during the deferment period or as an increase in the amount or number of your monthly payments when you resume making payments. This deferment does not apply, however, to new loans made on or after July 1, 1993.

To obtain a teaching deferment, you must submit a deferment form to your lender for each school year of teaching service. Under the FFEL and Direct Loan programs, a federally approved teacher shortage area can be a state region with a shortage of elementary or secondary school teachers. Or, it can be a grade level, subject matter, or discipline classification in which there is a statewide shortage of elementary or secondary school teachers. In any case, the shortage must be identified by the state education agency and approved by the U.S. Department of Education.

The principal at the school where you are teaching must certify on the deferment form that you are teaching in a federally designated teacher shortage area. If the state education agency has not informed principals that their schools were designated as having a shortage of teachers, you should contact your state education agency to get the form certified. Please remember that you must reapply each school year for a targeted teaching deferment.

If you continue to teach in the same shortage area for which you obtained the original deferment, you may continue to receive the deferment for a maximum of three years, even if your position is no longer considered to be in a teacher shortage area for those subsequent years. To receive the continuing deferment, you must provide the lender with a completed deferment form, certified by the school principal, indicating that you continue to teach full time in the same teacher shortage area for which the deferment was received the previous school year.

For more information about teaching deferments for the FFEL Program, you should consult your promissory note, and contact the lender or guarantor holding your loan, or the state education agency in the state where you are teaching. Direct Loan borrowers should contact the Direct Loan Servicing Center at 1-800-848-0979.

Forbearance

Forbearance is a temporary postponement or reduction of payments for a period of time because you are experiencing financial difficulty. You can receive forbearance if you're not eligible for a deferment. Unlike deferment, whether your loans are subsidized or unsubsidized, interest accrues, and you're responsible for repaying it. Your loan holder can grant forbearance in intervals of up to 12 months at a time for up to three years. You have to apply to your loan servicer for forbearance, and you must continue to make payments until you've been notified your forbearance has been granted.

Other Forms Of Payment Relief

Although you're asked to choose a repayment plan when you first begin repayment, you might want to switch repayment plans later if a different plan would work better for your current financial situation. Under the Federal Family Education Loan Program[SM], you can change repayment plans once a year. Under the Federal Direct Student Loan Program[SM], you can change plans any time as long as the maximum repayment period under your new plan is longer than the time your Direct Loans have already been in repayment. See Chapter 25, "Repaying Federal Student Loans," for more information.

Chapter 27

Loan Cancellation (Forgiveness) Of Federal Student Loans

What is forbearance?

If you are temporarily unable to make your monthly loan payments (for example, due to illness or financial hardship) but you do not meet the eligibility requirements for a deferment, your lender may grant you forbearance for a limited and specific period of time. Forbearance allows you to temporarily postpone or reduce your student loan payments. Interest continues to accrue (accumulate), however, and you are responsible for paying it, no matter what kind of loan you have. In some cases, your loan holder is required to grant forbearance if you meet certain requirements. For example, your loan holder must grant forbearance if any of the following apply:

- You are in a medical or dental internship or residency

- You have student loan payments that are 20 percent or more of your monthly income

- You have payments being made for you by the Department of Defense

You must request forbearance and in some cases must provide documentation showing that you meet the eligibility requirements. Contact your lender or loan servicing agency for more information.

What is the Public Service Loan Forgiveness Program?

Through the College Cost Reduction and Access Act of 2007, Congress created the Public Service Loan Forgiveness Program to encourage individuals to enter and continue to work

---

About This Chapter: Information in this chapter is from the following documents from the U.S. Department of Education: *Funding Education Beyond High School, The Guide to Federal Student Aid*, March 2010 (compiled in 2009); "Loan Forgiveness for Public Service Employees," February 2009; "Stafford Loan Forgiveness Program for Teachers," February 2011.

full time in public service jobs. Under this program, borrowers may qualify for forgiveness of the remaining balance due on their eligible federal student loans after they have made 120 payments on those loans under certain repayment plans while employed full time by certain public service employers. Since borrowers must make 120 monthly payments on their eligible federal student loans after October 1, 2007 before they qualify for the loan forgiveness, the first cancellations of loan balances will not be granted until October 2017.

What federal student loans are eligible for forgiveness under the Public Service Loan Forgiveness Program?

Any nondefaulted loan made under the William D. Ford Federal Direct Loan Program (Direct Loan Program) is eligible for loan forgiveness. The Direct Loan Program includes the following types of loans:

- Federal Direct Stafford/Ford Loans (Direct Subsidized Loans)

- Federal Direct Unsubsidized Stafford/Ford Loans (Direct Unsubsidized Loans)

- Federal Direct PLUS Loans (Direct PLUS Loans)—for parents and graduate or professional students

- Federal Direct Consolidation Loans (Direct Consolidation Loans)

How can other federal student loans qualify for loan forgiveness?

Although loan forgiveness under this program is available only for loans made and repaid under the Direct Loan Program, loans made under other federal student loan programs may qualify for forgiveness if they are consolidated into a Direct Consolidation Loan. However, only payments made on the Direct Consolidation Loan will count toward the required 120 monthly payments.

The following types of loans may be consolidated into the Direct Loan Program:

- Federal Family Education Loan (FFEL) Program loans, which include:

  - Subsidized Stafford Loans

  - Unsubsidized Stafford Loans

  - Federal PLUS Loans—for parents and graduate or professional students

  - Federal Consolidation Loans (excluding joint spousal consolidation loans)

- Federal Perkins Loans

- Certain Health Professions and Nursing Loans

It's A Fact!

To consolidate a Federal Perkins Loan or Health Professions/Nursing Loan into the Direct Loan Program, you must also consolidate at least one FFEL Program loan or Direct Loan. If you are unsure about what kind of loans you have, you can find information about your federal student loans in the U.S. Department of Education's National Student Loan Data System at http://nslds.ed.gov.

Source: From "Loan Forgiveness for Public Service Employees," a publication of the U.S. Department of Education, February 2009.

What are the borrower eligibility requirements for loan forgiveness under the Public Service Loan Forgiveness Program?

- The borrower must not be in default on the loans for which forgiveness is requested.

- The borrower must be employed full time by a public service organization when making the required 120 monthly loan payments (certain repayment conditions apply); at the time the borrower applies for loan forgiveness; and at the time the remaining balance on the borrower's eligible loans is forgiven.

What are the specific loan repayment requirements for loan forgiveness under this program?

- The borrower must have made 120 separate monthly payments after October 1, 2007 on the Direct Loan Program loans for which forgiveness is requested. Earlier payments do not count toward meeting this requirement. Each of the 120 monthly payments must be made for the full scheduled installment amount within 15 days of the due date.

- The 120 required payments must be made under one or more of the following Direct Loan Program repayment plans:

  - Income Based Repayment (IBR) Plan (not available to parent Direct PLUS Loan borrowers)

  - Income Contingent Repayment Plan (not available to parent Direct PLUS Loan borrowers)

  - Standard Repayment Plan with a 10-year repayment period

- Any other Direct Loan Program repayment plan, but only payments that are at least equal to the monthly payment amount that would have been required under the Standard Repayment Plan with a 10-year repayment period may be counted toward the required 120 payments.

For more information about the repayment plans available in the Direct Loan program, please visit: www.ed.gov/DirectLoan.

What types of public service jobs will qualify a borrower for loan forgiveness under this program?

The borrower must be employed full time (in any position) by a public service organization, or must be serving in a full-time AmeriCorps or Peace Corps position. For purposes of the Public Service Loan Forgiveness Program, the term "public service organization" means the following:

- A federal, state, local, or tribal government organization, agency, or entity (includes most public schools, colleges, and universities)

- A public child or family service agency

- A nonprofit organization under section 501(c)(3) of the Internal Revenue Code that is exempt from taxation under section 501(a) of the Internal Revenue Code (includes most not-for-profit private schools, colleges, and universities)

- A tribal college or university

- A private organization that is not a for-profit business, a labor union, a partisan political organization, or an organization engaged in religious activities (unless the qualifying activities are unrelated to religious instruction, worship services, or any form of proselytizing) and that provides the following public services:

It's A Fact!

The Public Service Loan Forgiveness Program provides for forgiveness of the remaining balance of a borrower's eligible loans after the borrower has made 120 payments on those loans. In general, only borrowers who are making reduced monthly payments through the Direct Loan Income Contingent or Income Based repayment plans will have a remaining balance after making 120 payments on a loan.

Source: From "Loan Forgiveness for Public Service Employees," a publication of the U.S. Department of Education, February 2009.

- Emergency management
- Military service
- Public safety
- Law enforcement
- Public interest law services
- Early childhood education (including licensed or regulated health care, Head Start, and state-funded prekindergarten)
- Public service for individuals with disabilities and the elderly
- Public health (including nurses, nurse practitioners, nurses in a clinical setting, and full-time professionals engaged in health care practitioner occupations and health care support occupations)
- Public education
- Public library services
- School library or other school-based services

Where can I find additional information?

For more detailed information about the Public Service Loan Forgiveness Program, refer to the final regulations for this program (34 C.F.R. 685.219) that the U.S. Department of Education issued on October 23, 2008. You may view the final regulations at http://www.ed.gov/legislation/FedRegister/finrule/2008-4/102308a.html.

What is the Stafford Loan Forgiveness Program for Teachers?

The Teacher Loan Forgiveness Program is intended to encourage individuals to enter and continue in the teaching profession. Under this program, individuals who teach full time for five consecutive, complete academic years in certain elementary and secondary schools that serve low-income families and meet other qualifications may be eligible for forgiveness of up to a combined total of $17,500 in principal and interest on their FFEL and/or Direct Loan program loans.

What are the eligibility requirements for the Loan Forgiveness Program for Teachers?

- You must not have had an outstanding balance on a FFEL or Direct Loan program loan as of October 1, 1998, or on the date that you obtained a Direct Loan Program loan or a FFEL Program loan after October 1, 1998.

> ## It's A Fact!
>
> As of August 14, 2008, an otherwise eligible borrower may qualify for forgiveness if the borrower has provided qualifying teaching services at one or more locations that are operated by an educational service agency.
>
> All elementary and secondary schools operated by the Bureau of Indian Education (BIE) or operated on Indian reservations by Indian tribal groups under contract with the BIE qualify as schools serving low-income students. These schools are qualifying schools for purposes of the Stafford loan forgiveness program.
>
> Source: From "Stafford Loan Forgiveness Program for Teachers," a publication of the U.S. Department of Education, February 2011.

- If you are in default on a FFEL and/or Direct Loan program loan(s), you are not eligible for forgiveness of that loan(s) unless you have made satisfactory repayment arrangements with the holder of the defaulted loan(s).

- The loan(s) for which you are seeking forgiveness was made prior to the end of your five academic years of qualifying teaching service.

- You have not received benefits through the AmeriCorps Program under Subtitle D of Title I of the National and Community Service Act of 1990 for the same teaching service for which you are seeking forgiveness on your FFEL and/or Direct Loan program loan(s).

- You must have been employed as a full-time teacher for five consecutive, complete academic years, at least one of which was after the 1997–1998 academic year, in an elementary or secondary school that meets the following requirements:

  - Is in a school district that qualifies for funds under Title I of the Elementary and Secondary Education Act of 1965, as amended

  - Has been selected by the U.S. Department of Education based on a determination that more than 30 percent of the school's total enrollment is made up of children who qualify for services provided under Title I

  - Is listed in the Annual Directory of Designated Low-Income Schools for Teacher Cancellation Benefits. If this directory is not available before May 1 of any year, the previous year's directory may be used.

If your five consecutive, complete years of qualifying teaching service began before October 30, 2004:

- You may receive up to $5,000 in loan forgiveness if, as certified by the Chief Administrative Officer of the school where you were employed, you were: a full-time elementary school teacher who demonstrated knowledge and teaching skills in reading, writing, mathematics, and other areas of the elementary school curriculum; or a full-time secondary school teacher who taught in a subject area that was relevant to your academic major.

- You may receive up to $17,500 in loan forgiveness if, as certified by the Chief Administrative Officer of the school where you were employed, you were: a highly qualified full-time mathematics or science teacher in an eligible secondary school; or a highly qualified special education teacher whose primary responsibility was to provide special education to children with disabilities, and you taught children with disabilities that corresponded to your area of special education training and have demonstrated knowledge and teaching skills in the content areas of the curriculum that you taught.

If your five consecutive, complete years of qualifying teaching service began on or after October 30, 2004:

- You may receive up to $5,000 in loan forgiveness if you were a highly qualified full-time elementary or secondary school teacher.

- You may receive up to $17,500 in loan forgiveness if, as certified by the Chief Administrative Officer of the school where you were employed, you were: a highly qualified full-time mathematics or science teacher in an eligible secondary school; or a highly qualified special education teacher whose primary responsibility was to provide special education to children with disabilities, and you taught children with disabilities that corresponded to your area of special education training and have demonstrated knowledge and teaching skills in the content areas of the curriculum that you taught.

If you were unable to complete an academic year of teaching, that year may still be counted toward the required five consecutive, complete academic years under the following conditions:

- You completed at least one-half of the academic year; and

- Your employer considers you to have fulfilled your contract requirements for the academic year for the purposes of salary increases, tenure, and retirement; and

It's A Fact!

If your school meets the eligibility requirements for at least one year of your teaching service, but does not meet these requirements during subsequent years, your subsequent years of teaching at the school may be counted toward the required five consecutive, complete academic years of teaching.

Source: From "Stafford Loan Forgiveness Program for Teachers," a publication of the U.S. Department of Education, February 2011.

- You were unable to complete the academic year for the following reasons:

  1. You returned to postsecondary education, on at least a half-time basis, in an area of study directly related to the performance of the teaching service described above

  2. You had a condition covered under the Family and Medical Leave Act of 1993 (FMLA)

  3. You were called or ordered to active duty status for more than 30 days as a member of a reserve component of the Armed Forces

---

It's A Fact!

Absence due to a period of postsecondary education, a condition covered under the FMLA, or active duty service, including the time needed for you to resume teaching no later than the beginning of the next regularly scheduled academic year, does not constitute a break in the required five consecutive, complete years of qualifying teaching service for the Stafford Loan Forgiveness Program for Teachers.

Source: From "Stafford Loan Forgiveness Program for Teachers," a publication of the U.S. Department of Education, February 2011.

How do I find a low-income school?

Each year, the U.S. Department of Education publishes a list of low-income elementary and secondary schools. To find out if a school is classified as a low-income school, check our online database at https://www.tcli.ed.gov/CBSWebApp/tcli/TCLIPubSchoolSearch.jsp for the year(s) you have been employed as a teacher. Questions about the inclusion or omission of a particular school must be directed to the state education agency contact in the state where the school is located and not to the U.S. Department of Education.

How do I apply for a teacher loan cancellation?

You apply for teacher loan cancellation after you have completed the five-year teaching requirement. You can find a copy of the Teacher Loan Forgiveness Application at http://ifap.ed.gov/dpcletters/attachments/GEN0811AttTLFAform.pdf. The Chief Administrative Officer of the school at which you performed your qualifying teaching service must complete the certification section. If you taught at more than one school during the same academic year, the Chief Administrative Officer from one of the schools may complete the certification section. If you taught at different schools during different academic years, the Chief Administrative Officers from all of the schools must certify your eligibility. If you need more than one Chief

Administrative Officer's certification, the additional certifications may be provided on a separate piece of paper and submitted with your completed form. Return the completed form to the address shown in Section 9 of the application. If you are applying for forgiveness of loans that are held by different loan holders, you must submit a separate form to each loan holder.

Can I postpone repayment while under consideration for cancellation?

You can get forbearance for up to 60 days while you're completing the loan discharge application which includes the time it takes for the lender and guarantor to review it.

The loan holder or guaranty agency must notify you within 135 days of their decision on your application. If your application is approved, new repayment terms based on any remaining loan balances will be provided to you. The lender may cancel up to $17,500 of the aggregate loan amount that is outstanding after you've finished your fifth year of teaching. (The aggregate loan amount includes both principal and interest.) However, the lender cannot refund the payments you made before you completed the fifth year of teaching service.

Your lender can grant forbearance for each year of your qualifying teaching service if the expected cancellation amount will satisfy the anticipated remaining outstanding balance on the loan at the time of the expected cancellation. Unless you give your lender or loan servicing agency other

What's It Mean?

Academic Year: One complete school year at the same school, or two complete and consecutive half years at different schools, or two complete and consecutive half years from different school years (at either the same school or different schools). Half years exclude summer sessions and generally fall within a 12-month period. For schools that have a year-round program of instruction, nine months is considered an academic year.

Elementary School/Secondary School: A public or nonprofit private school that provides elementary education or secondary education as determined by state law (or by the U.S. Department of Education if the school is not in a state).

Full-Time Employment As A Teacher: Determined by the state's standard. For a borrower teaching in more than one school, the determination of full time is based on the combination of all qualifying employment.

Teacher: A person who provides direct classroom teaching or classroom-type teaching in a nonclassroom setting, including Special Education teachers.

Source: From "Stafford Loan Forgiveness Program for Teachers," a publication of the U.S. Department of Education, February 2011.

instructions, your unsubsidized Stafford Loan balance will be cancelled first, followed by any outstanding subsidized Stafford Loan balance, and then any eligible outstanding Consolidation Loan balance. The lender may cancel only the outstanding portion of the Consolidation Loan that was used to repay subsidized or unsubsidized Stafford Loans that qualified for loan forgiveness.

To be a highly qualified teacher a public elementary or secondary school teacher must meet the following criteria:

- Have obtained full state certification as a teacher (including certification obtained through alternative routes to certification) or passed the state teacher licensing examination, and holds a license to teach in that state, except that when used with respect to any teacher teaching in a public charter school, the term means that the teacher meets the requirements set forth in the state's public charter school law

- Have not had certification or licensure requirements waived on an emergency, temporary, or provisional basis

An elementary school teacher who is new to the profession is considered highly qualified if s/he also meets the following criteria:

- Holds at least a bachelor's degree

- Has demonstrated, by passing a rigorous state test, subject knowledge and teaching skills in reading, writing, mathematics, and other areas of the basic elementary school curriculum (which may consist of passing a state-required certification or licensing test or tests in reading, writing, mathematics, and other areas of the basic elementary school curriculum)

A middle or secondary school teacher who is new to the profession is highly qualified if the teacher also meets the following criteria:

- Holds at least a bachelor's degree

- Has demonstrated a high level of competency in each of the academic subjects in which the teacher teaches by: passing a rigorous state academic subject test in each of the academic subjects in which the teacher teaches (which may consist of a passing level of performance on a state-required certification or licensing test or tests in each of the academic subjects in which the teacher teaches); or by successful completion, in each of the academic subjects in which the teacher teaches, of an academic major, a graduate degree, coursework equivalent to an undergraduate academic major, or advanced certification or credentialing.

An elementary, middle, or secondary school teacher who is not new to the profession is highly qualified if the teacher also meets the following criteria:

- Holds at least a bachelor's degree

- Meets the applicable standards of an elementary, middle, or secondary school teacher who is new to the profession; or demonstrates competence in all the academic subjects in which the teacher teaches based on a high objective uniform state standard of evaluation that meets the following criteria:

  - Is set by the state for both grade appropriate academic subject matter knowledge and teaching skills

  - Is aligned with challenging state academic content and student academic achievement standards and developed in consultation with core content specialists, teachers, principals, and school administrators

  - Provides objective, coherent information about the teacher's attainment of core content knowledge in the academic subjects in which a teacher teaches

  - Is applied uniformly to all teachers in the same academic subject and the same grade level throughout the state

  - Takes into consideration, but is not based primarily on, the time the teacher has been teaching in the academic subject

  - Is made available to the public upon request; and may involve multiple, objective measures of teacher competency

Where can I find a summary of this information?

You can download and print out information in a convenient trifold Stafford Loan Forgiveness Program for Teachers Portable Document Format (PDF), at http://studentaid.ed.gov/students/attachments/siteresources/35718_GPO_Stafford_12_2010_SCREEN.pdf. The color PDF version works best if printed as a two-sided sheet and then folded into a brochure. This brochure can be duplicated but not sold.

What if I have had student loans forgiven for community service?

Any student loan amounts forgiven by nonprofit, tax-exempt charitable or educational institutions are excluded from income for borrowers who take community service jobs that address unmet community needs. For example, a recent graduate who takes a low-paying job in a rural school will not owe any additional income tax if, in recognition of this service, his or her college or another charity forgives a loan it made to him or her to help pay college costs. This provision applies to loans forgiven after August 5, 1997.

Chapter 28

Federal Work Study And Education For Unemployed Workers Programs

The Federal Work-Study (FWS) Program

Under the FWS Program, you can work part time to earn money for your education. The FWS Program has the following characteristics:

- Provides part-time employment while you are enrolled in school

- Helps pay your educational expenses

- Is available to undergraduate and graduate students

- Is available to full-time or part-time students

- Is administered by schools participating in the FWS Program

- Encourages community service work and work related to your course of study, whenever possible

Available Jobs

The FWS Program provides jobs for students demonstrating financial need. The program encourages community service work and work related to the student's course of study.

About This Chapter: Information in this chapter is from the following publications: "Work-Study," a publication of the U.S. Department of Education, 2009–2010; "New Educational Opportunities for Unemployed Workers," a publication of the U.S. Department of Education and the U.S. Department of Labor, 2009; and "Questions and Answers for Unemployed Americans Interested in Education and Training Opportunities," a publication of the U.S. Department of Education and the U.S. Department of Labor, 2009.

Job Location

FWS jobs are available both on campus and off campus. If you work on campus, you'll usually work for your school. If you work off campus, your employer will usually be a private non-profit organization or a public agency, and the work performed must be in the public interest.

Some schools might have agreements with private for-profit employers for FWS jobs. These jobs must be relevant to your course of study (to the maximum extent possible). If you attend a proprietary school (i.e., a for-profit institution), there may be further restrictions on the types of jobs you can be assigned.

Earnings

You'll earn at least the current federal minimum wage. However, the amount might be higher depending on the type of work you do and the skills required for the position.

Your total FWS award depends on the following:

- When you apply

- Your level of financial need

- Your school's funding level

> ### It's A Fact!
>
> The U.S. Department of Education's office of Federal Student Aid provides a certain amount of work-study funds to participating schools; when all funds have been awarded, no additional work-study awards can be made for that year.
>
> Source: From "Work-Study," a publication of the U.S. Department of Education, 2009–2010.

Payment

Undergraduate Student: If you are an undergraduate student, you will be paid by the hour.

Graduate Student: If you are a graduate student, you will be paid by the hour or by salary, depending on the work you do.

Your school must pay you at least once a month. In addition, your school must pay you directly unless you request that the school do one of the following:

- Send your payments directly to your bank account

- Use the money to pay for your education-related institutional charges such as tuition, fees, and room and board

Hours

You cannot work any number of hours you want. The amount you earn can't exceed your total FWS award. When assigning work hours, your employer or financial aid administrator will consider your class schedule and your academic progress.

New Educational Opportunities For Unemployed Workers

Americans with more education and training have more secure jobs and higher earnings. With jobs hard to find, it may be a good time to consider going back to school.

The President recently announced that unemployed workers receiving unemployment benefits may qualify for a special hand in paying for education and training. And aid can be significant: In particular, the Federal Pell Grant program can provide up to $5,350 for educational costs at community colleges, colleges and universities, and many trade and technical schools. This is only one example of several federal student aid programs available to assist unemployed workers.

Information For Unemployed Americans Interested In Education And Training Opportunities

Federal Financial Aid And Training

The federal government has a variety of grants, loans, and work-study programs to help you pay for continuing education and training.

The President announced in May of 2009 that he encourages unemployed Americans to consider education and training opportunities during this period of economic hardship. In particular, the President highlighted the availability of federal student aid, including the Federal Pell Grant. If you are currently unemployed, you may be eligible for federal financial aid, including a Federal Pell Grant.

Unemployment And Eligibility

If you are currently unemployed, you may be eligible for federal financial aid. Eligibility for federal grant aid, such as Pell Grants, is need-based and depends on the total income of your family. Federal student loans are available regardless of your income level. Financial aid administrators at participating institutions have been urged to take an unemployed person's current economic circumstance into account when determining a student's eligibility for Pell Grants and other student assistance.

It's A Fact!
Applying for financial aid and finding education and training are not difficult.

Source: From "New Educational Opportunities for Unemployed Workers," a publication of the U.S. Department of Education and the U.S. Department of Labor, 2009.

A student must also meet certain other eligibility requirements, such as: not being in default on a federal student loan; having a high school diploma, General Education Development (GED) equivalency, or a demonstrated ability to benefit from the education or training offered; and being a U.S. citizen or eligible noncitizen.

State Workforce Agency Letters

If, while receiving unemployment benefits, you have received a letter from your state workforce agency encouraging you to consider seeking additional education and training, the letter does not guarantee you federal financial aid. However, you should bring that letter (or, if you no longer have the letter, other evidence you are currently receiving unemployment benefits) to a financial aid office at the school you are considering. The U.S. Department of Education is working with community colleges, colleges, and universities to help them meet your financial needs.

Unemployment Benefits And Services

If you are currently unemployed and in need of benefits and/or reemployment services, check with your state workforce agency for available benefits and services. Assistance is available to locate state workforce agencies and your local One-Stop Career Center by visiting www.careerinfonet. org or calling the U.S. Department of Labor toll-free number: 1-877-US-2-JOBS.

Other Financial Aid

In addition to the federal financial aid offered by the U.S. Department of Education, there may be opportunities from your state or the school that you are interested in may offer scholarships or other institutional aid. For example, some institutions have established special financial aid programs to address the needs of those who have recently lost a job or otherwise have become unemployed. Your local One-Stop Career Center will also have information on training funds available from the U.S. Department of Labor. Visit www.careeronestop.org/findos to locate a One-Stop Career Center near you.

Covered Expenses And Pell Grants

Federal Pell Grants are available if you are taking classes as part of a program that leads to an undergraduate degree or certificate. Federal student aid, including Pell Grants, can be used to cover a variety of costs, generally including the following:

- Tuition and fees normally assessed

- Books, supplies, transportation, and miscellaneous personal expenses

- Living expenses such as room and board

- An allowance for costs expected to be incurred for dependent care for a student with dependents

Pell Grant Amounts

The Federal Pell Grant Program is a need-based program and the amount a student is eligible for is determined when you complete a Free Application for Federal Student Aid (FAFSA). You may complete a FAFSA at http://www.fafsa.ed.gov/. For more information about the FAFSA, see Chapter 21, "Applying For Federal Student Aid."

More Information

Funding Education Beyond High School: The Guide to Federal Student Aid is a free publication that the U.S. Department of Education offers to explain the federal financial aid process. It is available at http://studentaid.ed.gov/students/publications/student_guide/index.html.

If you have additional questions, call 1-800-4-FED-AID or go to www.federalstudentaid .ed.gov.

It's A Fact!

You can get more information on federal financial aid at www.federalstudentaid.ed.gov.

Source: From "Questions and Answers for Unemployed Americans Interested in Education and Training Opportunities," a publication of the U.S. Department of Education and the U.S. Department of Labor, 2009.

Chapter 29

Education Tax Credits

American Opportunity Credit

Under the American Recovery and Reinvestment Act (ARRA), more parents and students will qualify over the next two years for a tax credit, the American Opportunity Credit, to pay for college expenses.

The new credit modifies the existing Hope Credit for tax years 2009 and 2010, making the Hope Credit available to a broader range of taxpayers, including many with higher incomes and those who owe no tax. It also adds required course materials to the list of qualifying expenses and allows the credit to be claimed for four postsecondary education years instead of two. Many of those eligible will qualify for the maximum annual credit of $2,500 per student.

The full credit is available to individuals whose modified adjusted gross income is $80,000 or less, or $160,000 or less for married couples filing a joint return. The credit is phased out for taxpayers with incomes above these levels. These income limits are higher than under the existing Hope and Lifetime Learning Credits.

Qualifying Expenses

The term qualified tuition and related expenses has been expanded to include expenditures for course materials. For this purpose, the term course materials means books, supplies, and equipment needed for a course of study whether or not the materials are purchased from the educational institution as a condition of enrollment or attendance.

About This Chapter: Information in this chapter is from the following publications of the U.S. Department of the Treasury: "American Opportunity Credit," 2010; "American Opportunity Credit: Questions and Answers," 2010; "Lifetime Learning Credit," 2009.

Whether an expenditure for a computer qualifies for the American Opportunity credit depends on the facts. An expenditure for a computer would qualify for the credit if the computer is needed as a condition of enrollment or attendance at the educational institution.

Calculating The American Opportunity Tax Credit

Taxpayers will receive a tax credit based on 100% of the first $2,000 of tuition, fees, and course materials paid during the taxable year, plus 25% of the next $2,000 of tuition, fees, and course materials paid during the taxable year.

The American Opportunity Tax Credit And Your Tax Return

You will be able to reduce your tax liability one dollar for each dollar of credit for which you're eligible. If the amount of the American Opportunity tax credit for which you're eligible is more than your tax liability, the amount of the credit that is more than your tax liability is refundable to you, up to a maximum refund of 40% of the amount of the credit for which you're eligible.

Eligibility

A taxpayer who pays qualified tuition and related expenses and whose federal income tax return has a modified adjusted gross income of $80,000 or less ($160,000 or less for joint filers) is eligible for the credit. The credit is reduced ratably if a taxpayer's modified adjusted gross income exceeds those amounts. A taxpayer whose modified adjusted gross income is greater than $90,000 ($180,000 for joint filers) cannot benefit from this credit.

Modified Adjusted Gross Income

The modified adjusted gross income, for the purposes of the American Opportunity tax credit, is the taxpayer's adjusted gross income increased by foreign income that was excluded, and by income excluded from sources in Puerto Rico or certain U.S. possessions.

Eligible Years

The American Opportunity tax credit is for amounts paid in 2009 and 2010 only. You may be eligible for the lifetime learning credit for any tuition and fees required for enrollment you pay after 2010.

The Tuition And Fees Tax Deduction

You cannot claim the tuition and fees tax deduction in the same year that you claim the American Opportunity tax credit or the Lifetime Learning credit. You must choose among them. You also cannot claim the tuition and fees tax deduction if anyone else claims the American Opportunity tax credit or the Lifetime Learning credit for you in the same year. A tax deduction of up to $4,000 can be claimed for qualified tuition and fees paid. Though the credit will usually result in greater tax savings, taxpayers should calculate the effect of both on the tax return to see which is most beneficial—the tax credit or the deduction. Often tax software will automatically compare the two for you.

New Benefit For 529 Plans

A qualified, nontaxable distribution from a Section 529 plan during 2009 or 2010 now includes the cost of the purchase of any computer technology or equipment or internet access and related services, if such technology, equipment, or services are to be used by the beneficiary of the plan and the beneficiary's family during any of the years the beneficiary is enrolled at an eligible educational institution.

Lifetime Learning Credit

The Lifetime Learning Credit may be claimed for the qualified tuition and related expenses of the students in the taxpayer's family (i.e., the taxpayer, the taxpayer's spouse, or an eligible dependent) who are enrolled in eligible educational institutions. A taxpayer cannot claim both a Lifetime Learning Credit and a Hope Credit (American Opportunity Credit) for the same student in the same year.

It's A Fact!

To claim the American Opportunity tax credit, use Form 8863, attached to Form 1040 or 1040A.

Source: From "American Opportunity Credit: Questions and Answers," a publication of the U.S. Department of the Treasury, 2010.

Eligibility

An individual paying qualified tuition and related expenses at a postsecondary educational institution may claim the credit, provided the institution is an eligible educational institution. Unlike the Hope Scholarship Credit, students are not required to be enrolled at least half time in one of the first two years of postsecondary education.

Nonresident aliens generally are not eligible to claim the Lifetime Learning Credit.

Dependents

An individual may claim the Lifetime Learning credit for his/her own qualified tuition and related expenses and the qualified tuition and related expenses of his/her spouse and other eligible dependents (including children) for whom the dependency exemption is allowed. Generally, a parent may claim the dependency exemption for his/her unmarried child if: (1) the parent supplies more than half the child's support for the taxable year, and (2) the child is under age 19 or is a full-time student under age 24.

An individual may claim a Lifetime Learning Credit for more than one family member. However, unlike the Hope Scholarship Credit (American Opportunity credit), the Lifetime Learning Credit is calculated on a per family, rather than a per student, basis. Therefore, the maximum available credit does not vary with the number of students in the family. For example, if a married individual whose modified adjusted gross income is $35,000 pays $5,000 of qualified tuition and related expenses to attend an eligible educational institution, the individual may claim a $1,000 Lifetime Learning Credit. If in the same year the individual also pays another $2,000 in qualified tuition and related expenses for his spouse to attend an eligible educational institution, the individual's Lifetime Learning Credit is still $1,000.

Course Load

The Lifetime Learning credit is available for a student taking only one course. For example, a student who has just graduated from high school and is taking a single course at a community college may claim the Lifetime Learning Credit if the student comes within the income limits and is not claimed as a dependent by someone else.

It's A Fact!

Qualified tuition and related expenses for graduate-level education are eligible for the Lifetime Learning Credit.

Source: From "Lifetime Learning Credit," a publication of the U.S. Department of the Treasury, 2009.

Claiming The Lifetime Learning Credit

Either the parent or the child, but not both, may claim the credit for the child's expenses in a particular year. If an individual claims the child as a dependent on his/her Federal income tax return for the year, only the individual may claim the Lifetime Learning Credit for the child's qualified tuition and related expenses. If no one claims the child as a dependent on a Federal income tax return for the year, only the child may claim the Lifetime Learning Credit for the child's expenses.

The parent may claim the credit on his/her federal income tax return even if the child files his/her own tax return. When a child is claimed as a dependent on the parent's return, any qualified tuition and related expenses paid by the child during the year are treated as if the parent had paid them and, therefore, are included in calculating the parent's Lifetime Learning Credit. A child may not claim a Lifetime Learning Credit on his/her tax return for any year if the child's parent claims the child as a dependent in that same year.

A married taxpayer who does not file a joint return is not eligible to claim the Lifetime Learning Credit.

Maximum Amount

The Lifetime Learning Credit is equal to 20% of the taxpayer's out-of-pocket expenses for qualified tuition and related expenses of all eligible family members, up to a maximum of $5,000 in expenses annually through 2002. Thus, the maximum Lifetime Learning Credit a taxpayer may claim through 2002 is $1,000. After 2002, the credit is equal to 20% of the taxpayer's out-of-pocket expenses up to a maximum of $10,000 in expenses. Thus, the maximum Lifetime Learning Credit a taxpayer may claim after 2002 is $2,000. The maximum credit does not change even if the taxpayer is claiming a credit for the expenses of more than one student in the family.

> ### It's A Fact!
> The term *qualified tuition and related expenses* for purposes of the Lifetime Learning Credit has the same meaning as it does for purposes of the Hope Scholarship Credit (American Opportunity credit).
>
> Source: "Lifetime Learning Credit," a publication of the U.S. Department of the Treasury, 2009.

Calculating The Lifetime Learning Credit

If a student (who is not claimed as a dependent on anyone's Federal income tax return) pays qualified tuition and related expenses using a combination of a Pell Grant, a loan, a gift from a family member, and some personal savings, the student may take into account only out-of-pocket expenses in calculating the Lifetime Learning Credit. Qualified tuition and related expenses paid with the student's earnings, a loan, a gift, an inheritance, or personal savings (including savings from a qualified state tuition program) are taken into account in calculating the credit amount. However, qualified tuition and related expenses paid with a Pell Grant or other tax-free scholarship, a tax-free distribution from an Education IRA, or tax-free employer-provided educational assistance are not taken into account in calculating the credit amount.

Eligible Years

Unlike the Hope Scholarship (American Opportunity) Credit, there is no limit to the number of years in which a Lifetime Learning Credit may be claimed for each student. Thus, for example, an individual who enrolls in one college-level class every year would be able to claim the Lifetime Learning Credit for an unlimited number of years, provided the individual meets the income limits and is taking the classes at institutions that meet the eligibility requirements.

Advance Tuition

Generally, the Lifetime Learning credit is available only for payments of qualified tuition and related expenses that cover an academic period beginning in the same calendar year as the year in which payment is made. (An academic period begins on the first day of classes, and does not include periods of orientation, counseling, or vacation.) An exception, however, allows a parent or student to claim a Lifetime Learning Credit for payments of qualified tuition and related expenses made during the calendar year to cover an academic period that begins in January, February, or March of the following taxable year. Because the Lifetime Learning Credit does not apply to expenses paid before July 1, 1998, this exception does not apply to tuition paid before that date to cover academic periods beginning before or after that date.

Part Five
Other Sources Of Financial Aid

Chapter 30

Finding A Scholarship

Where The College Scholarships Are

Develop Your Scholarship Strategy

Most student aid comes in the form of federal education loans and grants from colleges. However, scholarships—which don't have to be paid back—get a huge amount of attention from students and their families. If you decide to invest your time in a search for scholarships, it's important to have an organized system to find, apply for, and win scholarship money. It's also best to start early.

Start With A Personal Inventory

Most of the information you are asked for on a scholarship search questionnaire is easy to come up with—year in school, citizenship, state of residence, religion, ethnic background, disability, military status, employer, and membership organizations.

Beyond those questions, you have to give some thought to your academic, extracurricular, and career plans. You should ask yourself:

- Do I want to participate in a competition? If so, what are my talents and interests?

- What subject do I plan to major in?

- What career do I plan to pursue?

About This Chapter: Information in this chapter is from "Where The Scholarships Are," http://www.collegeboard .com/student/pay/scholarships-and-aid/8936.html. Copyright © 2011 The College Board. Reproduced with permission. The chapter also includes "How to Apply for a Scholarship" http://www.collegeboard.com/student/ pay/scholarships-and-aid/8937.html. Copyright © 2011 The College Board. Reproduced with permission.

- Do I want to apply for all types of aid or only scholarships?

Your answers to these questions help determine your scholarship eligibility. Take your time brainstorming and don't overlook anything—the more personal characteristics you discover, the more scholarships you could potentially apply for.

Research Local Scholarships First

Begin with your high school counseling office. Your counselors know about scholarships for students graduating from your high school. They may also be aware of scholarships for residents of your town, county, and state.

Your next stop should be the college aid section of your public library. Most libraries have a number of books about financial aid, including scholarship guides such as the College Board's *Scholarship Handbook*. They also may have information on local scholarships.

Then it's time to start looking at national scholarships such as those sponsored by the National Merit Scholarship Corporation, Gates Millennium Scholars, Intel Science Talent Search, the Coca-Cola Scholars Foundation, and the Robert C. Byrd Honors Scholarship Program. You can also learn more about the scholarship competitions the College Board co-sponsors in science, math, and technology. Use your library, or check online.

Check Membership Organizations And Employers

Organizations of all types and sizes sponsor scholarships—leave no stone unturned. Explore categories you might not have considered, such as religious, community service, fraternal, military, union, and professional.

And don't forget your parents. Many large companies offer scholarships or tuition programs for children of employees. If you are uncertain, ask your parents to check with their human resources departments.

It's A Fact!
You should never have to pay for scholarship information.

Source: From "Where The Scholarships Are," http://www.collegeboard.com/student/pay/scholarships-and-aid/8936.html. Copyright © 2011 The College Board. Reproduced with permission.

Use A Free Scholarship Search Service

A scholarship search company collects information on hundreds of awards and compares your student characteristics with scholarship restrictions. Based on your answers to a questionnaire, you receive a list of possible scholarships. It is up to you to decide which ones to try for.

You should never have to pay for scholarship information. If you're asked to pay a fee for exclusive scholarship leads, there's a good chance your scholarship service is really a scholarship scam.

Here are some free scholarship search services:

- Scholarship Search
- Fastweb
- Sallie Mae

Contact Your State Department Of Higher Education

Almost every state has a scholarship program for residents—the awards are usually limited to students who attend college in state. For example, the State of Florida offers Bright Futures Scholarships to qualified Floridians who decide to attend in-state colleges and universities. One of New York State's programs, the Tuition Assistance Program, offers grants to qualified New Yorkers who attend in-state colleges and universities.

Research Institutional Scholarships

Since the vast majority of all scholarship money is disbursed by colleges, it makes sense to research what kinds of scholarships are available at the colleges that interest you. Check out college websites, catalogs, and financial aid offices for this information. Institutional awards can be offered on a university-wide basis, or within a particular college or major. Eligibility for such awards can be based on merit, financial need, intended major, ethnicity, or a variety of other factors. Here are some questions you might want to ask about these awards:

- Are scholarships awarded automatically if a student matches certain criteria, such as grade point average (GPA) or Scholastic Aptitude Test (SAT®) score?

- What is the application procedure? What materials are required?

- Is the award renewable? What are the requirements to maintain the award?

Scholarship Application Tips

Once you've created a list of scholarships that interest you, read about how to apply for a scholarship for advice on creating a winning application.

How To Apply For A Scholarship

To Get Money, You Have To Ask For It

The scholarship application process is very similar to the college application process. First, you filter a large list of possible choices into a focused list that matches your needs. Then you create compelling applications that are supported by your achievements, essays, recommendations, and interviews. Here are some tips to help you create strong scholarship applications.

Scholarship Application Tips

There's a lot of advice out there about the best way to apply for scholarships—how to package yourself in your essay, what extracurricular activities to emphasize. The truth is, much of this advice can vary widely, depending on the author—what works for one applicant may not necessarily work for another. You'll discover that most of the scholarship secrets you read about boil down to using your common sense and following directions carefully.

Start Your Research Early: The more time you can put into your scholarship search, the more options you have. You need time to research scholarships, request information and application materials, and complete your application—and remember, some scholarships have deadlines early in the fall of senior year. Use the College Board's Scholarship Search at http://apps.collegeboard.com/cbsearch_ss/welcome.jsp to get started.

Read Eligibility Requirements Carefully: The more time you can put into your scholarship search, the more options you'll have. If you have a question about your eligibility for a particular scholarship, contact the scholarship sponsors.

Organize All Scholarship Materials: Create a separate file for each scholarship and file by application date. Keep a calendar of application deadlines and follow-up appointments.

Many scholarships require you to provide some combination of the following:

- Transcript

- Standardized test scores

- Financial aid forms, such as the FAFSA or CSS/Financial Aid PROFILE®

- Parents' financial information, including tax returns

- One or more essays

- One or more letters of recommendation

- Proof of eligibility (e.g., membership credentials)

You may also need to prepare for a personal interview. For students competing for talent-based scholarships, an audition, performance, or portfolio may be required.

Proofread Your Applications Carefully: Use your computer's spelling and grammar check features. Have a family member, teacher, or friend read your essays.

Don't Leave Items Blank: Contact scholarship sponsors if you aren't sure how to fill out any part of the application.

Follow Instructions To The Letter: Avoid going over the length limit for the essay. Don't send supporting materials that are not requested in the application.

Make Sure Your Application Is Legible: Type or print your application forms and essays.

Make Copies Of Everything You Send: If application materials are lost, having copies on hand makes it much easier to resend your application quickly.

Double-Check Your Application: If you're reusing material (such as a cover letter or essay) from another scholarship application, check to make sure you haven't left in any incorrect names or blank fields. Don't forget to sign and date your application.

Get Your Applications In Early: You miss out if you miss deadlines. Consider using certified mail or requesting a return receipt.

It's A Fact!

Private scholarships can actually reduce parts of your financial aid package.

Source: From "How to Apply for a Scholarship" http://www.collegeboard.com/student/pay/scholarships-and-aid/8937.html. Copyright © 2011 The College Board. Reproduced with permission.

How Scholarships Affect Your Financial Aid Package

Private scholarships can actually reduce parts of your financial aid package. How? Colleges must consider outside scholarships as a student's financial resource, available to pay for education costs. If a college financial aid office meets your full financial need, government regulations specify that any scholarship money you win lowers your need figure on a dollar-for-dollar basis.

What should matter to you is which types of your aid are reduced or eliminated—self-help aid (loans or work-study) or need-based grants. Colleges, following federal regulations, can adjust your aid package in a variety of ways—some subtract the value of unmet need first, others reduce self-help aid before reducing grants, still others use scholarship funds only to replace grant money. Some colleges even give you the option of using scholarships to reduce your expected family contribution.

Quick Tip

It's a good idea to contact the financial aid office of colleges that interest you and ask about their policies on outside scholarships.

Source: From "How to Apply for a Scholarship" http://www.collegeboard.com/student/pay/scholarships-and-aid/8937.html. Copyright © 2011 The College Board. Reproduced with permission.

Chapter 31

Avoiding Scholarship Scams

Common Scholarship Scams

Fraudulent scholarships can take many forms; some of the most common types are presented here. If you receive an offer that uses one of these tactics, be suspicious (see our suggestions for protecting yourself from scholarship scams). If you believe the offer is a scam, report it. Sometimes a scam persists for years before people catch on to it. Even when people realize they've been cheated, few are stubborn enough to try to take advantage of guarantees or to file a complaint.

Scholarships That Never Materialize

Many scams encourage you to send them money up front, but provide little or nothing in exchange. Usually victims write off the expense, thinking that they simply didn't win the scholarship.

Scholarships For Profit

This scam looks just like a real scholarship program, but requires an application fee. The typical scam receives 5,000 to 10,000 applications and charges fees of $5 to $35. These scams can afford to pay out a $1,000 scholarship or two and still pocket a hefty profit, if they happen to award any scholarships at all.

About This Chapter: Information in this chapter is from "Common Scholarship Scams" and "Protecting Yourself from Scholarship Scams," © 2011 FinAid Page, LLC (www.finaid.org). All rights reserved. Reprinted with permission.

The Advance-Fee Loan

This scam offers you an unusually low-interest educational loan, with the requirement that you pay a fee before you receive the loan. When you pay the money, the promised loan never materializes. Real educational loans deduct the fees from the disbursement check. They never require an upfront fee when you submit the application. If the loan is not issued by a bank or other recognized lender, it is probably a scam. Show the offer to your local bank manager to get their advice.

The Scholarship Prize

This scam tells you that you've won a college scholarship worth thousands of dollars, but requires that you pay a disbursement or redemption fee or the taxes before they can release your prize. If someone says you've won a prize and you don't remember entering the contest or submitting an application, be suspicious.

In a common variation the sponsor sends the student a check for the scholarship, but requires the recipient to send back a check for the taxes or some other fees. Or the sponsor sends a check for more than the scholarship amount and asks the recipient to send back a check for the difference. The scholarship check ultimately bounces, as it is a forgery, but by then the recipients' funds are long gone.

The Guaranteed Scholarship Search Service

Beware of scholarship matching services that guarantee you'll win a scholarship or they'll refund your money. They may simply pocket your money and disappear, or if they do send you a report of matching scholarships, you'll find it extremely difficult to qualify for a refund.

Investment Required For Federal Loans

Insurance companies and brokerage firms sometimes offer free financial aid seminars that are actually sales pitches for insurance, annuity, and investment products. When a sales pitch implies that purchasing such a product is a prerequisite to receiving federal student aid, it violates federal regulations and state insurance laws.

Free Seminar

You may receive a letter advertising a free financial aid seminar or interviews for financial assistance. Sometimes the seminars do provide some useful information, but often they are cleverly disguised sales pitches for financial aid consulting services (e.g., maximize your eligibility for financial aid), investment products, scholarship matching services, and overpriced student loans.

Protecting Yourself From Scholarship Scams

This advice can help you avoid becoming the victim of a scholarship scam.

Rules Of Thumb

1. If you must pay money to get money, it might be a scam.

2. If it sounds too good to be true, it probably is.

3. Spend the time, not the money.

4. Never invest more than a postage stamp to get information about scholarships.

5. Nobody can guarantee that you'll win a scholarship.

6. Legitimate scholarship foundations do not charge application fees.

7. If you're suspicious of an offer, it's usually with good reason.

Warning Signs Of A Scholarship Scam

Certain telltale signs can help you identify possible scholarship scams. Note that the following signs do not automatically indicate fraud or deception; however, any organization that exhibits several of these signs should be treated with caution.

Application Fees: Be wary of any scholarship which requests an application fee, even an innocuously low one like $2 or $3. Most scams have application fees of $10 to $25, but some have had fees as low as $2 and as high as $5,000. Don't believe claims that the fee is necessary to cover administrative expenses or to ensure that only serious candidates apply, or that applicants who do not receive any money may be entitled to a refund. Even if the outfit gives out a token scholarship, the odds of your winning it are less than your chances of winning the lottery. Legitimate scholarship sponsors do not require an application fee.

Loan Fees: If you have to pay a fee in advance of obtaining an educational loan, be careful. It might be called an application fee, processing fee, origination fee, guarantee fee, default fee, or insurance fee, but if it must be paid in advance, it's probably a scam. Legitimate educational loans deduct the origination and default fees from the disbursement check. They never require an up-front fee when you submit the application.

Other Fees: If you must pay to get information about an award, apply for the award, or receive the award, be suspicious. Never spend more than a postage stamp to get information about scholarships and loans.

Guaranteed Winnings: No legitimate scholarship sponsor will guarantee you'll win an award. No scholarship matching services can guarantee that you'll win any scholarships either, as they have no control over the decisions made by the scholarship sponsors. Also, when such guarantees are made, they often come with hidden conditions that make them hard to redeem or worth less than they seem.

Everybody Is Eligible: All scholarship sponsors are looking for candidates who best match certain criteria. Certainly there are some scholarships that do not depend on academic merit, some that do not depend on athletic prowess, and some that do not depend on minority student status, but some set of restrictions always applies. No scholarship sponsor hands out money to students simply for breathing.

The Unclaimed Aid Myth: You may be told that millions or billions of dollars of scholarships go unused each year because students don't know where to apply. This simply isn't true. Most financial aid programs are highly competitive. No scholarship matching service has ever substantiated this myth with a verifiable list of unclaimed scholarship awards. There are no unclaimed scholarships.

The most common version of this myth, that "$6.6 billion went unclaimed last year," is based on a 1976–77 academic year study by the National Institute of Work and Learning. The study estimated that a total of $7 billion was potentially available from employer tuition assistance programs, but that only about $300 million to $400 million was being used. This is a 30-year-old estimate that has never been substantiated. Furthermore, the money in question is not available to the general public, only to certain employees enrolled in eligible programs of study whose employers offer tuition assistance. This money goes unused because it can't be used. Popular variations on this myth include the figures $2.7 billion, $2 billion, $1 billion, and $135 million.

We Apply On Your Behalf: To win a scholarship, you must submit your own applications, write your own essays, and solicit your own letters of recommendation. There's no way to avoid this work.

Claims Of Influence With Scholarship Sponsors: Scholarship matching services do not have any control over the awarding of scholarships by third parties.

High Success Rates: Overstated claims of effectiveness are a good tip-off to a scam. For example, less than one percent of users of fee-based scholarship matching services actually win an award. If something sounds too good to be true, it probably is.

Excessive Hype: If the brochure or advertisement uses a lot of hyperbole (e.g., free money, win your fair share, guaranteed, first come, first served, and everybody is eligible), be careful. Also be wary of letters and postcards that talk about "recent additions to our file," immediate confirmation, and invitation number.

Unusual Requests For Personal Information: If the application asks you to disclose bank account numbers, credit card numbers, calling card numbers, or Social Security numbers, it is probably a scam. If they call and ask you for personal information to confirm your eligibility, verify your identity, or as a sign of good will, hang up immediately. They can use this information, in conjunction with your date of birth and the names of your parents, to commit identity theft and apply for new credit cards in your name. They can also use the numbers on the bottom of your checks (the bank routing number and the account number) to withdraw money from your bank account using a demand draft. A demand draft works very much like a check, but does not require your signature.

No Telephone Number: Most legitimate scholarship programs include a telephone number for inquiries with their application materials.

Mail Drop For A Return Address: If the return address is a mail drop (e.g., a box number) or a residential address, it is probably a scam.

Masquerading As A Federal Agency: If you receive an offer from an organization with an official-sounding name, check whether there really is a federal agency with that name. Don't trust an organization just because it has an official-looking "governmental" seal as its logo or has a prestigious-seeming Washington, DC return address.

Claims Of University, Government, Chamber Of Commerce, Or Better Business Bureau Approval: Be wary of claims of endorsement and membership, especially if the recommendation is made by an organization with a name similar to that of a well-known private or government group. The federal government, U.S. Department of Education, and the U.S. Chamber of Commerce do not endorse or recommend private businesses.

Suggesting That They Are A NonProfit, Charitable Organization When They Are Not: Don't assume from an organization's name that it has a charitable purpose. Although it is illegal in most states to use a misleading business name, enforcement of the law is lax. For example, an organization with Fund or Foundation in its name is not necessarily a charitable foundation and may even be a for-profit business.

Quick Tip

If a financial aid seminar is held in a local college classroom or meeting facility, don't assume that it is university sanctioned. Call the school's financial aid office to find out whether it is a university approved or sponsored event.

Unsolicited Opportunities: Most scholarship sponsors will only contact you in response to your inquiry. If you've never heard of the organization before, it's probably a scam.

Failure To Substantiate Awards: If the organization can't prove that its scholarships are actually awarded and disbursed, be cautious.

Typing And Spelling Errors: Application materials that contain typing and spelling errors or lack an overall professional appearance may be an indication of a scam. Many scams misspell the word "scholarship" as "scholorship."

Time Pressure: If you must respond quickly and won't hear about the results for several months, it might be a scam. A scholarship scam might say that grants are handed out on a first come, first served basis and urge you to act quickly. Few, if any, legitimate scholarship sponsors make awards on a rolling basis. Take the time you need to carefully consider their offer.

Notification By Phone: If you have won a scholarship, you will receive written notification by mail, not by phone.

Disguised Advertising: Don't believe everything you read or hear, especially if you see it online. Unless you personally know the person praising a product or service, don't believe the recommendation. One scam set up its own fake Better Business Bureau (BBB) and used it as a reference. Another offered a forged certificate of merit from the local BBB. Yet another distributed a paid advertisement as though it were an article written by the newspaper. A Ponzi scheme gave out a few scholarships initially as "sugar money" to help attract victims.

A Newly Formed Company: Most philanthropic foundations have been established for many years. If a company was formed recently, ask for references.

Gives You A Runaround Or Nonspecific Information: Demand concrete answers that directly respond to your questions. If they repeat the same lines again and again, the caller is probably reading a standard pitch from a boilerplate script.

Abusive Treatment: If the caller swears at you or becomes abusive when you ask questions, it's probably a scam.

A Florida Or California Address: A disproportionate number of scams seem to originate from Florida and California addresses.

Practical Tips For Students On Avoiding Scholarship Scams

Be cautious if fees are involved. Even if the organization turns out to be legitimate, it is never in your best interest to respond to an offer with an up-front fee.

Get an independent opinion from a trusted source, such as a financial aid administrator at a local college or university, the local reference librarian, or your high school guidance counselor.

Call Directory Assistance to see if the company has a listing. If they don't, they're unlikely to be legit. You can reach Directory Assistance by dialing 1 followed by the area code and 555-1212. (Use 1-800-555-1212 to see if they have a toll-free number.) You can also look for a listing online using 555-1212.com, BigBook, Switchboard, WhoWhere, WorldPages, Yahoo People Search, and Zip2.

Never give out personal information to strangers. Don't divulge your checking or savings account numbers, social security number, or other personal information, no matter how reasonable-sounding the request.

Get it in writing before responding. Get offers, cancellation and refund policies, and guarantees in writing before sending money. Then read all the fine print. Don't rely on verbal promises.

Don't respond to unsolicited offers.

Quick Tip

For more information, visit the Federal Trade Commission (FTC)'s scholarship scams section, which includes Six Signs That Your Scholarship is Sunk (Poster) and bookmark, and the FTC Consumer Alert about scholarship scams. Also a consumer alert about free grants. For warnings about scholarship matching services, also see Evaluating Scholarship Matching Services and the Looking for Student Aid brochure published by the U.S. Department of Education.

Ask the organization how it got your name. If they got your name from a reputable source, verify it with the source. The College Board, for example, only releases its mailing lists to colleges, universities, and carefully vetted nonprofit tax-exempt foundations. Scams often use carefully written scripts designed to elicit your Scholastic Aptitude Test (SAT) score or grade-point average (GPA) and then feed it back to you later in the conversation to reassure you as to their legitimacy.

Ignore offers that involve time pressure. If the company demands an immediate response, respond by hanging up the phone.

Trust your instincts. If you feel uneasy about an offer, don't spend any money until you've addressed your concerns. Your initial suspicious reaction to an offer is often correct.

Keep good records. Keep photocopies of your correspondence with the company and the company's promotional materials and take notes during any telephone conversations. If it does turn out to be a scam, include these materials with your complaint to law enforcement agencies.

Practical Tips For Schools On Protecting Students From Scholarship Scams

Safeguard student privacy. Carefully investigate any organization before releasing any information about your students to the organization. Remember that the Family Education Rights and Privacy Act (FERPA) may prohibit the release of this information.

Monitor the use of your student lists. If you do release a list of student names and addresses, such as a Dean's List or Honor Roll, include a few fake names and addresses to let you monitor how the list is used.

Prohibit the third-party release of student information. Require any organization that has access to your student list, such as yearbook publishers, to safeguard the privacy of your students. Prohibit them from releasing the list to any third party without your prior written permission in each case.

Promptly notify parents of any problems. If you find that the list is being abused, promptly notify the students and their parents of the problem.

Chapter 32

The Robert C. Byrd Honors Scholarship Program

This program, which is federally funded and state administered, is designed to recognize exceptionally able high school seniors who show promise of continued excellence in postsecondary education. The Department of Education awards funds to state education agencies (SEAs), which make scholarship awards to eligible applicants. Students receive scholarships for college expenses.

Students with questions or concerns regarding the Robert C. Byrd Honors Scholarship Program should contact the state education agency in their state of legal residence.

Eligibility

High school graduates who have been accepted for enrollment at institutions of higher education (IHEs), have demonstrated outstanding academic achievement, and show promise of continued academic excellence may apply to states in which they are residents. The Department provides grant funds to states on a formula basis.

An eligible student applicant must meet the following criteria during the same secondary academic year in which the scholarship is to be awarded:

- Be a graduate of a public or private secondary school or have received the recognized equivalent of a high school diploma (General Educational Development Tests, or GED)

- Be a legal resident of the state in which he or she applies

- Be a U.S. citizen or national of the United States or have evidence from the U.S. Immigration and Naturalization Service that he or she is a permanent resident or is in the United States for other than a temporary purpose

About This Chapter: Information in this chapter is from "Robert C. Byrd Honors Scholarship Program," a publication of the U.S. Department of Education, 2010.

- Has applied or been accepted for enrollment at an institution of higher education

- Certify that he or she is not ineligible to receive assistance as a result of default on a federal student loan or other obligation

- File, with the school that he or she plans to attend, a Statement of Selective Service Registration Status. A student attending a military academy is ineligible to receive a Byrd scholarship.

It's A Fact!

Effective August 14, 2008, the Robert C. Byrd Program's eligibility requirements in Section 419F of the Higher Education Act of 1965, as amended, were changed to include home schooled students as eligible applicants, regardless of how the home schooled student is treated under state law.

Applicant Information

Students must apply directly to the state education agency (SEA) in their state of legal residence. Application deadlines are set forth by the respective SEA. Students must request the application package from the state education agency and follow the instructions for application procedures.

Awards

The 50 states, DC, Puerto Rico, and the Insular Areas receive funding for this program. Scholarships are awarded to individuals who apply in their state or area for a period of not less than one or more than four years during the first four years of study at any institution of higher education eligible to participate in the program.

Performance Reports

Performance reports are mailed annually from the Department to the state education agency's contact person.

It's A Fact!

In Fiscal Year 2010, the average award per scholar for the Robert C. Byrd Honors Scholarship was $1,500.

Chapter 33

The Nursing Scholarship Program

The purpose of the Nursing Scholarship Program (NSP) is to provide scholarships to nursing students in exchange for a minimum two-year full-time service commitment (or part-time equivalent), at an eligible health care facility with a critical shortage of nurses. Scholarships are awarded competitively and consist of payment for tuition, fees, other reasonable costs, and a monthly support stipend.

Recipients of the NSP award are required to fulfill their NSP service commitments within the United States, the District of Columbia, the Commonwealth of Puerto Rico, the Territory of Guam, the Commonwealth of the Northern Marianas, the U.S. Virgin Islands, the Territory of American Samoa, the Republic of Palau, the Republic of the Marshall Islands, or the Federated States of Micronesia.

Benefits

- **Service:** NSP provides nurses with an opportunity to increase access to care by delivering nursing services in eligible health care facilities with a critical shortage of nurses.

- **Scholarship:** NSP provides funds to support nursing school tuition and fees; an annual payment for other reasonable costs to cover expenses for books, clinical supplies, and instruments; and monthly stipends to cover living expenses.

About This Chapter: Information in this chapter is from "Nursing Scholarship Program," a publication of the U.S. Department of Health and Human Services, 2010.

Eligibility Requirements

To be eligible for a scholarship, an NSP applicant must meet the following criteria:

- Be a U.S. citizen (either U.S. born or naturalized), U.S. national, or a lawful permanent resident.

- Be enrolled or accepted for enrollment as a full- or part-time student in an accredited nursing degree program at one of the following:

  - **An Associate Degree School Of Nursing:** A department, division, or other administrative unit in a junior college, community college, college, or university which provides primarily or exclusively a two-year program of education in professional nursing and allied subjects leading to an associate degree in nursing or to an equivalent degree and is an accredited program

  - **A Collegiate School Of Nursing:** A department, division, or the administrative unit in a college or university which provides primarily or exclusively a program of education in professional nursing and related subjects leading to a degree of bachelor of arts, bachelor of science, bachelor of nursing, graduate degree in nursing, or to an equivalent degree, and including advanced training related to such program of education provided by such school and is an accredited program

  - **A Diploma School Of Nursing:** A school affiliated with a hospital or university, or an independent school, which provides primarily or exclusively a program of education in professional nursing and allied subjects leading to a diploma or to an equivalent evidence of completion and is an accredited program

- Be enrolled in or accepted for enrollment in a school of nursing located in a state, the District of Columbia, or a U.S. Territory. The schools and educational programs for which scholarship support is requested must be in one of the 50 States, the District of Columbia, the Commonwealth of Puerto Rico, the Commonwealth of the Northern Marianas, the U.S. Virgin Islands, the Territory of Guam, the Territory of American Samoa, the Republic of Palau, the Republic of the Marshall Islands, or the Federated States of Micronesia. A student attending a school outside of these areas is not eligible for the Nursing Scholarship Program, even though the student may be a citizen/national/lawful permanent resident of the United States.

- Begin the nursing degree program on or before September 30, 2011

- Submit a complete application and signed contract

> ## It's A Fact!
> Students enrolled in LPN programs, self-paced study programs (online), bridge programs, and dual degree programs are not eligible for a scholarship award.

Accredited Program

The NSP considers a nursing program to be accredited if it is accredited by a national nurse education accrediting agency or state approval agency recognized by the Secretary of the U.S. Department of Education. Currently, these agencies include the Commission on Collegiate Nursing Education; the National League for Nursing Accrediting Commission; Kansas Board of Nursing; Maryland Board of Nursing; Missouri Board of Nursing; North Dakota Board of Nursing; and New York State Board of Regents, State Education Department, Office of the Professions (Nursing Education).

Ineligibility

An applicant will be deemed ineligible if the applicant has any of the following issues:

- Any judgment liens against his or her property arising from a debt owed to the United States

- A breach of a prior service obligation

- Is excluded, debarred, suspended, or disqualified by a federal agency

- An existing service obligation. An applicant who is already obligated to a Federal, State, or other entity for professional practice or service after academic training is not eligible for an NSP award. An exception may be made if the entity to which the obligation is owed provides documentation that there is no potential conflict in fulfilling the service commitment to the NSP and that the NSP service commitment will be served first. An NSP scholarship participant who subsequently enters into another service commitment and is not immediately available after completion of the participant's degree to fulfill his/her NSP service commitment will be subject to breach of contract provisions.

Individuals in a Reserve component of the Armed Forces including the National Guard are eligible to participate in the NSP. Reservists should understand the following:

- Military training or service performed by reservists will not satisfy the NSP service commitment. If a participant's military training and/or service, in combination with the participant's other absences from the service site, will exceed seven weeks per service year, the participant should request a suspension. The NSP service obligation end date will be extended to compensate for the break in NSP service.

- If the critical shortage facility (CSF) where the reservist is serving at the time of his/her deployment is unable to reemploy that reservist, the reservist will be expected to complete his/her NSP service obligation at another eligible critical shortage facility. The reservist must contact NSP to request a transfer and receive approval, in accordance with the transfer policy.

Program Requirements

Requirements While In School

It's A Fact!
A credit and excluded parties list system check will be performed as part of the application approval process.

- **Maintain Enrollment:** The NSP participant must maintain enrollment in the nursing program until the program is complete.

- **Maintain Good Academic Standing:** A scholarship participant must be in good academic standing, as defined by the institution's academic policies, for the duration of the academic year.

- **Notify NSP Of Any Changes In Enrollment Status:** A participant is required to notify the NSP promptly by phone and in writing via e-mail as soon as one of the following events is anticipated:

  - Repeat course work for which the NSP has already made payments

  - A change in the applicant's graduation date

  - A leave of absence approved by the school

  - Withdrawal or dismissal from school

  - A change from full-time student status to a less than full-time student status for participants who sign "Full-Time Student" Contracts (a change from part-time student status to less than part-time student status for participants who sign "Part-Time Student" Contracts).

  - Voluntary withdrawal from courses during an academic term

  - A transfer to another school or program

These events could have an adverse impact on a participant's receipt of NSP payments.

Change In Enrollment Status

A change in enrollment status can result in a reduction or discontinuation of benefits. A participant is required to notify the NSP promptly by phone and in writing as soon as one of the events listed above is anticipated. If a change in enrollment status has already occurred, the participant must submit a letter from the school verifying that the change has occurred.

Please be advised that if the NSP has any questions concerning a participant's eligibility for continued support, the NSP may delay the payment of all benefits to that participant pending clarification of the participant's continuing eligibility and status.

Service Requirements And Eligible Sites

Service Requirements After Graduation

Obtain A License: Graduates must obtain a license. The following criteria apply to an NSP graduate's license:

- Prior to commencing service at a CSF, NSP participants must be permanently licensed within six months of graduation to practice as a registered nurse (or if appropriate, as an advanced practice nurse) in the state where they will be serving.

- Credit towards fulfillment of the scholarship service commitment will not be given in the absence of a current, unencumbered permanent license in the state of service.

- In addition, advanced practice nurses are expected to pass a national certification examination for their specialty (that is administered by a nationally recognized certifying body) prior to commencing service.

- Service credit will NOT be given until the NSP has received documentation that all licensure and certification requirements have been met. Documents should be sent to:

  ATTN: Division of Nursing and Public Health, Nursing Scholarship Program
  Monitoring and Transition Team
  Fax: 1-855-444-6032

- Responsibility for obtaining the required state license (and national certification exam, if applicable) prior to the service start date rests with the NSP participant.

- NSP participants are expected to take the appropriate licensure/certification exams at the earliest possible date.

- If the participant is unsuccessful in obtaining a license or passing the certification exam(s) within six months of his or her graduation date, the participant should immediately contact the NSP in writing at the address above to request a suspension.

Obtain A Position At A Critical Shortage Facility: Graduates must obtain a position at a CSF. The following criteria apply:

- NSP participants will have up to six months from their date of graduation to obtain a nursing license and accept an offer of employment from an NSP-approved facility. Participants will have up to three months following the date of the acceptance of such job offer to commence full-time (or if approved by the Secretary, part-time) clinical services at the facility.

- Participants should contact the NSP prior to accepting employment to assure facility/ position eligibility. The NSP reserves the right to grant final approval of all service locations in order to ensure a participant's compliance with statutory requirements related to the service obligation. Once employment begins, participants are required to submit an initial Employment Verification Form and a Six-Month Employment Verification Form thereafter until the service obligation is completed.

- Participants may be recommended for default of their service obligation for failure to accept an offer of employment from an NSP-approved facility within six months of their date of graduation or commence full-time (or if approved by the Secretary, part-time) clinical services at the facility within three months following the date of the acceptance of the job offer.

Perform Full-Time or Part-Time Clinical Service: Graduates must perform clinical service. The following criteria apply:

- Participants may satisfy their service obligations on either a full-time or, with written approval from the Secretary or his/her designee, a part-time basis.

- Full-Time clinical practice is defined as a minimum of 32 hours per week for a minimum of 45 weeks per year. At least 26 hours per week must be spent providing clinical services, or direct patient care, to patients. The remaining six hours may be spent on administrative or other nonclinical activities.

- Part-Time clinical practice is defined as a minimum of 16 hours per week and up to a maximum of 31 hours per week, for a minimum of 45 weeks per year.

- Participants wishing to serve part time must first obtain approval from the Secretary or his/her designee and must extend their service obligation so that the aggregate amount of service performed will equal the amount of a full-time service obligation.

- At least 80 percent of the hours each week must be spent providing clinical services, or direct patient care, to patients. For example, a nurse scheduled to work 20 hours per week must spend at least 16 hours per week providing clinical services.

- The following criteria apply to absences:

  - No more than seven weeks per service year can be spent away from the approved NSP site for vacation, holidays, continuing professional education, illness, or any other reason.

  - For absences of greater than seven weeks in a service year, the participant must request a suspension of the NSP service obligation.

  - There is no guarantee that a request for a suspension will be approved. If a suspension is approved, the participant's service obligation end date will be extended accordingly.

Verify Service: Every NSP participant must submit a service verification form from their employer for each six months of service. The following criteria apply:

- The NSP will send a service verification form to each NSP participant. The form must be completed and signed by the participant and an appropriate official at the approved service site.

- By signing this form, the site will be certifying the participant's compliance or noncompliance with the full-time or part-time clinical practice requirement during that six-month period.

- The form will also record the participant's time spent away from the practice site during that six-month period.

- Participants who fail to complete and submit their six-month service obligation verification forms on time may jeopardize receiving service credit.

- Service Verification Forms should be submitted to the following:

  ATTN: Division of Program Operations
  Nursing Scholarship Program
  Fax: 1-855-444-6032

Leaving A Facility

The NSP expects that a participant will fulfill his or her obligation at the NSP-approved critical shortage facility; however, the NSP does understand that circumstances may arise that require a participant to leave the initial facility and complete service at another NSP-approved critical shortage facility. If a participant feels he or she can no longer continue working at the approved facility, the participant should contact the NSP immediately in writing. All transfers must be approved by the NSP. A transfer request should be submitted before the participant leaves his or her site. Leaving the assigned site without prior written approval may result in a default recommendation.

Types Of Sites For Service Obligation

By statute, NSP participants are required to serve for a minimum of two years at a health care facility with a critical shortage of nurses (CSF). NSP participants must provide full-time (or if approved by the Secretary, part-time) clinical service in a public or private nonprofit facility with a critical shortage of nurses located in a U.S. state, the District of Columbia, or U.S. territory. Please note that the designation and definition of a CSF is subject to change. A facility deemed to be a CSF today may not be a CSF in the future. When NSP participants are ready to begin their service obligation, they will be required to serve at what is deemed to be a CSF at that time. NSP participants who must relocate to accept a position in a different geographic area will not receive a relocation incentive or reimbursement.

Currently, Critical Shortage Facilities include the following types:

- **Disproportionate Share Hospital (DSH)**: A nonprofit hospital that has a disproportionately large share of low-income patients and receives an augmented payment from the state under Medicaid or a payment adjustment from Medicare. Hospital-based outpatient services are included under this definition.

- **Nursing Home**: A public or private nonprofit institution (or a distinct part of an institution), certified under section 1919(a) of the Social Security Act, that is primarily engaged in providing, on a regular basis, health-related care and service to individuals who, because of their mental or physical condition, require care and service (above the level of room and board) that can be made available to them only through institutional facilities, and is not primarily for the care and treatment of mental diseases.

- **State Or Local Public Health And/Or Human Services Department:** The state, county, parish, or district entity in a state that is responsible for providing population-focused health services which include health promotion, disease prevention, and intervention services provided in clinics or other health care facilities that are operated by the Department.

- **Federally Qualified Health Center:** A nonprofit entity that is receiving a grant, or funding from a grant, under section 330 of the Public Health Service Act, as amended, to provide primary health services and other related services to a population that is medically underserved. Federally-qualified health centers include Community Health Centers, Migrant Health Centers, Health Care for the Homeless Health Centers, and Public Housing Primary Care Health Centers.

- **Federally Qualified Health Center Look-Alike:** A nonprofit entity that is certified by the Secretary as meeting the requirements for receiving a grant under section 330 of the Public Health Service Act, but is not a grantee. For more information, please see Health Center Policy Information Notice 1999-10.

- **Native Hawaiian Health Center:** An entity: (a) which is organized under the laws of the state of Hawaii; (b) which provides or arranges for health care services through practitioners licensed by the state of Hawaii, where licensure requirements are applicable; (c) which is a public or nonprofit private entity; and (d) in which Native Hawaiian health practitioners significantly participate in the planning, management, monitoring, and evaluation of health services. For more information, please see the Native Hawaiian Health Care Act of 1988 (Public Law 100-579), as amended by Public Law 102-396.

- **Indian Health Service Health Center**: A nonprofit health care facility (whether operated directly by the Indian Health Service or by a tribe or tribal organization, contractor, or grantee under the Indian Self-Determination Act, as described in 42 Code of Federal Regulations (CFR) Part 136, Subparts C and H, or by an urban Indian organization receiving funds under Title V of the Indian Health Care Improvement Act) that is physically separated from a hospital, and which provides clinical treatment services on an outpatient basis to persons of Indian or Alaskan Native descent as described in 42 CFR Section 136.12.

- **Rural Health Clinic:** A public or private nonprofit entity that the Centers for Medicare and Medicaid Services has certified as a rural health clinic under section 1861(aa) (2) of the Social Security Act. A rural health clinic provides outpatient services to a nonurban area with an insufficient number of health care practitioners.

- **Critical Access Hospital (CAH):** A nonprofit facility that is (a) located in a state that has established with the Centers for Medicare and Medicaid Services (CMS) a Medicare rural hospital flexibility program; (b) designated by the State as a CAH; (c) certified by the CMS as a CAH; and (d) in compliance with all applicable CAH conditions of participation.

- **Skilled Nursing Facility (SNF):** A public or private nonprofit institution (or a distinct part of an institution), certified under section 1819(a) of the Social Security Act, that is primarily engaged in providing skilled nursing care and related services to residents requiring medical, rehabilitation, or nursing care and is not primarily for the care and treatment of mental diseases.

- **NonFederal, NonDisproportionate Share Hospital:** Any public or private nonprofit institution in a state that is primarily engaged in providing care, by or under the supervision of physicians, to inpatients: (a) diagnostic and therapeutic services for medical diagnosis, treatment, and care of injured, disabled, or sick persons, of (b) rehabilitation of injured, disabled, or sick persons. Hospital-based outpatient services are included under this definition.

- **Ambulatory Surgical Center:** A nonprofit entity in a state that provides surgical services to individuals on an outpatient basis and is not owned or operated by a hospital.

- **Home Health Agency:** A public agency or private nonprofit organization, certified under section 1861(o) of the Social Security Act, that is primarily engaged in providing skilled nursing care and other therapeutic services.

- **Hospice Program**: A public agency or private nonprofit organization, certified under section 1861(dd)(2) of the Social Security Act, that provides 24-hour care and treatment services (as needed) to terminally ill individuals and bereavement counseling for their immediate family members. This care is provided in individuals' homes, on an outpatient basis, and on a short-term inpatient basis, directly or under arrangements made by the agency or organization.

- **Federal Hospital:** Any federal institution in a state that is primarily engaged in providing, by or under the supervision of physicians, to inpatients: (a) diagnostic and therapeutic services for medical diagnosis, treatment, and care of injured, disabled, or sick persons; or (b) rehabilitation of injured, disabled, or sick persons. Hospital-based outpatient services are included under this definition.

Ineligible facilities include, but are not limited to the following:

- Free-standing clinics that do not qualify as a facility above
- Renal dialysis centers
- Private practice offices
- Assisted living facilities
- Clinics in prisons and correctional facilities
- Private for-profit facilities

Funding Awards

Among eligible applicants, the NSP uses various funding preferences and selection factors to determine scholarship awardees.

Funding Preferences

There is a funding preference for applicants of greatest financial need. An applicant's financial need is determined based on the applicant's Expected Family Contribution (EFC), which is provided on the Student Aid Report (SAR).

Among those applicants of greatest financial need (i.e., applicants with an EFC of zero), the following funding preferences will be used to make NSP awards:

- First funding preference will be given to qualified applicants who have a zero EFC and are enrolled or accepted for enrollment in an accredited undergraduate nursing program as full-time students.

- Second funding preference will be given to qualified applicants who have a zero EFC and are enrolled or accepted for enrollment in an accredited graduate nursing program as full-time students.

- Third funding preference will be given to qualified applicants who have a zero EFC and are enrolled or accepted for enrollment in an accredited undergraduate or graduate nursing program as part-time students.

To the extent that funds remain available, all other applicants will be considered in the order of decreasing need.

Selection Factors

The following selection factors will be considered when determining scholarship awardees:

- **Legal History:** An NSP applicant who has a history of not honoring a prior legal obligation, as evidenced by one or more of the following factors, may not be selected:

  - Default on a prior service obligation to the federal government, a state or local government, or other entity, even if the applicant subsequently satisfied that obligation through service, monetary payment, or other means.

  - Default on any federal payment obligations (e.g., student loans, federal income tax liabilities, mortgages, etc.) or nonfederal payment obligations (e.g., court-ordered child support payments)

- Write off of any federal or nonfederal debt as uncollectible.

- **Academic Performance:** Demonstrates the ability to excel and maintain good academic standing in school

- **Essay Questions:** Demonstrates a thorough commitment to a career in nursing; interest/ motivation in providing care to underserved communities; and relevant work experience and/or activities (i.e., community service, research, and internships) that have prepared the applicant to work with underserved populations.

- **Recommendation Letters:** Provides a detailed description of the applicant's performance in school; education/work achievements; community/civic or other nonacademic achievements; ability to work and communicate constructively with others from diverse backgrounds; and interest and motivation to serve underserved populations through work experience, course work, special projects, research, etc.

Expected Awards

The NSP for the 2011–2012 school year is expected to be highly competitive. The Program anticipates more applicants for scholarship awards than there are funds available. It is expected that approximately 450 awards will be made for the 2011–2012 school year. In the past, NSP funds have only allowed for funding of individuals in the first funding preference.

Breaching The Contract, Suspension, And Waiver

Breaching The Contract

A participant is in breach of the NSP contract if he or she has any of the following issues:

- Fails to maintain an acceptable level of academic standing in the nursing program
- Is dismissed from the nursing program for disciplinary reasons
- Voluntarily terminates the nursing program
- Fails to provide health services in an NSP service site for the applicable period of time as specified in his or her NSP contract

If a participant breaches the contract, he or she will be liable to the federal government to repay all funds paid to the participant, or on the participant's behalf, under the NSP and pay interest on such amounts at the maximum legal prevailing rate from the date of default. The amount owed, including interest, must be paid within three years of the date of the participant's default.

Failure to repay the NSP debt within three years will result in delinquency and has the following consequences:

- **Reporting:** The debt will be reported to credit reporting agencies. During the three-year repayment period, the debt will be reported to credit reporting agencies as current. If the debt becomes past due, it will be reported as delinquent.

- **Referral:** The debt will be referred to a debt collection agency and the Department of Justice. Any NSP debt past due for 45 days may be referred to a debt collection agency. If the debt collection agency is unsuccessful in receiving payment in full, the debt may be referred to the U.S. Department of Justice for enforced collection.

- **Administrative Offset:** Federal and/or state payments due to the participant (e.g., an income tax refund) may be offset by the U.S. Department of Treasury to repay a delinquent NSP debt. Also, recovery through Administrative Wage Garnishment may be enforced to repay a delinquent NSP debt.

- **Medicare/Medicaid Exclusion:** Delinquent defaulters who are unwilling to enter into, or stay in compliance with, an agreement to repay their scholarship debt can be excluded from participation in Medicare, Medicaid, and other federal health care programs.

Waivers And Suspensions

Requests for waivers and suspensions are processed and reviewed by the Office of Legal and Compliance (OLC). Suspensions are granted if compliance with a service obligation by the participant is temporarily impossible or would temporarily involve an extreme hardship such that enforcement of the obligation would be unconscionable. A waiver of a service obligation may be granted by the OLC when compliance by the participant is permanently impossible, or would cause permanent extreme hardship to the individual and would be against equity and good conscience to enforce.

Compliance would be considered impossible if the OLC determines that the participant suffers from a physical or mental disability resulting in his/her inability to perform the commitment incurred.

To determine whether performance of the obligation would impose an extreme hardship and be against equity and good conscience, the OLC will consider the following factors:

- The participant's present financial resources and obligation
- The participant's estimated future financial resources and obligation

- The extent to which the participant has problems of a personal nature, such as physical or mental disability, or terminal illness in the immediate family, which so intrude on the participant's present and future ability to perform as to raise a presumption that the individual would be unable to perform the obligation incurred.

Scholarship participants seeking a waiver (for a permanent situation) or suspension (for a temporary situation) of the service obligation must submit a written request to the following:

ATTN: Division of Program Operations

Nursing Scholarship Program

Fax: 1-855-444-6032

The request must state the underlying circumstances and be supported by appropriate documentation.

Chapter 34

The National Health Service Corps Scholarship

The National Health Service Corps (NHSC), through scholarship and loan repayment programs, helps Health Professional Shortage Areas (HPSAs) in the U.S. get the medical, dental, and mental health providers they need to meet their tremendous need for health care.

Since 1972, more than 30,000 clinicians have served in the Corps, expanding access to health care services and improving the health of people who live in urban and rural areas where health care is scarce.

About half of all NHSC clinicians work in Health Resources and Services Administration (HRSA)-supported Health Centers, which deliver preventive and primary care services to patients regardless of their ability to pay. About 40 percent of Health Center patients have no health insurance.

Scholarship

The NHSC scholarship is a competitive program that pays tuition and fees and provides a living stipend to students enrolled in accredited medical (Medical Doctor (MD) or Doctors of Osteopathy (DO)), dental, nurse practitioner, certified nurse midwife, and physician assistant training. Upon graduation, scholarship recipients serve as primary care providers for between two and four years in a community-based site in a high-need Health Professional Shortage Area (HPSA) that has applied to and been approved by the NHSC as a service site.

Awards are made to applicants most committed to serving underserved people and most likely to build successful careers in HPSAs and meet future needs for care throughout the nation.

About This Chapter: Information in this chapter is from "About the NHSC," "National Health Service Corps Scholarship," and "How to Apply," publications of the U.S. Department of Health and Human Services, 2011.

Loan Repayment

The NHSC Loan Repayment Program offers fully trained primary care physicians (MD or DO), family nurse practitioners, certified nurse midwives, physician assistants, dentists, dental hygienists, and certain mental health clinicians $60,000 to repay student loans in exchange for two years serving in a community-based site in a high-need HPSA that has applied to and been approved by the NHSC as a service site.

After completing their two years of service, loan repayors may apply for additional years of support.

The loan repayment program recruits both clinicians just completing training and seasoned professionals to meet the immediate need for care throughout the nation.

National Health Service Corps Scholarship

The National Health Service Corps scholarship pays tuition, required fees, and some other education costs, tax free, for as many as four years. Education costs may include books, clinical supplies, laboratory expenses, instruments, two sets of uniforms, and travel for one clinical rotation. Recipients also receive a monthly living stipend ($1,289 in 2010–2011), which is taxable.

Eligibility

To be eligible for the scholarship, you must meet the following criteria:

- Be a U.S. citizen or national

- Be a full-time student at an accredited school, pursuing a degree in:
  - Medicine (MD or DO)
  - Dentistry (Doctor of Dental Surgery [DDS] or Doctor of Dental Medicine [DMD])
  - Nurse practitioner
  - Certified nurse-midwife
  - Physician assistant (in primary care)

It's A Fact!

- The NHSC has more than 8,000 clinicians and more than 10,000 sites.

- More than seven million people receive health care from NHSC clinicians.

- There are more than 9,000 job vacancies for NHSC primary care medical, dental, and mental health clinicians.

Source: From "About the NHSC," a publication of the U.S. Department of Health and Human Services, 2011.

Service Commitment

National Health Service Corps scholars are committed to serve one year for each year of support (minimum of two years service) at an approved site in a high-need Health Professional Shortage Area soon after they graduate, serve a primary care residency (family medicine, general pediatrics, general internal medicine, obstetrics/gynecology, or psychiatry for physicians and general or pediatric for dentists) and are licensed.

Scholars compete for employment at the approved service sites of their choice from a listing of job vacancies in their discipline and specialty. The NHSC helps scholars select a compatible service site and pays for travel to and from interviews.

Service Locations

Many types of health care facilities are approved NHSC sites. About half of NHSC scholars fulfill their service commitment at federally supported health centers. Health center clinicians can be granted medical malpractice liability protection through the Federal Tort Claims Act.

Other types of NHSC approved sites include the following:

- Federally Qualified Health Centers (FQHC)

- FQHC Look-Alike

- Rural Health Center (RHC)

- Hospital Affiliated Primary Care Out-Patient Clinic

- Indian Health Service, Tribal Clinic, and Urban Indian Health Clinic (ITCU)

- Correctional Facility

- Private Practice (Solo/Group)

- Other Health Facility (Community Outpatient Facility, Community Mental Health Facility, State and County Departments of Health Clinic, Mobile Unit, Free Clinic, Immigration and customs Enforcement (ICE) Health Service Corps)

Scholars negotiate their salaries with the employing site, but the NHSC requires that they be paid at least as much as they would in an equivalent federal civil service position. A few scholars serve in an established private practice in a high-need Health Professional Shortage Area (HPSA). These arrangements must be approved by the NHSC and scholars working in them are not protected by the NHSC minimum salary requirement.

Sites that have applied to and been approved by the NHSC post vacancies on the NHSC Job Opportunities List. Sites that list vacancies for scholars must be located in the neediest HPSAs.

How To Apply

The National Health Service Corps Scholarship (NHSC) Program accepts applications once a year from students who are enrolled or accepted for enrollment at an accredited health professions training program in an eligible primary care discipline: medicine (MD or DO), dentistry, family nurse practitioner, certified nurse midwife, or physician assistant. You can apply before your first year or after you have finished one or more years of school.

The application is submitted online, with supplemental forms and documentation that must be either submitted online or mailed by the application deadline. You will need to submit the following:

- Proof of U.S. citizenship

- Transcript

- Resume detailing volunteer and work experience (no more than five pages)

- Verifications and evaluations from your school

- Essays in response to prompts

It's A Fact!

All NHSC approved sites accept Medicare and Medicaid and provide services on a sliding fee scale or other method that enables poor and uninsured patients to receive care whether or not they are insured or able to pay.

Criteria

If you meet the eligibility requirements and are dedicated to working where you are needed most, you are encouraged to apply to the NHSC Scholarship Program. Because the NHSC does not usually have enough funding to award scholarships to every worthy applicant, scholars are selected according to the following priorities:

1. Former NHSC scholars in need of additional years of support.

It's A Fact!

Applications submitted after the deadline are not reviewed.

---

2. Scholarship for Students of Exceptional Financial Need recipients enrolled in medical or dental school.

3. Students from disadvantaged backgrounds.

If you are selected to receive the NHSC scholarship, you will be notified by e-mail or postal letter by September 30 and must respond promptly that you accept. If you do not accept by the deadline specified in your notification, your offer expires.

If you are selected as an alternate, you will be notified by e-mail by September 30 that you are an alternate. If a scholarship becomes available, you will be notified immediately.

If you are not selected as a scholarship recipient or alternate, you will be notified by October 31.

Chapter 35

College-Bound Athletes

The NCAA And NCAA Eligibility Center

What Is The NCAA?

The NCAA, or National Collegiate Athletic Association, was established in 1906 and serves as the athletics governing body for more than 1,300 colleges, universities, conferences, and organizations. The national office is in Indianapolis, but the member colleges and universities develop the rules and guidelines for athletics eligibility and athletics competition for each of the three NCAA divisions. The NCAA is committed to the student athlete and to governing competition in a fair, safe, inclusive, and sportsmanlike manner.

The NCAA membership includes:

- 335 active Division I members;

- 288 active Division II members; and

- 432 active Division III members.

One of the differences among the three divisions is that colleges and universities in Divisions I and II may offer athletics scholarships, while Division III colleges and universities may not.

What Is The NCAA Eligibility Center?

The NCAA Eligibility Center will certify the academic and amateur credentials of all college-bound student athletes who wish to compete in NCAA Division I or II athletics. To

About This Chapter: Information in this chapter is from the "2010–2011 Guide for the College-Bound Student-Athlete," © National Collegiate Athletic Association. 2011. All rights reserved.

assist with this process, the Eligibility Center staff is eager to foster a cooperative environment of education and partnership with high schools, high school coaches, and college-bound student athletes. Ultimately, the individual student athlete is responsible for achieving and protecting his or her eligibility status.

How To Find Answers To Your Questions

The answers to most questions can be found in this chapter or by:

- Accessing the Eligibility Center's resource page on its website at www.eligibilitycenter.org, clicking on "Resources" and then selecting the type of student you are. You can then navigate through the resources to find helpful information.

- Contacting the Eligibility Center at the phone number in this chapter.

In addition, if you are sending transcripts or additional information to the Eligibility Center or have questions, please use the following contact information.

Eligibility Center Contact Information

NCAA Eligibility Center
Certification Processing
P.O. Box 7136
Indianapolis, IN 46207-7136

Package or overnight delivery
Certification Processing
1802 Alonzo Watford Sr. Drive
Indianapolis, IN 46202

Web address: www.eligibilitycenter.org

Eligibility Center customer service
U.S. callers (toll-free): 877-262-1492
International callers: 317-223-0700
Fax: 317-968-5100

When To Call The NCAA

Please contact the NCAA when you have questions such as these:

- What are the rules and regulations related to initial eligibility?

- What are the rules and regulations related to amateurism?

- What are the regulations about transferring from one college to another?

- What are the rules about athletics scholarships and how can they be reduced or canceled?

- I have an education-impacting disability. Are there any other requirements for me?

NCAA

P.O. Box 6222

Indianapolis, IN 46206-6222

317-917-6222 (customer service hours: Monday–Friday, noon–4 p.m. Eastern time)

Your Eligibility And You

Academic Eligibility Requirements

Division I: If you want to participate in athletics or receive an athletics scholarship during your first year, you must:

- graduate from high school

- complete these 16 core courses:
  - four years of English
  - three years of math (Algebra 1 or higher)
  - two years of natural or physical science (including one year of lab science if offered by your high school)
  - one extra year of English, math, or natural or physical science
  - two years of social science
  - four years of extra core courses (from any category above, or foreign language, non-doctrinal religion, or philosophy);

- earn a minimum required grade-point average in your core courses; and

- earn a combined Scholastic Aptitude Test (SAT) or American College Testing Program (ACT) sum score that matches your core course grade-point average and test score sliding scale (for example, a 2.400 core course grade-point average needs an 860 SAT).

Requirement To Graduate With Your High School Class

You must complete the 16 core course requirement in eight semesters, which begins when you initially started high school with your ninth-grade class. If you graduate from high school in eight semesters with your class, you may use one core course unit completed within one year after graduation (summer or academic year) to meet NCAA Division I initial eligibility requirements.

You may complete the core course at a location other than the high school from which you graduated and may initially enroll full time at a collegiate institution at any time after completion of the core course.

Division I Qualifier: Being a qualifier enables you to:

- practice or compete for your college or university during your first year of college;

- receive an athletics scholarship during your first year of college; and

- play four seasons in your sport if you maintain your eligibility from year to year.

Division I Nonqualifier: As a nonqualifier, you will not be able to:

- practice or compete for your college or university during your first year of college; or

- receive an athletics scholarship during your first year of college, although you may receive need-based financial aid.

You may be able to play only three seasons in your sport if you maintain your eligibility from year to year. To earn a fourth season you must complete at least 80 percent of your degree requirements before beginning your fifth year of college.

Division II: 2010–July 31, 2013: If you enroll in a Division II college and want to participate in athletics or receive an athletics scholarship during your first year, you must:

- graduate from high school;

- complete these 14 core courses:

  - three years of English

  - two years of math (Algebra 1 or higher)

  - two years of natural or physical science (including one year of lab science if offered by your high school)

  - two additional years of English, math, or natural or physical science

  - two years of social science

  - three years of extra core courses (from any category above, or foreign language, nondoctrinal religion or philosophy);

- earn a 2.000 grade-point average or better in your core courses; and

- earn a combined SAT score of 820 or an ACT sum score of 68. For individuals enrolling at a college or university in Puerto Rico, earn a combined Prueba de Aptitud Academica score of 730.

August 1, 2013, And After: If you enroll in a Division II college on or after August 1, 2013, and want to participate in athletics or receive an athletics scholarship during your first year, you must:

- graduate from high school;

- complete these 16 core courses:

  - three years of English

  - two years of math (Algebra 1 or higher)

  - two years of natural or physical science (including one year of lab science if offered by your high school)

  - three additional years of English, math, or natural or physical science

  - two years of social science

  - four years of additional core courses (from any category above, or foreign language, nondoctrinal religion, or philosophy);

- earn a 2.000 grade-point average or better in your core courses; and

- earn a combined SAT score of 820 or an ACT sum score of 68. For individuals enrolling at a college or university in Puerto Rico, earn a combined Prueba de Aptitud Academica score of 730.

Division II Qualifier: Being a qualifier enables you to:

- practice or compete for your college or university during your first year of college;

- receive an athletics scholarship during your first year of college; and

- play four seasons in your sport if you maintain your eligibility from year to year.

Division II Partial Qualifier: You will be considered a partial qualifier if you do not meet all of the academic requirements listed above, but you have graduated from high school and meet one of the following:

- the combined SAT score of 820 or ACT sum score of 68; or
- completion of the 14 core courses with a 2.000 core course grade-point average.

As a partial qualifier, you:

- can practice with your team at its home facility during your first year of college;
- can receive an athletics scholarship during your first year of college;
- cannot compete during your first year of college; and
- can play four seasons in your sport if you maintain your eligibility from year to year.

Division II Nonqualifier: You will be considered a nonqualifier if you did not graduate from high school, or, if you graduated and are missing both the core course grade-point average or minimum number of core courses and the required ACT or SAT scores.

As a nonqualifier, you:

- cannot practice or compete for your college or university during your first year of college;
- cannot receive an athletics scholarship during your first year of college, although you may receive need-based financial aid; and
- can play four seasons in your sport if you maintain your eligibility from year to year.

Division III: Division III colleges and universities develop student athlete potential through a holistic educational approach that includes rigorous academics, competitive athletics, and opportunity to pursue many interests and passions. Student athletes are responsible for their own paths and are provided with many opportunities to develop within a comprehensive educational experience. Division III minimizes the conflicts between athletics and academics through shorter playing and practicing seasons, a lower number of contests, no redshirting or out-of-season organized activities, and a focus on regional in-season and conference play.

Division III college-bound student athletes are not certified by the Eligibility Center because Division III colleges and universities each set their own admissions standards and there are no initial eligibility requirements in the division. College-bound student athletes should contact their Division III college or university regarding policies on admission, financial aid, and athletics eligibility.

Remember

Remember: Meeting the NCAA academic requirements does not guarantee your admission into a college. You must apply for college admission.

It's A Fact!

Not all classes you take to meet high school graduation requirements may be used as core courses. Courses completed through credit-by-exam will not be used.

Core Courses, Grade-Point Average, Tests, And Special Conditions

What Is A Core Course?

A core course must:

- be an academic course in one or a combination of these areas: English, mathematics, natural/physical science, social science, foreign language, nondoctrinal religion or philosophy;

- be four-year college preparatory;

- be at or above your high school's regular academic level (no remedial, special education, or compensatory courses); and

- be completed not later than the high school graduation date of your class [as determined by the first year of enrollment in high school (ninth grade) or the international equivalent].

Check your high school's list of NCAA courses located on the Resources page of the Eligibility Center website at www.eligibilitycenter.org or ask your high school counselor.

Keep Track Of Your Courses, Units, And Credits: By logging onto www.eligibilitycenter .org and clicking the "Resources" tab, then "U.S. Students" and "Are You on Track?" you will find the Divisions I and II worksheets, which will help you keep track of your completed core courses, units, grades, and credits you received for them, plus your ongoing core course grade-point average. Generally, you will receive the same credit from the Eligibility Center as you received from your high school. Examples are provided in the English and math sections of both worksheets:

One trimester unit = 0.34 units

One semester unit = 0.50 units

One year = 1.0 unit

Nontraditional Courses

What Are Nontraditional Courses? Nontraditional courses are those taught through the internet (online or virtual), distance learning, independent study, individualized instruction, correspondence, computer software programs, or other similar means.

There are many types of nontraditional educational programs available to high school students. When considering an online, distance learning, correspondence, or even a credit recovery program, there are several things to consider. However, the following themes should be kept in mind:

- There is no substitute for working hard and staying on course academically.

- NCAA rules require that all core courses are academic, four-year college preparatory courses. Also, courses that are taught through distance learning, online, credit recovery, etc. need to be comparable in length, content, and rigor to courses taught in a traditional classroom setting.

- All courses must include ongoing access between the instructor and student, as well as regular interaction for purposes of teaching, evaluating, and providing assistance. This may include, for example, exchanging of e-mails between the student and teacher, feedback on assignments, and the opportunity for the teacher to engage the student in individual instruction.

- Any course taken must have a defined time period for completion. For example, it should be clear whether the course is meant to be taken for an entire semester or during a more condensed time frame, such as six weeks, etc.

- Nontraditional courses should be clearly identified as such on the high school transcript.

A Note On Credit Recovery Courses: Many high schools offer credit recovery or credit retrieval programs for students to receive credit or new grades for courses that they took previously or to take courses for the first time to get ahead or catch up. If your high school offers credit recovery, students need to make sure the following conditions are met:

- The school must follow its credit recovery policies, whether the student is an athlete or not. The Eligibility Center may request the policy if necessary.

- The credit recovery course must be comparable to the regular course. There are many examples in which the course the student failed was a rigorous, college-preparatory course, and the credit recovery course is taught at a lower level and lacks adequate rigor.

- The credit recovery course must meet the NCAA legislated definition of a core course (including the new nontraditional definition).

- The credit recovery course should be clearly identified as such on the high school transcript.

Core Course Grade-Point Average

How Your Core Course Grade-Point Average Is Calculated: The Eligibility Center will calculate the grade-point average of your core courses on a 4.000 scale. The best grades from classes taken on your school's list of NCAA courses will be used. Grades from additional core courses you took will be used only if they improve your grade-point average.

To determine your points earned for each course, multiply the points for the grade by the amount of credit earned. Use the following scale unless your high school has a different scale on file with the Eligibility Center:

> **Remember**
>
> Remember: The Eligibility Center does not use plus or minus grades when figuring your core course grade-point average. For example, grades of B+, B, and B- will each be worth three quality points.

A: Four points

B: Three points

C: Two points

D: One point

Special High School Grades And Grade-Point Average: If your high school uses numeric grades (such as 92 or 93), those grades will be changed to your high school's letter grades (such as A or B). See your high school's grading scale by pulling up your school's list of NCAA courses at www.eligibilitycenter.org.

If your high school normally "weights" honors or advanced courses, these weighted courses may improve your core course grade-point average. Your high school must notify the Eligibility Center of such weighting. To see if your high school has a weighted scale that is being used for calculating your core course grade-point average, visit www.eligibilitycenter.org for an explanation of how these grade weights are handled.

Examples of total quality point calculation:

- An A grade (four points) for a trimester course (0.34 units): 4 points x 0.34 units = 1.36 total quality points

- An A grade (four points) for a semester course (0.50 units): 4 points x 0.50 units = 2.00 total quality points

- An A grade (four points) for a full-year course (1.00 units): 4 points x 1.00 units = 4.00 quality points

Calculate Your Core Course Grade-Point Average: To calculate your estimated core course grade-point average, divide the total number of points for all of your core courses by the total number of core-course units you have completed.

Note: Your calculation helps you keep track of your core course grade-point average. Should you have any questions, contact your high school counselor.

Test-Score Requirements

ACT And SAT Requirements: You must achieve the required score on the SAT or ACT before your full-time collegiate enrollment. You must do this whether you are a citizen of the United States or of a foreign country. Also, state-administered ACT exams will be accepted by the Eligibility Center. You may take the national test.

Prueba De Aptitud Academica (Division II): If you enroll in a Division II college or university located in Puerto Rico, you may use a minimum combined score on the Prueba de Aptitud Academica verbal and math reasoning sections of 730 to satisfy the test-score requirement.

Taking Tests More Than Once: You may take the SAT or the ACT more than one time. If you take either test more than once, you may use your best subscore from different tests to meet the minimum test-score requirements.

Table 35.1 provides an example.

Table 35.1. Multiple Test Scores

	Math	Verbal/Critical Reading	Total Score
SAT (10/09)	350	470	820
SAT (12/09)	420	440	860
Scores used	420	470	890

> ### It's A Fact!
>
> Important Change: All SAT and ACT scores must be reported to the Eligibility Center directly from the testing agency. Test scores will not be accepted if reported on a high school transcript.
>
> When registering for the SAT or ACT, input the Eligibility Center code of 9999 to make sure the score is reported directly to the Eligibility Center.

Your test score will continue to be calculated using the math and verbal/critical reading subsections of the SAT and the math, science, English, and reading subsections of the ACT. The writing component of the ACT or SAT will not be used to determine your qualifier status.

Students With Education-Impacting Disabilities: Special Conditions

A student with an education-impacting disability must meet the same requirements as all other students, but may be provided certain accommodations to help meet those requirements. If you are a student with a diagnosed education-impacting disability, you will need to let the Eligibility Center know about your education-impacting disability only if you plan on using core courses after your eighth semester of high school and you plan on attending an NCAA Division I college or university. It is important to note that the accommodations provided to students with education-impacting disabilities for NCAA Division I schools are different than for Division II schools.

For Division I only, a student must graduate on time in order to use the following accommodations:

- Use up to three additional approved core courses taken before full-time enrollment in college.

For Division II only, students may use the following accommodations:

- Use any approved core courses taken before full-time enrollment in college.

For Divisions I and II, students may use the following accommodations:

- Use courses for students with education-impacting disabilities that are designated on the high school's list of NCAA courses.

- May take a nonstandard test to satisfy test score requirements.

To document your education-impacting disability, send the following documentation by mail to:

NCAA Eligibility Center
EID Services
P.O. Box 7110
Indianapolis, IN 46207-7110

Or fax to 317-968-5100:

- Copy of your professional diagnosis; and

- Copy of your EIP, ITP, 504 plan, or statement of accommodations. (One of the above documents should be dated within the last three years.)

Note: Students should complete their Eligibility Center registration prior to submitting this documentation to the Eligibility Center. Please include your NCAA ID number, home address, telephone number, and high school graduation year.

Once approved, you will be notified in writing and will be provided with additional information regarding what accommodations are available.

Please note that NCAA academic requirements are the same for all students, including students with an education-impacting disability. Additionally, the information outlined above is for students who intend to enroll in an NCAA Division I or II college or university within the next few years. Because NCAA regulations are subject to change, the NCAA encourages you to consider how delaying your enrollment may impact your eligibility. For additional information, including a cover sheet and the "Buckley Statement," which you may wish to complete to allow the Eligibility Center to speak to others about your education-impacting disability status, please access the "Frequently Asked Questions for Students with Education-Impacting Disabilities" page on www.NCAA.org.

Nonstandard Tests: If you have an education-impacting disability, you may also take a nonstandard test to satisfy test score requirements. Follow these guidelines:

- Register for accommodations as described by ACT or SAT, submitting a properly documented and confirmed diagnosis.

- Follow procedures governed by ACT or SAT. (The test may not be administered by a member of your high school athletics department or any NCAA school's athletics department.)

- If you take a nonstandard ACT or SAT, you may take the test on a date other than a national testing date, but you still must achieve the required test score.

- Your high school counselor can help you register to take a nonstandard test.

Core Courses: If you are a high school student with an education-impacting disability and have received help (for example, taken special classes or received extra time for tests) because of that education-impacting disability, you are eligible for the following:

- You may use a course that your high school has designed for students with education-impacting disabilities, if it appears on your high school's list of NCAA courses.

- You may take core courses any time before your enrollment as a full-time student in college, even during the summer after your last high school year. Remember, for Division I, you must document your education-impacting disability with the NCAA to receive this accommodation.

The GED

The General Education Development (GED) test may, under certain conditions, satisfy the graduation requirement, but it will not satisfy core course grade-point average or test score requirements. Contact the NCAA for information about GED submission.

Home School Students

Home-schooled students who plan to enroll in a Division I or II college must register with the Eligibility Center and must meet the same requirements as all other students.

International Students

If you are an international college-bound student athlete or if you have received any secondary schooling outside of the United States, please refer to the *Guide to International Academic Standards*, located in the "International Students" section on the Resources page of the Eligibility Center's website, www.eligibilitycenter.org.

Your Amateurism And You

If you want to participate in NCAA Division I or II athletics, you must also be certified as an amateur student athlete. The Eligibility Center will determine the amateurism eligibility of all freshman and transfer college-bound student athletes for initial participation at an NCAA Division I or II college or university. In Division III, certification of an individual's amateurism status is completed by each college or university, not the Eligibility Center.

When you register with the Eligibility Center, you will be asked questions about your athletics participation. The information you will provide will be reviewed and a determination will be made as to whether your amateurism status should be certified or if a penalty should be assessed before certification. If a penalty is assessed, you will have an opportunity to appeal the decision.

The following precollegiate enrollment activities may be reviewed:

1. Contracts with a professional team.

2. Salary for participating in athletics.

3. Prize money.

4. Play with professionals.

5. Tryouts, practice, or competition with a professional team.

6. Benefits from an agent or prospective agent.

7. Agreement to be represented by an agent.

8. Delayed initial full-time collegiate enrollment to participate in organized sports competition.

It's A Fact!

Additional information regarding NCAA amateurism rules is available on the Eligibility Center's website by logging on to www.eligibilitycenter.org, then clicking on the "Resources" link at the top of the page.

Athletically Related Financial Aid

Athletics scholarships are awarded by NCAA Divisions I and II institutions. Division III institutions do not award financial aid based on athletics ability, but you may be eligible to receive academic scholarships or need-based financial aid. It is important to understand several points about athletics scholarships. (**Note:** The information below is a summary and does not include all Divisions I and II financial aid rules. Contact your college or university to get more detailed information about NCAA financial aid rules.)

- Athletics scholarships in Divisions I and II are initially awarded for up to one academic year. In Division I, they may be renewed annually up to a total of five years of athletics aid within six years after initial enrollment in college. In Division II, they may be renewed up to a total of 10 semesters/15 quarters of athletics aid. But please keep in mind that your athletics aid can be reduced or not renewed at the end of each year.

- Athletics scholarships can be renewed, reduced, increased, or canceled from year to year for almost any reason. If your scholarship is going to be reduced or cancelled at any time, your college or university must first provide you with an opportunity to appeal that decision.

- Athletics scholarships are awarded in a variety of amounts, ranging from full scholarships (including tuition, fees, room, board, and books) to very small scholarships that, for example, provide only required course-related books.

- You must report all scholarships you receive to your college financial aid office. The total amount of financial aid a student athlete can receive and the total amount of athletics aid a team can award may be limited. These limits can affect whether a student athlete may accept additional financial aid from other sources. Ask financial aid officials at the college or university about other financial aid you may be eligible to receive and about the impact of that aid on athletics aid limits.

Quick Tip

An athletics scholarship is a tremendous benefit to most families, but you should have a plan to pay for those college costs not covered by a scholarship (e.g., travel between home and school). You should also consider how you will finance your education if your athletics scholarship is reduced or canceled.

Chapter 36

College Funding For Students With Disabilities

Attending college can be an exciting and enriching experience. It can also be a costly one. In addition to tuition, fees, books, and supplies, other expenses to think about include room and board, health insurance, transportation, and spending money. A combination of financial aid and other outside funding resources can help you meet college costs.

Common forms of financial aid include grants, loans, work-study, and scholarships. Some are available specifically to students with disabilities. Many students use a combination of these financial aid resources. It is important to remember that financial aid results in a partnership of the student, parents, postsecondary educational institutions, state and federal governments, and/or private organizations. Such a partnership requires cooperation, communication, and an understanding by each of their responsibilities within the financial aid process.

The financial aid office at the school you plan to attend is a good place to begin your search for financial aid information. An administrator there can tell you about student aid available from your state, the school itself, and other sources.

Federal Student Aid Programs

The programs described below are administered by the U.S. Department of Education and provide billions of dollars each year to students attending postsecondary schools. Not all schools participate in all federal student aid programs. Check with your high school guidance

About This Chapter: Information in this chapter is excerpted from "College Funding for Students with Disabilities," © 2011 University of Washington. Reprinted with permission from University of Washington DO-IT (Disabilities, Opportunities, Internetworking, and Technology). The complete text of this brochure, including information about disability-related scholarships, awards, and other resources, is available at http://www.washington.edu/doit/Brochures/PDF/financial-aid.pdf.

counselor or the financial aid officer at a postsecondary institution to make sure your destination school participates in the federal program(s) you are interested in.

Federal Pell Grants are available to undergraduate students only and they do not have to be repaid.

Federal Stafford Loans are based on financial need, are available to both undergraduate and graduate students, vary in maximum value each year of study, and must be repaid. The interest rate is variable. If you qualify (based on need) for a subsidized Stafford loan, the government will pay the interest on your loan while you are in school, during grace periods, and during any deferment periods.

Federal PLUS Loans are unsubsidized loans made to parents. If you are independent or your parents cannot get a PLUS loan, you are eligible to borrow additional Stafford Loan funds. The interest rate is variable.

Campus-Based Programs are administered by participating schools. Three of these programs are described below.

- Federal Supplemental Educational Opportunity Grants are grants available for undergraduates only and range in value.

- Federal Work-Study provides jobs to undergraduate and graduate students, allowing them to earn money to pay education expenses.

- Perkins Loans are low-interest loans that must be repaid; the maximum annual loan amount is greater for graduate students than for undergraduate students.

For more information on federal student aid programs consult http://www.studentaid.ed.gov/ or call the Federal Student Aid Information Center at 800-433-3243 or 800-730-8913 (TTY). An online application can be found at http://www.fafsa.ed.gov/.

Supplemental Security Income (SSI) And Plan For Achieving Self Support (PASS)

SSI is a program that pays monthly benefits to people with low incomes and limited assets who are 65 years of age or older, are blind, or have other disabilities. Children can qualify if they meet Social Security's definition of disability for SSI children and if their income and assets fall within the eligibility limits.

As its name implies, Supplemental Security Income supplements a person's income up to a certain level. The level varies from one state to another and may increase each year to reflect changes in cost of living. Your local Social Security office can tell you about SSI benefit levels in your state.

Parent income and assets are considered when deciding if a child under eighteen qualifies for SSI. This applies to children who live at home or who are away at school but return home occasionally and are subject to parental control. When a child turns eighteen, parent income and assets are no longer considered when determining eligibility for SSI. Therefore, a child who was not eligible for SSI before his or her eighteenth birthday may become eligible at age eighteen.

The Social Security Administration may also approve a Plan for Achieving Self Support (PASS), in which a student is able to set aside income and resources that are being used toward a specific vocational goal (such as college tuition) and still receive SSI payments. However, be aware that earnings from employment may affect SSI benefits.

For more information on SSI and PASS, contact your local Social Security Administration office or consult http://www.ssa.gov/disability/.

State Vocational Rehabilitation Services

Your state vocational rehabilitation (VR) office helps people with disabilities prepare for, obtain, and retain employment. Vocational rehabilitation programs are custom designed for each individual. Typically, you may be eligible for services if a VR counselor determines that you meet the following three conditions:

1. You have a physical or mental disability. The VR counselor must verify the disability by getting copies of medical records or by having you complete tests, examinations, or evaluations to verify the disability.

2. Your disability prevents you from getting or keeping a job.

3. You require vocational rehabilitation services to get or keep a job that matches your strengths, resources, priorities, concerns, abilities, capabilities, interests, and choices.

A state VR agency provides a wide range of services for helping clients get or keep jobs. VR services include assessment services, counseling and guidance, training (school), job- related services, rehabilitation technology (assistive technology), independent living, and a variety of support services.

Quick Tip

To locate a state vocational rehabilitation office near you, consult the state government listings in your phone book under "Vocational Rehabilitation" or consult http://www.disability.gov/employment/jobs_&_career_planning/vocational_rehabilitation.

Other State Programs

Nearly all states offer financial assistance in the form of state grants and loans. Details and information can be obtained from a college financial aid office or a high school guidance counselor. To find out which agency in your state may offer financial assistance for higher education, consult http://wdcrobcolp01.ed.gov/Programs/EROD/org_list.cfm?category_ID =SHE.

General Scholarships And Awards

Scholarships and awards provide monetary gifts based on a student's achievements, interests, background, or other criteria. A good first step in your scholarship search is to check with your parents' employers, local organizations, your high school guidance counselor, your college or university's financial aid office, the department chairman at your chosen school, and your college or the local library. Below you'll find other resources and tips that may help you locate financial aid.

Employers: Parents can check with personnel administrators to see if their employers offer financial aid, tuition reimbursement, or scholarships for employees' children. If you are employed or volunteering, ask your company if they offer scholarships.

Organizations: Many professional or social organizations offer scholarships. The Elks Club, for example, offers millions of dollars each year in scholarships for graduating high school students. Some labor unions (AFLCIO, Teamsters, etc.) offer scholarships for members and their dependent children. If you are not a member of an organization, check with organizations that are related to your chosen field of study. For example, if you plan to study aeronautical engineering, check with the American Institute of Aeronautics and Astronautics regarding college scholarships they offer.

Religious Groups: Your church or synagogue may have scholarships available. Also check with the headquarters of your religious affiliation.

Chamber Of Commerce: Your local Chamber of Commerce may offer small grants or scholarships to local students, often to those pursuing a career in business.

Take the PSAT: The Preliminary Scholastic Aptitude Test (PSAT)/National Merit Scholarship Qualifying Test (NMSQT) is co-sponsored by the College Board and National Merit Scholarship Corporation (NMSC). The PSAT/NMSQT gives you practice for the Scholastic Aptitude Test (SAT), as well as a chance to qualify for scholarship and recognition programs.

Search The Web: Run searches for "scholarships," "financial aid," "grants," etc.

AmeriCorps: AmeriCorps is a network of national service programs that engage more than 50,000 Americans each year in intensive service to meet critical needs in education, public safety, health, and the environment. AmeriCorps jobs are open to U.S. citizens, nationals, or lawful permanent residents aged seventeen or older. Members serve full or part time over a 10- to 12-month period. Participants receive an education award to pay for college or graduate school, or to pay back student loans. For more information, call 1-800-942-2677 (TTY 1-800-833-3722) or consult http://www.americorps.org/.

Chapter 37

Institutional Education Grants

Institutional Grant Aid: Public Institutions

Institutional grants that meet financial need increased much more rapidly than other financial aid at public four-year colleges and universities over the decade from 1999–2000 to 2009–10. These grants increased from 28% to 42% of total institutional discounts.

- The $410 average grant per full-time equivalent (FTE) student that exceeded financial need in 2009–10 at public four-year colleges went to students who, according to the need analysis methodology, could afford to pay the total cost of attendance without aid, or who had other aid that met their measured need.

- Tuition waivers may be based on either state or institutional policies and are generally awarded to special categories of students such as veterans, foster children, or displaced workers. Many of these individuals have financial need, as do many recipients of athletic grants.

- Institutional policies may contribute to the increase in the percentage of institutional grant aid that meets need, but that increase is at least partially caused by a combination of rising tuition and the impact of the recession on employment and family incomes.

- In 2007–08, about a quarter of public four-year colleges and universities discounted their tuition by less than 8%, while at the other end of the spectrum, about a quarter discounted their tuition by 24% or more. (Baum, Lapovsky, and Ma, *Tuition Discounting*, The College Board, 2010)

About This Chapter: Information in this chapter is from "Institutional Grant Aid" http://trends.collegeboard.org/downloads/student _aid/PDF/Institutional_Grants_over_Time.pdf. Trends in Student Aid. Copyright © 2010 The College Board. Reproduced with permission.

- In 2007–08, 15% of all undergraduates at public nondoctoral and 26% of all undergraduates at public doctoral four-year institutions received institutional grants. (NCES, NPSAS *Student Financial Aid Estimates*, 2009)

It's A Fact!

Colleges provide institutional grants to help make up the difference between college costs and what a family can be expected to contribute through income, savings, loans, and student earnings. Other institutional grants, known as merit awards or merit scholarships, are awarded on the basis of academic achievement. Some merit awards are offered only to students whose families demonstrate financial need; others are awarded without regard to a family's finances.

Source: From "Institutional Grants," a publication of the U.S. Department of Education, 2006.

Over two-thirds of institutional grant aid at private nonprofit four-year colleges and universities helps meet the financial need of students who could not otherwise afford to enroll. Another 10% is in the form of athletic awards or tuition waivers.

- The terms institutional grant aid, scholarships, and tuition discounts all refer to subsidies awarded to selected students that diminish the amount of tuition and fees they are required to pay.

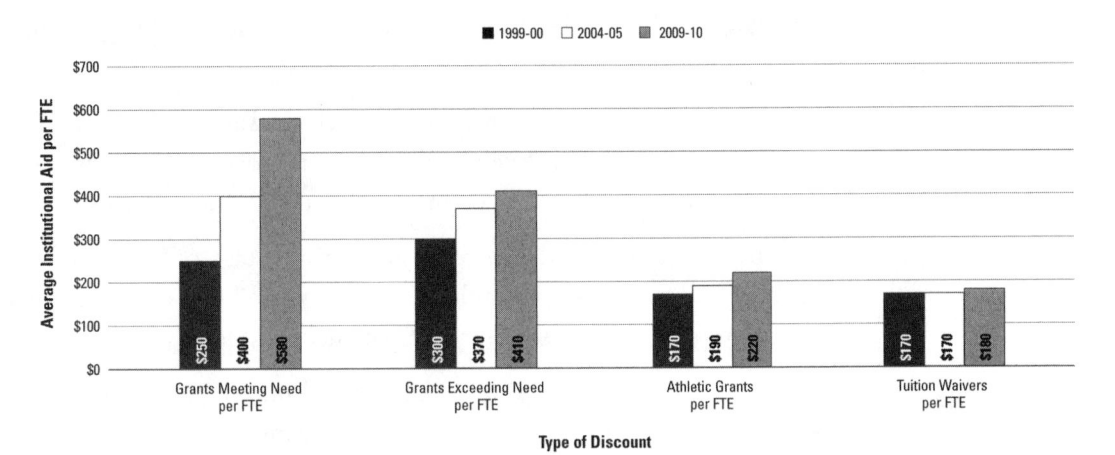

Figure 37.1. Institutional Grant Aid at Public Four-Year Colleges and Universities in Constant 2009 Dollars, 1999–2000, 2004–05, and 2009–10. (NOTE: Both grants awarded based on need and grants awarded without regard to financial circumstances that serve to meet documented need are considered "meeting need." The scale for Figure 37.1 is one-tenth of the scale for Figure 37.2. SOURCES: Annual Survey of Colleges, 2000–2010; calculations by the authors.)

> ## Quick Tip
>
> Some grants come with special privileges or obligations. You'll want to find out about the types of grants awarded by each college you are considering.
>
> Source: From "Institutional Grants," a publication of the U.S. Department of Education, 2006.

- In 2009–10, private nonprofit four-year institutions awarded an average of $6,440 per FTE student in grant aid meeting need and $2,060 in aid that exceeded financial need. This compares to $580 and $410, respectively, at public four-year institutions.

- Athletic grants and tuition waivers account for a small percentage of the discounts awarded by private nonprofit colleges and universities.

- As the cost of attending college rises more rapidly than family incomes, more students have financial need and more of the aid distributed for purposes other than meeting need ends up meeting need.

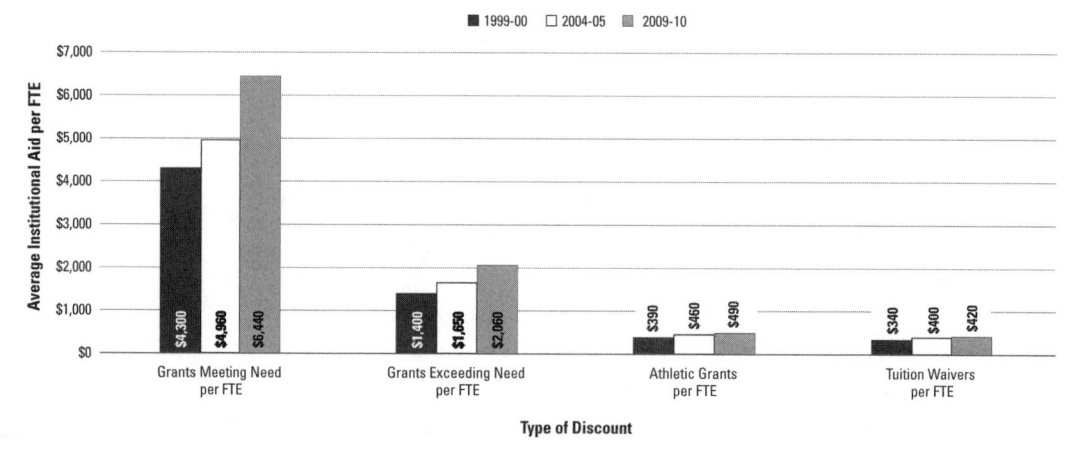

Figure 37.2. Institutional Grant Aid at Private Nonprofit Four-Year Colleges and Universities in Constant 2009 Dollars, 1999–2000, 2004–05, and 2009–10. (NOTE: Both grants awarded based on need and grants awarded without regard to financial circumstances that serve to meet documented need are considered "meeting need." The scale for Figure 37.1 is one-tenth of the scale for Figure 37.2. SOURCES: Annual Survey of Colleges, 2000–2010; calculations by the authors.)

- In 2007–08, about a quarter of private nonprofit four-year colleges and universities discounted their tuition by less than 25%, while at the other end of the spectrum, about a quarter discounted their tuition by 41% or more. (Baum, Lapovsky, and Ma, *Tuition Discounting*, The College Board, 2010)

- In 2007–08, 52% of all undergraduates at private nondoctoral and at private doctoral institutions received institutional grants. (NCES, NPSAS *Student Financial Aid Estimates*, 2009)

Chapter 38

Private Education Loans

Student Lending Analytics 2009 SLA Guide To Private (Or Alternative) Loans

1. **Exhaust all other sources of funding before looking for a private (last resort) loan.** Complete the Free Application for Federal Student Aid (FAFSA). Be sure to pursue scholarships, federal grants, work-study, and federal loan programs (Stafford, PLUS, and Grad PLUS) before applying for a private loan. Why? Federal loans typically carry lower fixed interest rates and they offer more flexible repayment options. For a useful comparison of PLUS and Private Loans, see number three.

2. **Find a cosigner…you will need it.** Find a creditworthy cosigner (for example, a parent, grandparent, aunt, uncle, or other relative) to increase the probability of having your loan approved while ensuring that you receive the lowest interest rate possible. Some lenders require a cosigner while others indicate that over 90% of their loans have a cosigner on the application. Without a cosigner, a private loan will be extremely difficult to obtain and even if you are lucky enough to be approved, you will likely pay dearly for this loan.

3. **Evaluate your alternatives; it can save you thousands.** Review your school's list of preferred private loan lenders (if available). Student Lending Analytics also provides the SLA Student Loan Ratings to assist you in finding the best private student loan. Be aware that obtaining a private loan requires credit approval and that certain lenders may restrict their lending activities to certain types of institutions or regional areas. Check

About This Chapter: This chapter includes the "2009 SLA Guide to Private (or Alternative) Loans," and "2009 SLA Private Loan Series: The Promissory Note," © 2009 Student Lending Analytics (http://studentlendinganalytics .typepad.com). Reprinted with permission.

your eligibility with lenders before applying. After doing your homework, complete applications for three to four lenders to provide you with some choices.

- Read about Fair Isaac's new policy change to learn about how shopping for loans over a 30-day period will protect your credit scores [www.myfico.com; search "student loans."]

- Read "Why Shopping For Student Loans Can Make A Big Difference!" to learn why it makes sense to comparison shop [Student Lending Analytics Blog, April 23, 2009; www. studentlendinganalytics.com].

- Once you have three to four choices, use a payment calculator, input interest rates, fees, and loan term to calculate which loan will work best for you.

4. **Your local credit union may be worth a shot.** With conservative financial management, credit unions have largely avoided the carnage that has afflicted the U.S. banking system. If you are a member of a credit union or belong to an affinity group that would qualify you for membership in a credit union, check out their private student loan offerings. Many universities have long-standing relationships with credit unions too.

5. **Certain states have private loan programs you may want to consider.** Be aware that certain states, such as Alaska, Connecticut, Hawaii, Maine, Massachusetts, Minnesota, New Jersey, North Carolina, North Dakota, Texas, and Vermont offer private loans to state residents and/or those attending schools in those states. Be sure to evaluate your state program's website for eligibility, interest rates, and loan terms. Compare these state programs with other alternatives. DO NOT assume because they are associated with the state that they are automatically the best private loan. Be aware that many of these programs have limited funds available, so be sure to apply early.

6. **Understand thy interest rate.** Interest rates on private student loans consist of an index (London Inter-Bank Offer Rate (LIBOR) or Prime Rate) and a Margin (e.g. +5%). To determine the starting interest rate on your loan, determine the lender's current Index and add the Margin. Be aware that almost all private loans are variable rate loans, which means that rates are adjusted monthly or quarterly and will go UP over the life of the loan. If history is any guide, expect that the average interest rate on your loan will be 2–3% higher than your starting interest rate.

7. **Select the repayment option that your financial situation allows for:**
- Want to save thousands of dollars in loan costs? Make interest payments on your loan while in school. Notify the lender that you would like to receive statements while in school to make these payments.

- Don't want to (or cannot) make payments while in school? Be sure that your lender (not all do) offers an in-school deferment option, which will allow you to postpone payments until after you graduate.

- Want to have the lowest monthly payment? Know the standard loan term offered by the lender. The longer the term, the lower the monthly payment but the more interest that you will pay over the life of the loan. Remember, despite having standard terms of 15–25 years, you always have the option to pay off your loan sooner without penalty.

8. **Once you take out this private loan, be aware that IT WILL NEED TO BE PAID BACK.** Like federal student loans, private loans may not be dischargeable in bankruptcy so be sure that you borrow responsibly and not beyond what you can reasonably expect to pay back.

9. **Sweat the details...read the Promissory Note.** Lurking inside that document could be a clause that allows a lender to raise your interest rates by 2–3% if you are late on one payment.

10. **Having second thoughts...you can always cancel the loan if you move quickly enough!** Review the Promissory Note closely to determine the loan cancellation terms, in terms of the timing and the steps required to cancel the loan.

2009 SLA Private Loan Series: The Promissory Note

Most people's eyes glaze over at just the mention of the topic of this information: the promissory note. Its multiple page legalese with six point font is easy to overlook. Most borrowers know it only as the document they have to sign to get "The Money." With most lenders now offering e-signature to speed the application process along, it is likely that fewer and fewer borrowers are actually reading its contents. This is unfortunate since the promissory note unlocks many secrets of the private student loan world. While promissory notes from various lenders share many similarities, there are also distinct differences that borrowers should be aware of when evaluating their options.

Let's tackle a few key questions that the promissory note answers:

What is the interest rate on my loan and how is it determined?

- Private loan interest rates typically have a variable rate, which incorporate an Index + Margin

    - The typical indices used for loans, which are spelled out in the promissory note, are one-month or three-month LIBOR or Prime Rate

    - Lenders will adjust this index on either a monthly or quarterly basis

    - To this index is added a margin (e.g. 7.0%), which typically remains constant over the life of the loan.

    - To calculate the actual starting interest rate, add the Index (e.g. 3.25% for Prime Rate) to the Margin (e.g. 3.75%) to get an actual rate of 7.0%.

- If the promissory note does not contain specifics about the current index and/or margin, then the lender is required to provide such information in a Disclosure Statement prior to the loan being consummated.

- **Example:** SunTrust indicates on the title page of their promissory note for cosigners listed the following:

    - **Margin:** 8.5%

    - **Variable Interest Rate:** One-month LIBOR + Margin

    - SunTrust's current one-month LIBOR figure can be found on their website in the footnotes at the bottom of a page describing their Academic Answer student loan: The current one-month LIBOR index was 0.625% on 4/1/09.

- So, if this loan were consummated in April, the starting interest rate on the loan would be 9.125%.

- **SLA Advice:** DO NOT sign a promissory note until you receive the interest rate and fees associated with your loan IN WRITING. If it doesn't appear on the promissory note, contact the lender directly and demand to have them send the interest rate and fees to you IN WRITING.

What fees will I be charged on the loan?

- This information is disclosed in both the promissory note and the Disclosure Statement which is required to be provided prior to loan consummation.

- Typical fees include (most common are first three listed):

  - **Origination And Repayment Fees:** Check to see if these fees will be added to loan principal which is typical. If so, be aware that these fees will incur finance charges for the life of the loan.

  - **Late Fees:** Fees assessed after a payment is not received during a certain number of days past the due date

  - **Payment Return Fee:** Fees if payment is returned or refused by bank for any reason

  - Fees to access loan payment history

  - Fees to expedite payment on the loan

  - Fees to send documents via express delivery or fax

  - Fees tied to forbearance

- **Example:** Wells Fargo includes the following specific disclosure of Other Charges in their promissory note: "I agree to pay the following charges for additional services I request (a) $5.00 per loan rating, loan verification, duplicate bill, or any document or letter, including (but not limited to) those indicating loan payment in full, loan status, or loan payment history for past 12 months, or copies of any Promissory Note or disclosures; (b) $10.00 per full loan payment history; (c) $15.00 per hour research fee (one hour minimum). I will also pay a handling charge of $15.00 for each payment on this loan that is returned for any reason, including (but not limited to) insufficient funds or stop payment order. I agree to have the charge(s) added to my next billing statement."

- **SLA Advice:** If the promissory note only includes general language about fees, contact the lender and indicate that you need to know all of the SPECIFIC loan fees PRIOR to signing the promissory note.

What repayment options are available to me?

- Most lenders offer borrowers three options to repay their loans, which are spelled out in the promissory note:

  - Interest only while in school

  - Immediate repayment while in school (principal and interest)

  - Full deferral: no payments while in school

- **Example:** From the SunTrust promissory note: "If the Student has elected the "Immediate Repayment" repayment option, there is no Deferment Period and my Loan payments will begin after the final Disbursement Date. If the Student has elected the "Interest Only" repayment option, then interest payments on my loan will begin after the first Disbursement Date and principal and interest payments on the Loan will begin after the Deferment End Date. If the Student has elected the "Full Deferral" repayment option, no payments of the Loan are required during the Deferment Period and principal and interest payments on the Loan will begin after the Deferment End Date on the date reflected in my Monthly Billing Statement."

- **SLA Advice:** While this decision may be glossed over when you apply for the loan, it should not be. If at all humanly possible, choose to pay interest on your loans during your in-school period since this will significantly reduce your total loan cost. I also recognize that this can be a challenge to students having constrained budgets. Having said that, there is certainly value to having a loan that has the flexibility to allow you to defer payments should situations warrant this need. Check with the lender to determine your flexibility to change your repayment option while you are in school. At a minimum, be sure that the lender is sending you statements during your in-school period so that you stay abreast of the loan.

It's A Fact!

Sallie Mae's Smart Option Loan is unique in that it does NOT offer a full deferral of payments.

Source: From "2009 SLA Private Loan Series: The Promissory Note," © 2009 Student Lending Analytics (http://studentlendinganalytics.typepad.com). Reprinted with permission.

How do I cancel my loan if I am unhappy with the final terms?

- All lenders allow borrowers to cancel their loan, however the deadlines and means to cancel the loan can differ between lenders as these examples indicate:

  - **Sallie Mae, from promissory note:** "Upon receipt of the Disclosure, I will review it and if I am not satisfied with the terms of my loan as approved, I may cancel this Note and all disbursements. To cancel this Note, I will call you at 1-888-2SALLIE within 10 business days of the date of the Disclosure and I will not cash any loan checks, or if funds are transmitted electronically or by master check, I will instruct the School, within 10 business days of the date of the Disclosure, to return the funds to you."

  - **Wells Fargo, from promissory note:** "To cancel, I must contact you within three days of receiving the Loan Disclosures and take the following steps: not endorse or cash any loan disbursements check, notify the School of the loan cancellation, and ensure that any loan disbursements are returned to you."

How will the lender apply by monthly payments should I wish to pay down my principal?

- Most lenders will take your monthly payment and pay down your loan in the following order:

  - Late fees and other charges

  - Accrued Interest

  - Principal

- Be aware that some lenders may have different policies:

  - **Example:** Sallie Mae indicates the following policy in their promissory note: "Payments will be applied first to applicable fees, charges, and costs; then to accrued interest; and the remainder to principal, as permitted by applicable law. Payments in excess of the amount due will advance the next payment due date by the number of whole payments satisfied by the extra funds. (For example, if my monthly payment is $100, I am not delinquent, and I pay $400 for the month of January, my next payment due date will be May.")

- **SLA Advice:** Contact the lender directly if you are interested in paying down principal (making extra payments) on your student loan. Find out what notice you need to provide them to ensure that payments are applied to principal rather than used to pay off future payments.

317

How frequently should I expect my monthly payment to change?

- Unlike a fixed rate loan, a variable rate loan will change as the underlying index changes (Prime Rate or LIBOR). For those borrowers who sign up for electronic payment of their loans, this can often be a surprise that the monthly payment on their private loan changes.

- Lenders take three approaches to setting monthly payment amounts from most to least confusing:

  - **Example:** Sallie Mae adjusts their Index monthly while resetting monthly payment due by the borrowers on a quarterly basis. Here is how they explain this confusing feature of their loans: "You will revise the repayment schedule so that it provides for consecutive monthly payments of principal and interest in the amounts necessary to repay, over the number of months remaining in the Repayment Period, any accrued but unpaid interest, as well as the unpaid principal and interest at the Variable Rate then in effect, with the payment amount changing in the months of February, May, August, and November, as necessary. The statements that you send me will reflect any changes in the amounts of these monthly payments."

  - Other lenders change the monthly payment due by borrowers at the same interval that they change their Index

  - Other lenders keep monthly payments fixed on an annual basis, readjusting them just once a year to minimize borrower confusion.

A question no borrowers want to consider: What happens if I default on my loan?

- First, borrowers need to be aware of what constitutes a default. Many would be surprised to see the following conditions that lenders indicate in their promissory notes constitute default (note that there are few instances where a lender actually forces a borrower into default with one late payment but they DO have that power):

  - **Wells Fargo:** "I fail to make any monthly payments to you within 10 days after it is due."

  - **Discover:** "If you do not make any payment before or on the date it is due."

  - **Citibank:** "Fail to make my monthly payment to you when due."

- In terms of what happens after the borrower defaults, the short answer is nothing good. Here is a sampling of what lenders tell us in their promissory notes:

- **Citibank:** "If I default, I will also be responsible to pay reasonable collection costs, including reasonable attorney's charges, court costs, and collection charges to the extent allowed by the law."

- **Chase:** "To the extent permitted by applicable law, if you default, we can, at our option: (a) accelerate the Repayment Start Date prior to the Deferment End Date; or (b) demand that you pay all you owe under this Agreement at once; and (c) take any reasonable action to prevent loss by us; and (d) exercise any other legal or equitable remedies available to us. To the extent permitted by law, if you default you will pay our actual collection fees and costs, our actual outside attorneys' fees, and other court costs."

Chapter 39

AmeriCorps Education Awards

About AmeriCorps

AmeriCorps is an opportunity to make a big difference in your life and in the lives of those around you. It's a chance to apply your skills and ideals toward helping others and meeting critical needs in the community.

Each year, AmeriCorps offers 75,000 opportunities for adults of all ages and backgrounds to serve through a network of partnerships with local and national nonprofit groups. Whether your service makes a community safer, gives a child a second chance, or helps protect the environment, you'll be getting things done through AmeriCorps.

AmeriCorps members address critical needs in communities all across America. As an AmeriCorps member, you can do the following:

- Tutor and mentor disadvantaged youth
- Fight illiteracy
- Improve health services
- Build affordable housing
- Teach computer skills
- Clean parks and streams
- Manage or operate after-school programs
- Help communities respond to disasters
- Build organizational capacity

About This Chapter: Information in this chapter is from the following 2010 publications of Americorps.gov: "What is AmeriCorps?" "Segal AmeriCorps Education Award," "Amount, Eligibility, and Limitations," "Using the Segal AmeriCorps Education Award," "Postponing Student Loan Payments And Getting Interest Paid," and "Tax Implications."

Benefits Of Service

As an AmeriCorps member, you'll gain new skills and experiences—and you'll also find the tremendous satisfaction that comes from helping others. In addition, full-time members who complete their service earn a Segal AmeriCorps Education Award to pay for college or graduate school, or to pay back qualified student loans; members who serve part time receive a partial Award. Some AmeriCorps members may also receive a modest living allowance during their term of service.

The College Cost Reduction and Access Act of 2007 created two new federal programs: a new Public Service Loan Forgiveness program and a new Income-Based Repayment plan (IBR) for the repayment of federal loans. The new Income-Based Repayment plan helps to make repaying education loans more affordable for low-income borrowers, such as an AmeriCorps member living on a stipend; AmeriCorps service is also recognized as equivalent to a public service job for the purposes of the Public Service Loan Forgiveness program.

AmeriCorps Programs

AmeriCorps is made up of three main programs: AmeriCorps State and National, AmeriCorps VISTA, and AmeriCorps NCCC (National Civilian Community Corps).

AmeriCorps State And National: AmeriCorps State and National supports a broad range of local service programs that engage thousands of Americans in intensive service to meet critical community needs.

AmeriCorps VISTA: AmeriCorps VISTA provides full-time members to community organizations and public agencies to create and expand programs that build capacity and ultimately bring low-income individuals and communities out of poverty.

AmeriCorps NCCC: The AmeriCorps National Civilian Community Corps (NCCC) is a full-time residential program for men and women, ages 18–24, that strengthens communities while developing leaders through direct, team-based national and community service.

Segal AmeriCorps Education Award

After successfully completing a term of service, AmeriCorps members who are enrolled in the National Service Trust are eligible to receive a Segal AmeriCorps Education Award. You can use your education award to pay education costs at qualified institutions of higher education, for educational training, or to repay qualified student loans. The Edward M. Kennedy Serve America Act made changes to the maximum amount of the Segal AmeriCorps

Education Award. The amount is now tied to the maximum amount of the U.S. Department of Education's Pell Grant. For terms of service that are approved using 2009 funds (or earlier funds) the award continues to be $4,725.00 for a year of full-time service, and is prorated for part-time service based on the full-time amount. For terms of service that are supported with 2010 funds the award value increased to $5,350.00. For terms of service that are supported with 2011 funds the award value increased to $5,550.00 You can make payments from your award in full or part, and can take up to seven years after your term of service has ended to use your award. To confirm the award amount for which you are eligible, call your program or project sponsor.

AmeriCorps VISTA

If you successfully complete a term of service in VISTA, you are eligible to receive either a Segal AmeriCorps Education Award or an end-of-service stipend of $1,500. The Segal AmeriCorps Education Award option is subject to available education trust allocations to AmeriCorps VISTA. You must select the Segal AmeriCorps Education Award option prior to the start of service.

Amount Of The Segal AmeriCorps Education Award

One of the important changes to the Segal AmeriCorps Education Award under the Serve America Act is how the value of the award is determined. Beginning with terms of service that are supported with 2010 funds, the amount of a full-time education award will be equivalent to the maximum value of the Pell Grant for the award year in which the term of service was funded. Because AmeriCorps State and National programs are funded on a different schedule than VISTA and NCCC, VISTA and NCCC members will be eligible for the new amount sooner than AmeriCorps State and National members.

- Because the AmeriCorps State and National education award amount is dependent upon the year in which the Corporation approved the program's positions, members must contact their program to ascertain the education amount for which they are eligible.

- All VISTA and NCCC members who enrolled between October 1, 2009 and September 30, 2010 will be eligible for awards based on a full-time award amount of $5,350.

- All VISTA and NCCC members who enroll between October 1, 2010 and September 30, 2011 will be eligible to receive awards based on the maximum value of the Pell Grant this year—$5,550.

- Because the maximum value of the Pell Grant can change every year, the amount of a full-time award can change in the future. However, once a member earns an award, the value of that award will not increase.

- For all programs, award amounts for part-time terms of service vary based upon the length of the required term of service.

- Payments made from Segal AmeriCorps Education Awards are considered taxable income in the year that the corporation makes the payment to the school or loan holder.

- A member serving in a full-time term of service is required to complete the service within 12 months.

Eligibility

You are eligible for a Segal AmeriCorps Education Award if you successfully complete your term of service in accordance with your member contract with one of the following approved AmeriCorps programs:

- AmeriCorps State and National

- AmeriCorps VISTA

- AmeriCorps NCCC

Alternative To The Segal AmeriCorps Education Award

As an alternative to the Segal AmeriCorps Education Award, AmeriCorps VISTA members may choose to take a postservice cash stipend instead.

Only AmeriCorps VISTA alumni who choose the stipend and have student loans may be eligible for up to 15% cancellation on certain types of loans. To determine what student loans may be eligible for cancellation and to receive forms, contact the U.S. Department of Education at 1-800-433-3243. AmeriCorps VISTA members who choose the education award may not claim a partial cancellation.

It's A Fact!

For All Members: You can check with your program or project sponsor to confirm the value of the award for which you are eligible.

Source: From "Amount, Eligibility, and Limitations," a publication of Americorps.gov, 2010.

Award Limitations

Currently, the maximum number of terms that you can serve are four for AmeriCorps State and National, three for VISTAs, and two for NCCC. Full-time, half-time, reduced half-time, quarter-time, and minimum-time terms of service each count as one term of service.

- Generally, if you are released for cause before completing your term of service and do not receive an education award, that term of service counts as one of your terms.

- The Trust does not make payments to anyone other than qualified schools and loan holders. See your financial aid counselor for information on how they handle disbursements and reimbursements.

- If you withdraw from the school at which you have used the education award, the school may be required to refund the Trust. If any refund is owed, it is credited to your education award account, and is subject to the award's original expiration date (seven years from the date the award was earned). For general information on how withdrawing from school may affect your student financial aid, ask your financial aid counselor or refer to the U.S. Department of Education's *Federal Student Aid Handbook*.

- Under certain circumstances, you can use the education award to study outside the U.S. Contact the National Service Trust/AmeriCorps Hotline at 1-800-942-2677 for further information.

- You have seven years to use the education award from the date of your completion of service. You can divide up your award and use portions of it at different times, as long as it is for authorized expenditures within the specified time period. You could, for example, apply a portion of it to existing qualified student loans, and save the remainder to pay for authorized college costs a few years down the road.

Award Transfers

The Serve America Act now allows for the transfer of AmeriCorps State and National and Silver Service education awards under certain conditions. The person who earned the award has to have been at least 55 years old when they began the term of service and the person to whom the award is transferred has to be the transferring individual's child, grandchild, or foster child.

To transfer an award, an individual must have done or do the following:

- Have earned an education award in an AmeriCorps State and National or a Silver Scholar term of service

- Have been at least 55 years of age before beginning the term of service for which the award is attached

- Have begun this term of service on or after October 1, 2009

- Transfer the award before the expiration date

- Designate all or a portion of the unused award for the transfer

- Complete the required paperwork authorizing the transfer, which includes providing information and certifying eligibility to make the transfer

Using The Segal AmeriCorps Education Award

You can use your Segal AmeriCorps Education Award, Silver Scholar Education Award, or Summer of Service Education Award in any of the following ways—or a combination of them.

Repay Qualified Student Loans: The national service legislation defines a qualified student loan as a loan backed by the federal government under Title IV of the Higher Education Act (except PLUS Loans to parents of students), or under Titles VII or VIII of the Public Health Service Act.

Segal AmeriCorps Education Awards may not be used to repay any other type of loan, even if the loan was obtained for educational purposes. You can use your Segal AmeriCorps Education Award to repay defaulted student loans as long as the loans meet the definition of qualified student loan.

Pay Current Educational Expenses At A Qualified School: Current educational expenses, as authorized under 42 U.S.C. § 12604(c), include the following:

- The cost of attendance (COA) for a degree- or certificate-granting program of study at a qualified school

- Educational expenses for nondegree courses offered by qualified schools, such as continuing education courses

It's A Fact!

You may also use your Segal AmeriCorps Education Award to repay a student loan made to you by a state agency, including state institutions of higher education.

Source: From "Using the Segal AmeriCorps Education Award," a publication of Americorps.gov, 2010.

Your school is qualified if it is a Title IV institution of higher education. This means that it participates in the U.S. Department of Education's Title IV Student Aid Programs. Students who attend the school are eligible for federal student aid.

Current educational expenses are expenses that were incurred after you became an AmeriCorps member.

For degree or certificate programs of study, the cost of attendance (COA) may include tuition, books and supplies, transportation, room and board, and other expenses. A school's financial aid office determines each student's COA based upon standard federal legislation and guidance.

Pay Current Educational Expenses While Participating In An Approved School-To-Work Program: The school-to-work program sunsetted in 2001 and is therefore not an available use for the education award.

Postponing Student Loan Payments And Getting Interest Paid

Forbearance: Individuals who are serving in a term of service in an approved AmeriCorps or Silver Scholar position may be eligible to postpone the repayment of their qualified student loans through an action called loan forbearance. While your loan is in forbearance during your term of service, interest continues to accrue. However, If you successfully complete your term of service the National Service Trust will pay all or a portion of the interest that accrued on your qualified student loans during your service period.

You can request to postpone the repayment of your qualified student loans during your service period. You can easily and quickly request the forbearance online through My AmeriCorps. After you finish your term of service, you will be responsible for repaying your loan according to the terms of the loan.

Eligibility For Forbearance: Individuals in approved AmeriCorps or Silver Scholar positions are eligible for forbearance for most federally guaranteed student loans. If your loan holder tells you that your student loan does not qualify for forbearance based upon your national service, ask if your service qualifies you for some other type of forbearance or for a deferment.

The corporation cannot approve or disapprove forbearance requests; it can only verify that you are in an approved national service position. Only the loan holder can determine your loan's eligibility for forbearance. If your loan is in default, it may not be eligible for forbearance. However, if you have loans that had gone into default before you began your national service, you can attempt to negotiate an arrangement with the loan holder or collection agency to bring the loan out of default so forbearance can be granted and interest can be paid.

How To Apply For Forbearance: After you have enrolled in an AmeriCorps project, you can go into your account in My AmeriCorps. In your home page, click on the "Create Forbearance" link at the top of the page to bring up the page to request forbearance. Follow the instructions. You will select your current term of service and identify the holder of your student loan. When you click on "submit," a request will be sent electronically to your loan company. This request will verify your involvement in AmeriCorps and request that your qualified loans be put in forbearance during your service period.

Your loan holder will notify you when they have acted upon your request. You should contact your loan holder if you have not heard from them within four weeks of submitting your information online.

If your loan company has not registered in My AmeriCorps, they will not be on the list of institutions in the system. You should click on the institution "Not Found" link and follow the directions.

Interest Payments: Individuals who have successfully completed a term of service in AmeriCorps or Silver Scholars are eligible to have the Trust pay as much as 100% of the interest that accrued on their qualified student loan during their service. The portion that the Trust will pay is determined by the type of service (full or part time) and the length of your service period. The Trust will only pay interest on qualified student loans.

The Trust will not pay interest if you fail to complete your term of service. Exceptions will be made only if you fail to complete your term of service for compelling personal circumstances and you have earned a prorated award. It is up to your individual program to determine compelling personal circumstances. Examples that might be considered are a serious illness or injury, death of your immediate family member, or early closing of your project. An interest payment can only be made after you have completed your service and have earned an award.

Interest payments are in addition to your education award; they are not deducted from your education award amount. Interest payments are based upon the interest that accrued only during the time you were serving in the AmeriCorps program.

How To Apply For An Interest Payment: After you have completed your service and received notification of your award, you can go into your account in My AmeriCorps. In your home page, click on the "Create Interest Accrual" link at the top of the page to bring up the page to request the payment. Follow the instructions. You will select the appropriate term of service and type of loan and identify the holder of your student loan. When you click on "submit," a notice will be sent electronically to your loan company. A record of your request will appear in your account home page.

Remember

Remember that interest payments, as well as payments made from your education award account, are considered by the Internal Revenue Service (IRS) to be taxable income in the year in which a payment is made.

Source: From "Postponing Student Loan Payments And Getting Interest Paid," a publication of Americorps.gov, 2010.

This notice will verify your involvement in national service and request that the loan holder provide AmeriCorps with the amount of interest that accrued between your start date and end date of your service period. The loan company will provide additional information, then certify and submit the information electronically to AmeriCorps.

When the interest payment has been made, it will show up in your account. It should also show up in your account statement that the loan company provides to you. These payment requests may need to be processed manually through paper forms and may take several weeks to complete.

Tax Implications

Segal AmeriCorps Education Award: The Segal AmeriCorps Education Award, unlike most other forms of scholarships and fellowships, is subject to federal tax in the year the payment is made. When and how much of the education award you redeem may have an impact on your overall income tax responsibility.

If the Trust makes a payment on qualified student loans to your school or lender for the entire amount of a full-time education award in one calendar year, you will be responsible for any income taxes owed in that calendar year on the entire amount. If you redeem only a portion of your education award in one calendar year, you will be responsible for any taxes owed on that portion. Interest that is paid on qualified student loans is also subject to income taxes in the year it is paid.

The Trust DOES NOT deduct taxes from your education award or interest payments. If your education award and interest payments total more than $600.00 in a calendar year, in January of the following year, the Corporation will send you a Form 1099 to be used in preparing your income tax return. The total sum of interest payments and the Segal AmeriCorps Education Award payments are listed together on the 1099 form.

Living Allowance: You are responsible for any income taxes owed on any AmeriCorps living allowances you receive. The living allowance amount received in a calendar year is subject to income taxes for that calendar year. For example, if you receive a partial living allowance in 2009 and the rest in year 2010, the portion received in 2009 is subject to 2009 income taxes, and the portion received in 2010 is subject to 2010 income taxes.

After the calendar year in which you earned any living allowance, your AmeriCorps project will send you a W-2 form indicating the amount of the allowance you earned in that year. Most AmeriCorps VISTA and AmeriCorps NCCC members receive their W-2 forms from the corporation.

Tax Relief: While you are responsible for taxes on your education award and other AmeriCorps benefits, you may be eligible for other tax relief through the Taxpayer Relief Act of 1997. Issues about income taxes are very complicated. The important point to remember is that you should consider the tax consequences of any decisions you make about when and how to use your education award. Contact a tax professional or the Internal Revenue Service for details.

It's A Fact!

IRS Publication 970, *Tax Benefits for Education*, explains tax benefits that may be available to members who are using education awards to pay for current educational expenses or to repay qualified student loans.

Source: From "Postponing Student Loan Payments And Getting Interest Paid," a publication of Americorps.gov, 2010.

Chapter 40

The Peace Corps Offers Leadership Experience And Financial Benefits

The Peace Corps traces its roots and mission to 1960, when then Senator John F. Kennedy challenged students at the University of Michigan to serve their country in the cause of peace by living and working in developing countries. From that inspiration grew an agency of the federal government devoted to world peace and friendship.

Since that time, nearly 200,000 Peace Corps volunteers have served in 139 host countries to work on issues ranging from AIDS education to information technology and environmental preservation.

Today's Peace Corps is more vital than ever, working in emerging and essential areas such as information technology and business development, and contributing to the President's Emergency Plan for AIDS Relief. Peace Corps volunteers continue to help countless individuals who want to build a better life for themselves, their children, and their communities.

Financial Benefits And Loan Deferment

During service, Peace Corps volunteers receive pay to cover living and housing expenses, earn money for their transition after service, get vacation time, and have options for possible deferment or partial cancellation of student loans. Peace Corps covers the travel costs to and from the country of service.

About This Chapter: This chapter includes information from the following publications of peacecorps.gov: "About Us," September 2010; "Financial Benefits and Loan Deferment," October 2010; "Instructions for Student Loans," March 2011; "Loan Deferment FAQ," July 2010; and "Educational Benefits," November 2010.

> ## It's A Fact!
> Unlike other international volunteer programs, there is not a fee to participate in the Peace Corps.
>
> Source: From "Financial Benefits and Loan Deferment," a publication of peacecorps.gov, October 2010.

Pay And Living Expenses

The Peace Corps provides volunteers with a living allowance that enables them to live in a manner similar to the local people in their community, covering housing, food, and incidentals.

Transition Funds

Returning from overseas requires some adjustment. To assist with the transition back home, volunteers are paid $7,425 (before taxes) at the close of 27 months of service. This money is yours to use as you wish: for travel, a vacation, making a move, or securing housing.

Vacation Time

Volunteers receive two vacation days per month of service, a total of 48 days over two years. Many use this time to travel to nearby countries, expanding their opportunities for adventure and cross-cultural experiences. Some invite family or friends to visit so they can share their experience of the host country with loved ones. And of course, volunteers can use this time for a visit home (at their own expense).

Deferment Of Student Loans

Volunteers may defer repayment of student loans under several federal programs, i.e., Stafford (formerly known as guaranteed student loans), Perkins, direct, and consolidation loans. Some commercial loans may also be deferred during Peace Corps service. Because the rules that authorize deferment are complicated and subject to change, it is best to talk to a Peace Corps recruiter about how this benefit applies to your situation.

Cancellation Of Student Loans

Only volunteers with Perkins loans are eligible for a partial cancellation benefit. Fifteen percent of your Perkins loans can be cancelled upon the completion of each 365 days of service during your first two years of service, and 20 percent can be cancelled upon completion of each of the third and fourth years. Therefore, four full years of service would equal a 70 percent cancellation of your existing loan.

Instructions For Student Loans

Volunteers who have outstanding debts under one of the federally administered or guaranteed student loan programs qualify for certain relief during their Peace Corps service. The regulations that authorize this relief are complicated, and different rules apply to each type of loan. The information in this chapter will help you to take advantage of the full range of benefits to which you are entitled.

Loan Deferment

It is your responsibility to apply for student loan deferment. YOU must contact your lending institution(s) and request appropriate forms. Take your deferment papers to staging with you; do not send them to the Peace Corps. The Peace Corps cannot verify that you are a volunteer until you arrive at staging.

Student loans may be deferred for the full period of your volunteer service, up to 27 months. Your lender may grant you a deferment for the full 27 months, or require you to reapply for a deferment every 12 months. You must contact your lender to determine the length of your deferment. If you extend your service, deferral of up to three years is available, but you must apply for this separately. Your country director will certify deferment forms for the second and possibly third years of service.

When determining benefits that are available, you must consider each type of loan and the principal and interest components individually. You can defer principal payments on Perkins Loans (National Direct Student Loans [NDSLs]) and Federal Direct Loans (including Federal Consolidation Loans, Stafford Loans, and Guaranteed Student Loans [GSLs]).

Interest Payments

Even though your principal payment is deferred, you must make interest payments on the following unsubsidized loans during your Peace Corps Service: Stafford Loans, Federal Consolidation Loans that include unsubsidized loans, and Federal Direct Loans. You may opt to apply to your lender for forbearance on the interest payment for these loans.

Quick Tip

Take extra deferment forms with you if your deferment must be certified annually.

Source: From "Instructions for Student Loans," a publication of peacecorps.gov, March 2011.

The Department of Education pays the interest during the period of deferment for subsidized Stafford Loans and subsidized Federal Consolidation Loans.

The Department of Education does not charge interest during the period of deferment for Perkins Loans and subsidized Federal Direct Loans.

As a volunteer, you may authorize payments of up to $206.25 per month from your readjustment allowance to cover interest due on your student loans.

Privacy Act Waiver

The Peace Corps strongly recommends signing the Privacy Act Waiver enclosed in the Invitation Kit. The Privacy Act Waiver gives the Peace Corps the ability to discuss and release financial information to a family member or friend that you designate. If questions arise about your student loan in your absence (i.e. request for service verification for deferment or payments made to your loan from your readjustment allowance) it is advantageous to have a local contact to handle these issues. If you do not have a signed Privacy Act Waiver on file with Peace Corps, we will not discuss your student loan or financial issues with anyone other than yourself.

The Peace Corps' Role

The Peace Corps' role in the loan deferment process is limited to certification of your dates and country of service and authorization of deductions from your monthly readjustment allowance. The Peace Corps does not grant or deny deferments of loans.

Loan Types And Benefits

Perkins Loans: The following information applies to Perkins Loans.

- Volunteers qualify for a 15 percent loan cancellation for each of their first two years of service and a 20 percent loan cancellation for their third and fourth years of service. Up to 70 percent of a Perkins Loan may be canceled. It is important to note that a volunteer must serve one complete year (365 days) in order to qualify for this cancellation benefit. Partial years of service will not qualify.

It's A Fact!

PLEASE NOTE that training time is included in the year of service that is eligible for the partial Perkins loan cancellation benefit.

Source: From "Instructions for Student Loans," a publication of peacecorps.gov, September 2008.

- If you consolidate your Perkins loan with other student loans, you will lose the cancellation benefit. Once a Perkins loan is consolidated, it is no longer considered a Perkins loan and therefore is ineligible for cancellation. If you are looking to combine several student loans, do not include the Perkins loan if you are interested in the cancellation benefit.

- The Department of Education does not charge interest during the deferment period.

- Volunteers qualify for a deferment of principal payments during their Peace Corps service and for six months immediately after their service ends. For Perkins Loans obtained before July 1, 1993, this relief is limited to three years of Peace Corps service, but for loans obtained on or after that date, it is available for the entire period of a volunteer's service.

Stafford Loans Guaranteed Student Loans or GSLs: The following information applies to Stafford Loans.

- Volunteers qualify for a deferment of principal payments for up to three years during Peace Corps service.

- The Department of Education pays interest on subsidized Stafford Loans during the deferment period.

Federal Direct Loans: The following information applies to Federal Direct Loans.

- Volunteers qualify for a deferment of principal payments for up to three years during Peace Corps service.

- The Department of Education does not charge interest on subsidized Federal Direct Loans during the deferment period.

- Volunteers with unsubsidized Federal Direct Loans must pay interest during service or apply to the Department of Education for forbearance.

Federal Consolidation Loans

- Volunteers with Federal Consolidation Loans qualify for a deferment of principal payments for up to three years during service.

- The Department of Education pays interest on subsidized Federal Consolidation Loans.

- Volunteers with Federal Consolidation Loans that include unsubsidized loans must pay interest during the deferment period or apply to their lender.

- If you have consolidated your loans or are thinking about doing so before you leave, it is important to discuss with your lender how this will affect your Peace Corps loan deferment/cancellation benefit. Some loans may not qualify for deferment once consolidated but will instead be placed in a forbearance status where the borrower is still expected to pay interest payments during their service. Be sure to verify all the details with your lender before attending staging.

Loan Deferment Information

Responsibility

You (or your power of attorney) are completely responsible for your loans. All matters of deferment, payment, reactivation, and cancellation of loans following your service are your responsibility.

The Peace Corps does not pay student loans. However, the Peace Corps does make it possible to apply a portion of your readjustment allowance each month toward debt repayment. Many volunteers use this to pay the interest on their unsubsidized loans; arrangements can be made during preservice training.

Loan Cancellation

Only volunteers with Perkins loans are eligible for a partial cancellation benefit. Fifteen percent of your Perkins loans can be cancelled upon the completion of each full year of service during your first two years of service, and 20 percent can be cancelled upon completion of each of the third and fourth years. Therefore, four full years of service would equal a 70 percent cancellation of your existing loan. You can apply for cancellation at the end of each completed 12 months of consecutive service. A volunteer must serve one complete year (365 days) in order to qualify for this cancellation benefit. Partial years of service will not qualify. Please note that you cannot receive partial cancellation of your Perkins loan if you have consolidated it with any other loan.

Deferment

Getting your student loans deferred while serving in the Peace Corps depends upon the policies of your lending institution(s). The Peace Corps does not have the power to grant loan deferments; we can only verify that you are in the Peace Corps serving as a volunteer. It is at the discretion of your lender whether or not deferments are granted for Peace Corps service. Check with your lending institution(s) to determine if Peace Corps service makes you eligible for deferment.

> ## It's A Fact!
>
> The Peace Corps does not defer student loans, nor does it provide loan deferment applications. To get your loans deferred, you must apply to your lending institution(s). Always contact your lenders directly to get the specific details of what they require.
>
> Source: From "Loan Deferment FAQ," a publication of peacecorps.gov, July 2010.

Forbearance Versus Deferment

Deferment means that your loans do not have to be repaid until after your service. If your loans are subsidized, you will not have to pay interest. Forbearance also means that you do not have to repay your loans until after your service, but interest may accrue. To determine what is necessary to ensure your loans are deferred, contact your lending institution(s) and ask them what forms you must complete.

Necessary Forms

Different lenders require different forms so all forms must be obtained directly from the lending institution(s). The Peace Corps does not have a universal loan form. Complete the form(s) provided by your lending institution(s) and bring it/them with you to your staging (predeparture orientation). At staging, Peace Corps staff will provide a letter verifying that you have officially begun your service in the Peace Corps. You may then mail your deferment form(s) and verification letter(s) to your lender(s).

Sometimes lending institutions mistakenly send incorrect forms. You must read the application carefully to determine whether or not you fit the criteria. Two forms that often cause confusion are for Direct Loans. One form is an economic hardship deferment request; the other is the Peace Corps or public service deferment request. The public service deferment request form states at the top that you must have received your loan before July 1, 1993, to receive this type of deferment. Only you will know if you fit the criteria indicated. Most volunteers apply for economic hardship deferment since most current volunteers received their loan(s) after July 1, 1993. However, if, for example, you received loans that fall within the periods specified by both forms, it may be best to complete both forms. Some volunteers who received part of their loans before July 1, 1993, have filled out one form and discovered that loans after that period did not get deferred. Always read your application forms carefully to determine if they are applicable to you.

Applying For Deferment During A Grace Period

You should always contact your lenders to find out when they would like your application for deferment. Some volunteers have sent their deferment application(s) to their lender(s) during the grace period, and the loans were not deferred. If your lender says you must wait until the six-month grace period expires, wait until that time. Bring extra forms with you and have an official in-country sign them or leave the forms with your power of attorney.

Interest

In some cases, interest can accrue on a deferred loan. Check with your lending institution(s) to discuss what will happen with your loans, once deferred. Interest on subsidized loans is paid by the Department of Education, provided your loan(s) is/are successfully deferred. Failure to do so may result in a defaulted loan. Interest on unsubsidized loans may have to be paid by the volunteer during service.

Quick Tip

Do not mail your deferment forms to the Peace Corps; you should bring them with you to your staging (predeparture orientation).

The Peace Corps will not mail out your forms. They will be given back to you at staging, and you are responsible for mailing them to your lending institution(s).

Source: From "Loan Deferment FAQ," a publication of peacecorps.gov, July 2010.

Form Certification

When you arrive at staging, have your deferment forms with you. Make sure that you have contacted all of your lenders to request the forms or that you have downloaded them from the internet as directed by the lender. A certifying officer will sign your forms at staging and give you a letter that certifies your projected dates of service. It is recommended that you make copies of all forms and the certification letter for your records or to send to your power of attorney.

Annual Renewal Of Deferment

Many loans require renewal each year. Check with your lender(s) to find out if you must renew your loan deferment.

To reapply for a loan deferment while serving in the Peace Corps, you can do one of two things: either bring extra forms with you and fill them out in-country, having an in-country official certify them for you, or designate someone at home as your power of attorney and have this person sign for you and send the forms to Peace Corps headquarters to be signed by the certifying officer.

Privacy Act Waiver

If you want your parents or another designated party to reapply for your deferment, they will need to request loan deferment paperwork from Peace Corps. They can only make this request if you have signed the Privacy Act Waiver included in the Invitation Kit and submitted it at your staging event. If you have given this signed consent, the designated party can contact Volunteer & PSC Financial Services to request the appropriate documentation for the continuation of your deferment. The address is: Paul D. Coverdell Peace Corps Headquarters Attn: Certifying Officer Volunteer & PSC Financial Services 1111 20th Street, 2nd Floor, NW Washington, DC 20526 800-424-8580 x1784.

Applying For Deferment After Service

Whether or not you can apply for a loan deferment after your Peace Corps service depends on the policies of your lending institution(s), but they will likely say it is too late. You are encouraged to make all of your arrangements before you leave the United States for service in the Peace Corps.

Educational Benefits

Peace Corps or graduate school? Two unique programs offer the best of both worlds.

Before And During Your Service

Master's International allows volunteers to incorporate Peace Corps service as credit in a master's degree program in a variety of fields at more than 80 academic institutions nationwide. Prospective students apply separately to Peace Corps and to a participating graduate school. Once accepted by both, students will study on campus, usually for one year, and then spend the next two years earning academic credit while working overseas in a related Peace Corps project. Most schools provide students in this program with opportunities for research or teaching assistantships, scholarships, or tuition waivers for the credits earned while serving in the Peace Corps.

Following Your Service

Fellows/USA offers returned volunteers scholarships or reduced tuition, stipends, and internships at more than 50 participating campuses in a variety of subject areas, combining graduate study with substantive, degree-related internships that help meet the needs of underserved American communities. Fellows teach in public schools, work in public health facilities, and contribute to community development projects at nonprofit organizations. Volunteers can apply for Fellows/USA any time after they complete their Peace Corps service.

Chapter 41

Military Service And Education Benefits

ROTC Programs

Founded in 1926, ROTC stands for Reserve Officer Training Corps. It's a college program offered at more than 1,000 colleges and universities across the United States that prepares young adults to become officers in the U.S. military. In exchange for a paid college education and a guaranteed postcollege career, cadets commit to serve in the military after graduation. Each service branch has its own take on ROTC.

Army ROTC

Army ROTC is one of the most demanding and successful leadership programs in the country. The training a student receives in Army ROTC teaches leadership development, military skills, and career training. Courses take place both in the classroom and in the field and are mixed with normal academic studies. Additional summer programs, such as Jump School, may also be attended. Upon completion, an Army ROTC graduate is awarded officer status in the Army.

Navy And Marine Corps ROTC

As the largest single source of Navy officers, the Navy ROTC program plays an important role in preparing young adults for leadership and management positions in the increasingly technical Navy. Offered at more than 160 leading colleges and universities throughout the

About This Chapter: Information in this chapter is from the following publications of the U.S. Department of Defense: "ROTC Programs," 2011; "Service Academies And Senior Military Colleges," 2011; "Military Myth Versus Reality," 2011; "Education Benefits," 2011. The chapter also contains "Military Scholarships," a publication of the U.S. Department of Education, 2010–2011.

U.S., the Navy ROTC offers a mixture of military training and normal academic study. Courses take place both in the classroom and in the field. Upon completion, an NROTC graduate is awarded officer status and the ability to choose an officer career in surface warfare, naval aviation, submarine, or special warfare.

Aspiring Marine Corps officers also participate in Navy ROTC. The ROTC academic curriculum for a Marine Corps-option student requires classes in national security policy and the history of American military affairs, in addition to the regular academic requirements for the student's degree.

Air Force ROTC

The Air Force ROTC mission is to produce leaders for the Air Force and build better citizens for America. Headquartered in Montgomery, Alabama, the Air Force ROTC commands 144 units at college and university campuses throughout the United States. Air Force ROTC offers a four-year program and a two-year program, both based on Air Force requirements and led by active-duty Air Force officers. Courses are a mix of normal college classes and Air Force ROTC curriculum, which covers everything from leadership studies to combat technique. Upon completion, a student enters the Air Force as an officer.

Coast Guard Student Reserve

Unlike other service branches, the Coast Guard does not have an ROTC program. However, high school seniors and college and vocational students between the ages of 17 and 30 can enroll in the Coast Guard Student Reserve Program, though some Reserve and Officer programs allow you to be older. Enlistees train for two summers and serve one weekend a month during the school year. Schooling continues uninterrupted. They receive pay for their weekend service and, after training is complete, begin Reserve duty. For more information, contact a recruiter.

It's A Fact!
- Qualified service members can receive more than $70,000 in tuition benefits.
- The military operates more than 300 schools, teaching more than 10,000 courses.
- The military offers retired personnel up to $100/month reimbursement for tutorial assistance.

Source: From "Military Myth Versus Reality," a publication of the U.S. Department of Defense, 2011.

Service Academies And Senior Military Colleges

For students who would like to experience a military environment while getting a first-class education, the four Service academies—the U.S. Military Academy (Army) in West Point, New York; the U.S. Naval Academy (Navy/Marine Corps) in Annapolis, Maryland.; the U.S. Air Force Academy (Air Force) in Colorado Springs, Colorado; and the U.S. Coast Guard Academy (Coast Guard) in New London, Connecticut—offer an outstanding education and full four-year scholarships. Tuition, books, board, and medical and dental care are all fully paid for all four years. The competition to get in is fierce. Admissions criteria include the following:

- High school academic performance

- Standardized test scores (Scholastic Aptitude Test (SAT) or American College Testing Program (ACT))

- Athletics and extracurricular activities

- Leadership experience and community involvement

- A congressional letter of recommendation (not required by the Coast Guard Academy)

Graduates of all four academies receive a bachelor of science degree and are commissioned as officers in their respective service branch. In all cases, there is a service obligation of a minimum of five years.

Similarly, the senior military colleges (SMCs) offer a combination of higher education with military instruction. SMCs include Texas A&M University, Norwich University, The Virginia Military Institute, The Citadel, Virginia Polytechnic Institute and State University (Virginia Tech), North Georgia College and State University, and the Mary Baldwin Women's Institute for Leadership. SMCs are among the most prestigious and famous education institutions in the world and they offer financial aid packages for eligible students. Every cadet must participate in the Reserve Officer Training Corps (ROTC) program, but only those cadets who receive an ROTC scholarship are required to enter military service following graduation. For example, about half of Virginia Military Institute's cadets earn commissions as second lieutenants (Army, Marine Corps, Air Force) or ensigns (Navy).

An additional option for students is U.S. Merchant Marine academies. The United States Merchant Marine is the fleet of civilian-owned merchant ships that transport cargo and passengers on behalf of the United States. In times of war, the Merchant Marine is an auxiliary to the Navy and can be called upon to deliver service members and supplies for the military.

Midshipmen at the Merchant Marine Academy in Kings Point, New York receive full scholarships in exchange for a service obligation in the Merchant Marine Reserve or Navy Reserve. The other Merchant Marine academies also produce shipboard officers for vessels integral to shipping and transportation needs, but a service commitment is not always required.

Education Support

The military offers many educational benefits that service members can take advantage of during or after service. From financial aid and college funds to programs that convert military training into college credit, there have never been more ways for service members to further their education.

Tuition Assistance

The rising cost of tuition can be hard to manage, but the Military's Tuition Assistance Program provides service members the opportunity to enroll in courses at accredited colleges, universities, junior colleges, and vocational-technical schools. Each service has unique programs that can help with tuition for anything from professional certifications to a graduate degree. To qualify, there are usually conditional requirements—such as having a minimum time remaining on your service contract and a cap on credit hours (or dollars) per year. Some programs, such as the Coast Guard's College Student Pre-Commissioning Initiative, also require that you attend a school from a designated list.

Tuition Assistance pays for up to 100 percent of the cost of tuition or expenses, up to a maximum of $250 per credit and a personal maximum of $4,500 per fiscal year per student. This program is the same for full-time-duty members in all military services. Selected Reserve and National Guard units also offer Tuition Assistance Programs, although the benefits may vary from the Active Duty's program.

It's A Fact!

- You must have a high school diploma or equivalent to enlist.
- A General Education Development test (GED) may be accepted with special approval.

Source: From "Military Myth Versus Reality," a publication of the U.S. Department of Defense, 2011.

Quick Tip

For more information about the GI Bill, including maximum allowances state-by-state, visit the Veterans Affairs GI Bill site at http://gibill.va.gov/post-911/or speak with a recruiter.

Source: From "Education Benefits," a publication of the U.S. Department of Defense, 2011.

The Post-9/11 GI Bill

The Post-9/11 GI Bill became effective on Aug. 1, 2009, and has the most comprehensive education benefits package since the original GI Bill was signed into law in 1944. Veterans who have served after Sept. 10, 2001, with at least 90 days of continuous service, are eligible. The Post-9/11 GI Bill also gives Reserve and Guard members who have been activated for more than 90 days since 9/11 access to the same benefits as their active-duty counterparts.

As of Aug. 1, 2011, the Post-9/11 GI Bill will now pay all public school in-state tuition and fees. The full benefit amount an individual can receive is calculated from the following numbers:

- Tuition and fees payment (not to exceed the highest public in-state undergraduate tuition and fees in each state)

- Living stipend (equivalent to basic housing allowance in that ZIP code for an E-5 with dependents)

- Allowance for books and supplies ($1,000 per year)

The actual benefit amount will vary based on an individual's total length of service. For example, those who have served at least 36 months or 30 continuous days prior to discharge for a service-connected disability can get maximum tuition and fees, a monthly housing stipend, and an annual stipend for books and supplies. Those who have served at least 90 days, but less than six months, receive 40 percent of the maximum benefit. These benefits are payable for up to 15 years following a member's honorable discharge or retirement from service.

Another aspect of the Post-9/11 GI Bill is the Yellow Ribbon Program. Colleges and universities that participate in this program contribute additional funds toward educational costs that exceed the maximums allowed by the Post-9/11 GI Bill. Institutions may set the amount they wish to contribute, which is matched by Veterans Affairs. This can be very beneficial for students at private colleges and universities or graduate programs, or those attending with out-of-state status.

The Post-9/11 GI Bill also offers service members the ability to share educational benefits with family members. In exchange for an additional service commitment, a service member may be able to transfer all or part of his or her earned benefits to spouses and children (including stepchildren). This is a first for the GI Bill and opens up new opportunities for service members and their families.

College Fund Programs (GI Bill "Kicker")

College Fund Programs offer an additional amount of money that can be added to the Post-9/11 GI Bill. The Army, Marine Corps, and Navy all have College Fund Programs; however, each service branch determines who qualifies for the College Fund and the amount received. College Fund Programs are offered to service members when they first join the military. Two mandatory qualifications are you must have a high school diploma and you must be enrolled in the Post-9/11 GI Bill. Depending on your service, test scores and occupation, there may also be additional requirements.

Loan Repayment Programs

The Army, Navy, and Air Force offer loan repayment programs that help enlisted personnel pay off college loans accrued prior to service. While each program has unique processes and requirements, they're all enlistment incentives designed to help recent college graduates manage education debt.

Army: In the full-time-duty Army, soldiers can qualify to have their loan repaid by the military at the rate of one-third of the loan for each year of full-time duty served (maximum loan repayment is $65,000). The Army even helps soldiers pay off student loans they've taken out, provided they attended schools on approved Perkins, Stafford, or other Department of Education guaranteed student loans.

Navy: In the full-time-duty Navy, a $65,000 Loan Repayment Program is also available. Qualifications include no prior military service, a high school diploma, and a loan guaranteed under the Higher Education Act of 1965. A candidate must qualify for the Navy Nuclear Field or other designated critical rating as defined by the U.S. Navy, and other restrictions apply. If an individual does qualify, either of these programs is a great way to get out of debt!

It's A Fact!

The Air Force doesn't have a College Fund Program, but it does have a community college.

Source: From "Education Benefits," a publication of the U.S. Department of Defense, 2011.

Air Force: The College Loan Repayment Program (CLRP) is a program created for all non-prior-service members considering enlistment in the Air Force. For young people who have taken some college courses and have accumulated debt, this could very well be the perfect opportunity. Participants must sign up for this program when signing the enlistment contract. Under CLRP, the repayment maximum is $10,000 per recruit.

Servicemembers Opportunity Colleges (SOC)

Servicemembers Opportunity Colleges (SOC) are a great way for servicemembers and their families to gain an education while serving, as it enables them to get college degrees through an association of accredited colleges, universities, and technical institutes. SOC member schools acknowledge and transfer credits, making it possible for servicemembers to continue college studies as they move to new duty stations.

SOC offers servicemembers the following:

- A personal degree plan

- Assurance that no single SOC school need contribute more than 25 percent of total degree coursework

- College credit for military experience and for accredited military training courses

- College credit for national tests such as the College Level Examination Program (CLEP)

Hundreds of thousands of people are enrolled each year in SOC. Coursework can be done in the classroom or at a distance by computer or correspondence. Two-year, four-year, and graduate-level programs are available. The Army has a special version of SOC called the Concurrent Admissions Program (ConAP), which helps link new soldiers to a college at the time of enlistment.

Community College Of The Air Force (CCAF)

The Community College of the Air Force (CCAF) is an accredited two-year college open to enlisted Air Force men and women. CCAF offers nearly 70 different associate degree programs in many scientific and technical fields including computer science technology, avionic systems technology, air and space operations technology, allied health sciences, paralegal, information management, and more.

Every CCAF degree requires courses in the service member's technical job specialty, leadership/management/military studies, general education, and physical education. Service members can accumulate credits while on Active Duty at Air Force technical training schools and when they enroll in colleges near their duty stations that offer accredited courses. Enlisted members of the Air Guard and Air Force Reserve are also eligible to participate in CCAF. CCAF also awards credit for exams offered by the military's testing programs.

Testing Programs

The military administers thousands of academic exams to service members each year. These tests can earn service members college credit for skills acquired during military training and operations and are available to all active-duty, Reserve, and Guard personnel, as well as their families. The testing is available at a discount and is divided into the following:

College Level Equivalency Program (CLEP) General Exams: Each exam measures the knowledge presumably gained during the first two years in college.

CLEP Subject Exams: For every one of these timed, computer-based exams that a service member passes, he or she generally receives three hours of college credit (6 or 12 hours are possible in some situations).

DANTES Subject Standardized Test (DSST): Passing a DSST exam also earns service members college credit. DANTES has no time limit and is a paper-based test.

Excelsior College Exams (ECE): Excelsior College (formerly known as Regents College) is a virtual university that counts many military personnel among its worldwide graduates. Excelsior College Exams are accepted for college credit by hundreds of colleges and universities. ECE are administered free to active-duty personnel through DANTES Test Centers.

It's A Fact!

As of August 1, 2011, service members can receive reimbursement for some licensing and certification exams, and they can also be reimbursed for fees related to the SAT, Law School Admission Test (LSAT), ACT and other college and graduate school entrance tests.

Source: "Education Benefits," a publication of the U.S. Department of Defense, 2011.

Military Scholarships

Army Reserve Officer Training Corps

Army Reserve Officer Training Corps (ROTC) scholarships are offered at hundreds of colleges. Application packets, information about eligibility, and the telephone number of an ROTC advisor in your area are available from:

College Army ROTC
Telephone: 1-800-USA-ROTC (1-800-872-7682)
Website: www.goarmy.com/rotc

Air Force Reserve Officer Training Corps

The Air Force Reserve Officer Training Corps (AFROTC) college scholarship program targets students pursuing certain foreign language and technical degrees, although students entering a wide variety of majors may be accepted. Information about AFROTC scholarships is available from:

College Scholarship Section
Telephone: 1-866-4-AFROTC (1-866-423-7682)
Website: www.afrotc.com

Naval Reserve Officers Training Corps

The Naval Reserve Officers Training Corps (NROTC) offers both two-year and four-year scholarships. For information and applications, contact:

Naval Service Training Command
Telephone: 1-800-NAV-ROTC (1-800-628-7682)
Website: https://www.nrotc.navy.mil

Part Six
If You Need More Information

Chapter 42

Directory Of Financial Aid Resources

Federal Student Aid

To obtain a copy of the U.S. Department of Education's current *Guide to Federal Student Aid*, visit the Federal Student Aid website at http://www.federalstudentaid.ed.gov. Order copies of the guide in English and Spanish in bulk from the U.S. Department of Education at:

Online: www.FSAPubs.gov

E-mail: orders@FSApubs.gov

Call in your request toll-free: 1-800-394-7084 or 1-877-433-7827 (1-877-4-ED-PUBS)

If 877 services are not available in your area, call 1-800-872-5327 (1-800-USA-LEARN). Those who use a telecommunications device for the deaf (TDD) or a teletypewriter (TTY), should call 1-800-437-0833.

You can order up to five copies of the guide by calling the Federal Student Aid Information Center at 1-800-433-3243 (1-800-4-FED-AID).

The guide is also available online (PDF and HTML) on the Federal Student Aid website at www.FederalStudentAid.ed.gov/pubs.

On request, the guide is available in alternate formats, such as Braille, large print, or CD. For more information, please contact the Federal Student Aid Information Center at 1-800-433-3243 (1-800-4-FED-AID). TTY users should call 1-800-730-8913.

About This Chapter: "Federal Student Aid" is excerpted from: U.S. Department of Education, Federal Student Aid, Student Aid Awareness and Applicant Services *Funding Education Beyond High School: The Guide to Federal Student Aid 2010–11*, Washington, D.C., 2010. Other resources listed in this chapter were compiled from many sources deemed accurate. Inclusion does not constitute endorsement, and there is no implication associated with omission. All contact information was verified in May 2011.

Useful Websites

Student Aid On The Web

http://www.FederalStudentAid.ed.gov

Click on Students, Parents, and Counselors

At this website you can do the following:

- Find information on federal student aid and access publications online.

- Use "MyFSA" to create a personalized folder to record your interests, career, and college searches to help you decide on a career and locate schools offering majors in that field. Track your progress in the college planning and application process by applying to schools online, access other sources of nonfederal aid, and store your personal information to populate fields on *FAFSA on the Web*[SM].

- Use FAFSA4caster[SM] to get an early estimate of your eligibility for federal student aid, and an early start in the financial aid process.

- Obtain a Federal Student Aid PIN to sign your *FAFSA on the Web* and access your personal information.

- Apply for federal student aid online using *FAFSA on the Web* (the online version of the Free Application for Federal Student Aid, or FAFSA[SM]).

- Keep track of your federal student aid through the National Student Loan Data System[SM].

College.gov

www.college.gov

This website is designed to motivate high school students with inspirational stories and information about planning, preparing, and paying for college.

Free Help Completing The FAFSA

www.FederalStudentAid.ed.gov/completefafsa

This website explains how to complete the FAFSA and the purpose of FAFSA questions.

The William D. Ford Federal Direct Loan Program (Direct Loan)

U.S. Department of Education as lender

www.ed.gov/DirectLoan

Use this website to find out more information on the Direct Loan Program℠, such as repayment options and interactive calculators.

Direct Loan Servicing Online

www.dl.ed.gov

Use this website to make Direct Loan online payments, view account balance, change billing options, enroll in electronic services, and much more.

U.S. Department Of Labor's Occupational Outlook Handbook (information on various careers and their earning potential)

www.bls.gov/oco

Frequently Requested Telephone Numbers

Federal Student Aid Information Center (FSAIC)

1-800-4-FED-AID (1-800-433-3243)

TTY users can call 1-800-730-8913

Callers in locations without access to 1-800 numbers may call 319-337-5665 (this is not a toll-free number).

The FSAIC staff will answer your federal student aid questions for FREE, and provide you with the following:

- Information about federal student aid programs
- Help completing the FAFSA
- Help in making corrections to your Student Aid Report (SAR), which contains your application results
- Information about the process of determining financial need and awarding aid
- Information about your federal student loans

You can also use an automated response system at this number to find out if your FAFSA has been processed and to request a copy of your SAR. Or you can write to the FSAIC at the address above.

Direct Loan Servicing

1-800-848-0979

TTY users can call 1-800-848-0983

Direct Loan Consolidation

1-800-557-7392

TTY users can call 1-800-557-7395

Inspector General Hotline

To report student aid fraud (including identity theft), waste or abuse of U.S. Department of Education funds.

1-800-MIS-USED (1-800-647-8733)

Website: http://www.ed.gov/misused

E-mail: oig.hotline@ed.gov

Other National Sources Of Student Aid

American Indian College Fund

8333 Greenwood Boulevard

Denver, CO 80221

Toll-Free: 800-776-3863

Phone: 303-426-8900

Fax: 303-426-1200

Website: http://www.collegefund.org

AmeriCorps

1201 New York Avenue NW

Washington, DC 20525

Toll-Free: 800-942-2677

Toll-Free TTY: 800-833-3722

Phone: 202-606-5000

TTY: 202-606-3472

Fax: 606-330-2530

Website: http://www.americorps.gov

E-mail: questions@americorps.org

Hispanic College Fund

1301 K Street NW, Suite 450-A West

Washington, DC 20005

Toll-Free: 800-644-4223

Phone: 202-296-5400

Fax: 202-296-3774

Website: http://www.hispanicfund.org

E-mail: hcf-info@hispanicfund.org

Hispanic Scholarship Fund

55 Second Street, Suite 1500

San Francisco, CA 94105

Toll-Free: 877-HSF-INFO

(877-473-4636)

Fax: (415) 808-2302

Website: http://www.hsf.net

Horatio Alger Association of Distinguished Americans

99 Canal Center Plaza, Suite 320
Alexandria, VA 22314
Phone: 703-684-9444
Fax: 703-548-3822
Website: http://www.horatioalger.org

National Association for the Advancement of Colored People (NAACP)

4805 Mount Hope Drive
Baltimore, MD 21215
Toll Free: 877-NAACP-98
(877-622-2798)
Phone: 410-580-5777
Website: http://www.naacp.org

National Health Service Corps

Toll-Free: 800-221-9393
Website: http://nhsc.bhpr.hrsa.gov
E-mail: callcenter@hrsa.gov

National Merit Scholarship

1560 Sherman Avenue, Suite 200
Evanston, IL 60201-4897
Phone: 847-866-5100
Fax: 847-866-5113
Website: http://www.nationalmerit.org

Peace Corps

Phone: 800-424-8580
Website: http://www.peacecorps.gov

Robert C. Byrd Honors Scholarship Program

U.S. Department of Education, OPE
Higher Education Programs, State Service
1990 K Street NW, 6th Floor
Washington, DC 20006-8512
Phone: 202-502-7750
Fax: 202-502-7861

Scholarship America

One Scholarship Way
P.O. Box 297
Saint Peter, MN 56082
Toll-Free: 800-537-4180
Phone: 507-931-1682
Website: http://scholarshipamerica.org

SLM Corporation (Sallie Mae, Inc.)

Toll-Free: 888-2-SALLIE
(888-272-5543)
Toll-Free TDD: 888-833-7562
Phone: 317-570-7397
Fax: 800-848-1949
Website: http://www.collegeanswer.com;
http://www.salliemae.com

Teach for America

315 West 36th Street, 7th Floor
New York, NY 10018
Toll-Free: 800-832-1230
Phone: 212-279-2080
Fax: 212-279-2081
Website: http://www.teachforamerica.org
E-mail: admissions@teachforamerica.org

United Negro College Fund

8260 Willow Oaks Corporate Drive
P.O. Box 10444
Fairfax, VA 22031-8044
Phone: 800-331-2244
Website: http://www.uncf.org

Volunteers in Service to America (VISTA)

1000 Wisconsin Avenue NW
Washington, DC 20007
Website: http://www.friendsofvista.org

Online Scholarship Search Services

Adventures In Education

Website: http://www.adventuresineducation
.org/HighSchool/Scholarships/index.cfm

BrokeScholar

Website: http://www.brokescholar.com

College Board

Website: http://apps.collegeboard.com/
cbsearch_ss/welcome.jsp

College Data

Website: http://www.collegedata.com

CSO College Center

Website: http://www.csocollegecenter.org

FastAid

Website: http://www.fastaid.com

FastWeb

Website: http://www.fastweb.com

GoCollege

Website: http://www.gocollege.com

NextStudent

Website: http://www.nextstudent.com/
scholarships/

Peterson's Financial Aid

Website: http://www.petersons.com/finaid

Sallie Mae's Scholarship Search

Website: http://go.salliemae.com/
scholarship

ScholarshipExperts

http://www.scholarshipexperts.com/

Scholarships.com

Website: http://www.scholarships.com

Additional Information About Planning For Higher Education

Adventures In Education

Texas Guaranteed Student Loan Corporation
P.O. Box 83100
Round Rock, TX 78683-3100
Toll-Free: 800-252-9743
Phone: 519-219-5700
Website: http://www.tgslc.org

American Association of Community Colleges

One Dupont Circle NW, Suite 410
Washington, DC 20036
Phone: 202-728-0200
Fax: 202-833-2467
Website: http://www.aacc.nche.edu

American College Testing (ACT)

Phone: 319-337-1000
Website: http://www.actstudent.org

American Council on Education

One Dupont Circle NW
Washington DC, 20036
Phone: (202) 939-9300
Website: http://www.acenet.edu

College Board

45 Columbus Avenue
New York, NY 10023-6917
Phone: 212-713-8000
Website: http://www.collegeboard.com

Council for Opportunity in Education

1025 Vermont Avenue NW, Suite 900
Washington, DC 20005
Phone: 202-347-7430
Fax: 202-347-0786
Website: http://www.coenet.us

Distance Education and Training Council

1601 18th Street NW, Suite 2
Washington, D.C. 20009
Phone: 202-234-5100
Fax: 202-332-1386
Website: http://www.detc.org

eCampusTours

Website: http://www.ecampustours.com
E-mail: info@campustours.com

FinAid Page, LLC

P.O. Box 2056
Cranberry Township, PA 16066-1056
Phone: 724-538-4500
Fax: 724-538-4502
Website: http://www.finaid.org

Let's Get Ready!

50 Broadway, Suite 806
New York, NY 10004
Phone: 646-808-2760
Website: http://www.letsgetready.org

Mapping Your Future

Website: http://www.mappingyourfuture.org

National Association for College Admission Counseling

1050 North Highland Street, Suite 400
Arlington, VA 22201
Toll-Free: 800-822-6285
Phone: 703-836-2222
Fax: 703-243-9375
Website: http://www.nacacnet.org

National Association for Equal Opportunity in Higher Education

209 Third Street SE
Washington, DC 20003
Phone: 202-552-3300
Fax: 202-552-3330
Website: http://www.nafeo.org

National Association of Student Financial Aid Administrators

1101 Connecticut Avenue NW, Suite 1100
Washington, DC 20036-4303
Phone: 202-785-0453
Fax: 202-785-1487
Website: http://www.nasfaa.org

National Center for Education Statistics

1990 K Street NW
Washington, DC 20006
Phone: 202-502-7300
Website: http://nces.ed.gov

National Collegiate Athletic Association (NCAA)

700 West Washington Street
P.O. Box 6222
Indianapolis, IN 46206-6222
Phone: 317-917-6222
Fax: 317-917-6888
Website: http://www.ncaa.org

Nelnet College Planning

Phone: 866-866-7372
Website:
http://www.collegeplanning.nelnet.net
E-mail: collegeplanning@nelnet.net

Saving For College

1151 Pittsford Victor Road, Suite 103
Pittsford, NY 14534
Website: http://www.savingforcollege.com

U.S. Department of Education

830 1st Street NE
Washington, DC 20202-5269
Toll-Free: 800-4-FED-AID
(800-433-3243)
Toll-Free TTY: 800-730-8913
Phone: 319-337-5665
Website: http://www.students.gov

Chapter 43

Directory Of State Higher Education Agencies

These agencies provide information on state education programs, colleges and universities, student aid assistance programs, grants, scholarships, continuing education programs, and career opportunities. For updated information, you can search the U.S. Department of Education's database at: http://www.ed.gov/Programs/bastmp/SHEA.htm (the URL is case-sensitive). You can contact agencies by calling the telephone numbers or online at the websites listed.

Alabama

Alabama Commission
on Higher Education
P.O. Box 302000
Montgomery, AL 36130-2000
Toll-Free: 800-960-7773
Phone: 334-242-1998
Fax: 334-242-0268
Website: http://www.ache.state.al.us

Alaska

Alaska Commission on Postsecondary
Education
P.O. Box 110510
Juneau, AK 99811-0510
Toll-Free: 800-441-2962
Phone: 907-465-2962
Website:
http://www.alaskaadvantage.state.ak.us

About This Chapter: Excerpted from U.S. Department of Education, Federal Student Aid, Student Aid Awareness and Applicant Services *Funding Education Beyond High School: The Guide to Federal Student Aid 2010–11*, Washington, D.C., 2010. All contact information was verified and updated in May 2011.

Arizona

Arizona Commission for Postsecondary
Education
2020 North Central Avenue, Suite 650
Phoenix, AZ 85004
Phone: 602-258-2435
Fax: 602-258-2483
Website: http://www.azhighered.org
E-mail: acpe@azhighered.gov

Arkansas

Arkansas Department of Higher Education
114 East Capitol Avenue
Little Rock, AR 72201
Toll-Free: 800-54-STUDY (800-547-8839)
Phone: 501-371-2000
Website: http://www.adhe.edu
E-mail: ADHE_Info@adhe.edu

California

California Student Aid Commission
P.O. Box 419026
Rancho Cordova, CA 95741-9026
Toll-Free: 888-224-7268
Fax: 916-464-8002
Website: http://www.csac.ca.gov
E-mail: studentsupport@csac.ca.gov

Colorado

Colorado Commission on Higher Education
1560 Broadway
Denver, CO 80202
Phone: 303-866-2723
Fax: 303-866-4266
Website: http://www.highered.colorado.gov
E-mail: CCHE@state.co.us

Connecticut

Connecticut Department
of Higher Education
61 Woodland Street
Hartford, CT 06105-2326
Phone: 860-947-1800
Fax: 860-947-1310
Website: http://www.ctdhe.org

Delaware

Delaware Higher Education Commission
Carvel State Office Building, 5th Floor
820 North French Street
Wilmington, DE 19801-3509
Toll-Free: 800-292-7935
Phone: 302-577-3240
Fax: 302-577-6765
Website: http://www.doe.k12.de.us/info
suites/students_family/dheo/default.shtml
E-mail: dhec@doe.k12.de.us

District of Columbia

Office of the State Superintendent of
Education
810 First Street NE, 9th Floor
Washington, DC 20002
Phone: 202-727-6436
Website: http://www.seo.dc.gov

Florida

Office of Student Financial Assistance,
Florida Department of Education
Toll-Free: 888-827-2004
Website:
http://www.floridastudentfinancialaid.org
E-mail: OSFA@fldoe.org

Georgia

Georgia Student Finance Commission
2082 East Exchange Place
Tucker, GA 30084
Toll-Free: 800-505-GSFC
(800-505-4732)
Phone: 770-724-9000
Fax: 770-724-9089
Website: http://www.gsfc.org

Hawaii

University of Hawaii System
Office of Student Affairs
2444 Dole Street, Bachman 207
Honolulu, HI 96822
Phone: 808-956-8753
Website: http://www.hawaii.edu/
admissions/aid.html

Idaho

Idaho State Board of Education
P.O. Box 83720
Boise, ID 83720-0037
Phone: 208-334-2270
Fax: 208-334-2632
Website: http://www.boardofed.idaho.gov/
scholarships
E-mail: board@osbe.idaho.gov

Illinois

Illinois Student Assistance Commission
1755 Lake Cook Road
Deerfield, IL 60015-5209
Toll-Free: 800-899-4722
Website: http://www.collegeillinois.org
E-mail: collegezone@illinois.gov

Indiana

State Student Assistance
Commission of Indiana
W462 Indiana Government
Center South
402 West Washington Street
Indianapolis, IN 46204
Toll-Free: 888-528-4719
Phone: 317-232-2350
Fax: 317-232-3260
Website: http://www.in.gov/ssaci

Iowa

Iowa College Student Aid Commission
603 East 12th Street, Floor 5
Des Moines, IA 50319
Toll-Free: 877-272-4456
Phone: 515-725-3400
515-725-3401
Website: http://www.iowacollegeaid.org
E-mail: info@iowacollegeaid.gov

Kansas

Kansas Board of Regents
1000 SW Jackson Street, Suite 520
Topeka, KS 66612-1368
Phone: 785-296-3421
Fax: 785-296-0983
Website: http://www.kansasregents.org

Kentucky

Kentucky Higher Education Assistance
Authority
Toll-Free: 800-928-8926
Phone: 502-696-7200
Website: http://www.kheaa.com

Louisiana

Louisiana Office of Student Financial
Assistance
P.O. Box 91202
Baton Rouge, LA 70821-9202
Toll-Free: 800-259-5626
Phone: 225-219-1012
Fax: 225-208-1496
Website: http://www.osfa.state.la.us
E-mail: custserv@osfa.la.gov

Maine

Finance Authority of Maine
5 Community Drive
P.O. Box 949
Augusta, ME 04332-0949
Toll-Free: 800-228-3734
Phone: 207-623-3263
TTY: 207-626-2717
Fax: 207-623-0095
Website:
http://www.famemaine.com
E-mail:
education@famemaine.com

Maryland

Maryland Higher
Education Commission
839 Bestgate Road, Suite 400
Annapolis, MD 21401
Toll-Free: 800-974-0203
Toll-Free TTY: 800-735-2258
Phone: 410-260-4500
Fax: 410-260-3200
Website: http://www.mhec.state.md.us
E-mail: osfamail@mhec.state.md.us

Massachusetts

Massachusetts Department of Higher
Education
Office of Student Financial Assistance
454 Broadway, Suite 200
Revere, MA 02151
Phone: 617-727-9420
Fax: 617-727-0667
Website: http://www.osfa.mass.edu
E-mail: osfa@osfa.mass.edu

Michigan

Student Financial Services Bureau
P.O. Box 30047
Lansing MI 48909-7547
Toll-Free: 888-447-2687
Website:
http://www.michigan.gov/mistudentaid
E-mail: sfs@michigan.gov

Minnesota

Minnesota Office of Higher Education
1450 Energy Park Drive, Suite 350
St. Paul, MN 55108-5227
Toll-Free: 800-657-3866
Toll-Free TTY: 800-627-3529
Phone: 651-642-0567
Fax: 651-642-0675
Website: http://www.ohe.state.mn.us;
www.getreadyforcollege.org

Mississippi

Mississippi Office of
Student Financial Aid
3825 Ridgewood Road
Jackson, MS 39211-6453
Toll-Free: 800-327-2980
Phone: 601-432-6997
Website: http://www.mississippi.edu/
riseupms/financialaid-state.php
E-mail: sfa@mississippi.edu

Missouri

Missouri Department of
Higher Education
205 Jefferson Street
P.O. Box 1469
Jefferson City, MO 65102-1469
Toll-Free: 800-473-6757
Phone: 573-751-2361
Fax: 573-751-6635
Website: http://www.dhe.mo.gov
E-mail: info@dhe.mo.gov

Montana

Montana Guaranteed Student
Loan Program
P.O. Box 203101
Helena, MT 59620-3101
Toll-Free: 800-537-7508
Fax: 406-444-1869
Website: http://www.mgslp.org

Nebraska

Nebraska Coordinating Commission for
Postsecondary Education
P.O. Box 95005
Lincoln, NE 68509-5005
Phone: 402-471-2847
Fax: 402-471-2886
Website: http://www.ccpe.state.ne.us

Nevada

Office of the State Treasurer
101 North Carson Street, Suite 4
Carson City, NV 89701
Toll-Free: 1-888-477-2667
Phone: 775-684-5600
Fax: 775-684-5781
Website:
http://www.nevadatreasurer.gov

New Hampshire

New Hampshire Postsecondary Education
Commission
3 Barrell Court, Suite 300
Concord, NH 03301
Phone: 603-271-2555
Website: http://www.nh.gov/
postsecondary/financial/index.html

New Jersey

New Jersey Higher Education
Student Assistance Authority
P.O. Box 540
Trenton, NJ 08625-0540
Toll-Free: 800-792-8670
Website: http://www.hesaa.org
E-mail: clientservices@hesaa.org

New Mexico

New Mexico Higher Education Department
2048 Galisteo
Santa Fe, New Mexico 8750
Toll-Free: 800-279-9777
Phone: 505-476-8400
Fax: 505-476-8453
Website: http://www.hed.state.nm.us

New York

New York State Higher Education
Services Corporation
99 Washington Avenue
Albany, NY 12255
Toll-Free: 888-697-4372
Phone: 518-473-1574
Website: http://www.hesc.org

North Carolina

College Foundation of North Carolina
P.O. Box 41966
Raleigh, NC 27629-1966
Toll-Free: 866-866-2362
Fax: 919-821-3139
Website: http://www.cfnc.org
E-mail: programinformation@CFNC.org

North Dakota

North Dakota University System
10th Floor, State Capitol
600 East Boulevard Avenue, Department 215
Bismarck, ND 58505-0230
Phone: 701-328-2960
Fax: 701-328-2961
Website: http://www.ndus.edu
E-mail: ndus.office@ndus.edu

Ohio

Ohio Board of Regents
30 East Broad Street, 36th Floor
Columbus, OH 43215-3414
Toll-Free: 888-833-1133 (for information
specifically about Ohio programs)
Toll-Free: 877-428-8246 (for information
about other sources of financial aid)
Phone: 614-466-6000
614-466-5866
Website: http://www.regents.ohio.gov/sgs/
index.php

Oklahoma

Oklahoma State Regents for Higher
Education
655 Research Parkway, Suite 200
Oklahoma City, OK 73104
Toll-Free: 800-858-1840
Phone: 405-225-9100
Website: http://www.okhighered.org
E-mail: communicationsdepartment@
osrhe.edu

Oregon

Oregon Student Assistance Commission
1500 Valley River Drive, Suite 100
Eugene, OR 97401
Toll-Free: 800-452-8807
Toll-Free TTY: 800-735-2900
Phone: 541-687-7400
Fax: 541-687-7414
Website: http://www.osac.state.or.us;
www.getcollegefunds.org

Pennsylvania

Pennsylvania Higher Education
Assistance Agency
P.O. Box 8157
Harrisburg, PA 17105-8157
Toll-Free: 800-692-7392
Toll-Free TDD: 800-654-5988
Fax: 717-720-3786
Website: http://www.pheaa.org

Rhode Island

Rhode Island Higher Education
Assistance Authority
560 Jefferson Boulevard, Suite 100
Warwick, RI 02886-1304
Toll-Free: 800-922-9855
Phone: 401-736-1100
TDD: 401-734-9481
Fax: 401-732-3541
Website: http://www.riheaa.org
E-mail: info@riheaa.org

South Carolina

South Carolina Commission on Higher
Education
1333 Main Street, Suite 200
Columbia, SC 29201
Phone: 803-737-2260
Fax: 803-737-2297
Website: http://www.che.sc.gov
E-mail: cbrown@che.sc.gov

South Dakota

South Dakota Board of Regents
306 East Capitol Avenue, Suite 200
Pierre, SD 57501-2545
Phone: 605-773-3455
Fax: 605-773-5320
Website: http://www.sdbor.edu
E-mail: info@sdbor.edu

Tennessee

Tennessee Student Assistance Corporation
404 James Robertson Parkway, Suite 1510
Parkway Towers
Nashville, TN 37243-0820
Toll-Free: 800-342-1663
Phone: 615-741-1346
Fax: 615-741-6101
Website: http://www.collegepaystn.com
E-mail: TSAC.AidInfo@tn.gov

Texas

Texas Higher Education Coordinating
Board
Texas Financial Aid Information Center
Toll-Free: 888-311-8881
Website: http://www.collegefortexans.com

Utah

Utah Higher Education Assistance
Authority
P.O. Box 145112
Salt Lake City, UT 84114-5112
Toll-Free: 877-336-7378
Phone: 801-321-7294
Fax: 801-366-8430
Website: http://www.uheaa.org

Vermont

Vermont Student Assistance Corporation
10 East Allen Street
P.O. Box 2000
Winooski, VT 05404
Toll-Free: 800-642-3177
Toll-Free TDD: 800-281-3341
Phone: 802-655-9602
TDD: 802-654-3766
Fax: 802-654-3765
Website: http://www.vsac.org
E-mail: info@vsac.org

Virginia

State Council of Higher Education for
Virginia
101 North 14th Street, 10th Floor
James Monroe Building
Richmond, VA 23219
Toll Free: 877-516-0138
Phone: 804-225-2600
Fax: 804-225-2604
Website: http://www.schev.edu
E-mail: communications@schev.edu

Washington

Washington State Higher Education Co-
ordinating Board
917 Lakeridge Way
P.O. Box 43430
Olympia, WA 98504-3430
Toll-Free: 888-535-0747
Phone: 360-753-7800
Website: http://www.hecb.wa.gov
E-mail: info@hecb.wa.gov

West Virginia

West Virginia Higher Education Policy
Commission
1018 Kanawha Boulevard E, Suite 700
Charleston WV 25301-2800
Toll-Free: 888-825-5707
Phone: 304-558-4614
Fax: 304-558-5719
Website: http://www.hepc.wvnet.edu
E-mail:
financialaiddirector@hepc.wvnet.edu

Wisconsin

Wisconsin Higher Educational Aids
Board
P.O. Box 7885
Madison, WI 53707-7885
Phone: 608-267-2206
Fax: 608-267-2808
Website: http://www.heab.wisconsin.gov
E-mail: HEABmail@wisconsin.gov

Wyoming

Wyoming Department of Education
2300 Capitol Avenue
Hathaway Building, 2nd floor
Cheyenne, WY 82002-0050
Phone: 307-777-7690
Fax: 307-777-6234
Website: http://www.k12.wy.us/grants.asp

U.S. Territories

American Samoa

American Samoa Community College
P.O. Box 2609
Pago Pago, American Samoa 96799
Phone: 684-699-9155
Fax: 684-699 6259
Website: http://www.amsamoa.edu
E-mail: info@amsamoa.edu

Commonwealth of the Northern Mariana Islands

Northern Marianas College
Financial Aid Office
Phone: 670-234-5498x1527
Website: http://www.nmcnet.edu
E-mail: daisym@nmcnet.edu

Federated States of Micronesia

Federated States of Micronesia Department of Education
FSM National Government
P.O. Box PS 87
Palikir, Pohnpei, FM
Phone: 691-320-2609
Fax: 691-320-5500
Website: http://www.literacynet.org/micronesia/doe.html
E-mail: ccantero@otan.dni.us

Guam

University of Guam
UOG Station
Mangilao, Guam 96923
Phone: 671-735-2288
Website: http://www.uog.edu
E-mail: finaid@uguam.uog.edu

Puerto Rico

Puerto Rico Council
on Higher Education
P.O. Box 1900
San Juan, Puerto Rico 00910-1900
Phone: 787-641-7100
Fax: 787-641-2573
Website: http://www.ces.gobierno.pr

Republic of Palau

Republic of Palau Ministry of Education
Palau National Scholarship Board
P.O. Box 1608
Koror, Republic of Palau 96940
Phone: 680-488-3608
Fax: 680-488-3602
Website: http://www.palaumoe.net
E-mail: pnsb@palaunet.com

Republic of the Marshall Islands

Marshall Islands Scholarship Grant and Loan Board
P.O. Box 1436
Majuro, Marshall Islands 96960
Phone: 692-625-5770
Fax: 692-625-7325
Website: http://www.rmischolarship.net

Virgin Islands

Government of the United States Virgin Islands
Department of Education
Office of the Commissioner
1834 Kongens Gade
Saint Thomas, VI 00802
Phone: 340-774-0100
Fax: 340-779-7153
Website: http://www.doe.vi

Index

Index

Page numbers that appear in *Italics* refer to tables or illustrations. Page numbers that have a small 'n' after the page number refer to information shown as Notes at the beginning of each chapter. Page numbers that appear in **Bold** refer to information contained in boxes on that page (except Notes information at the beginning of each chapter).

A